MUSIC REFERENCE
AND
RESEARCH MATERIALS

MUSIC

REFERENCE

AND

RESEARCH

MATERIALS

AN ANNOTATED BIBLIOGRAPHY

Compiled by

VINCENT DUCKLES

THE FREE PRESS OF GLENCOE
COLLIER-MACMILLAN LIMITED, *London*

For information, address:
The Free Press of Glencoe
A Division of The Macmillan Company
The Crowell-Collier Publishing Company
60 Fifth Avenue, New York, N.Y. 10011
Collier-Macmillan Canada, Ltd., Toronto, Ontario

Library of Congress Catalog Card Number: 64-16955

INTRODUCTION

A bibliography can be regarded as the relatively inert by-product of scholarly activity, or it can be treated as an active ingredient in the learning process. The latter perspective has been adopted in this guide to *Music Reference and Research Materials*. While no one but a professional bibliographer may be expected to come for his leisure reading to a list of books, most of us can respond with interest to an organized survey of the literature of a particular field. A bibliography, in fact, offers one of the best means of gaining an over-all impression of a subject area. It throws the essential patterns of a discipline into relief, casting light on what has been accomplished and drawing attention to the shadows where work still needs to be done. This guide has been designed to illuminate the bibliographical resources for musical scholarship. It is, above all, intended to serve a teaching purpose. Implicit in its organization is the concept that bibliography is an approach to knowledge, a way in which the student can progress toward mastery in his chosen field of specialization within the larger dimensions of the field of music. The guide was developed, through a series of editions beginning in 1949, as a text for a graduate seminar entitled "An Introduction to Musical Scholarship" given in the Music Department of the University of California at Berkeley. If its pattern has been determined to some extent by the way in which music bibliography is taught in a specific institution, its structure is still flexible enough to permit other teachers to use it in their own way.

The work is actually intended to fulfill the requirements of two groups: graduate students who need to become acquainted with the resources for musical research, and music reference librarians whose job it is to help others find the information they want. While the needs of the two have much in common, there are points at which their interests diverge. Much more is listed here than will be required for reference services in any but a large music research library, and there is material included which the scholar would rarely need to consult unless he moved outside of the traditional framework of historical musicology.

The present volume is much larger than any of its predecessors, yet it remains a selective list. One limitation in coverage, strictly enforced, is the selection of titles that pertain directly or exclusively to *music*. This criterion eliminates a great deal of valuable reference material, particularly important in areas that lie on the borderline between musicology and other disciplines: liturgics, the theater arts, literature, the dance, etc. No musicologist can afford to neglect such general reference tools as the *Encyclopedia of Religion and Ethics*, or Cabrol's *Dictionnaire d'archéologie chrétienne et de liturgie*, or, in another area, the *Census of Medieval and Renaissance Manuscripts in the U.S. and Canada*, by Seymour de Ricci, or Paul O. Kristeller's valuable survey of the catalogs of *Latin Manuscript Books before 1600*. The fact that these tools are indispensable only serves to demonstrate that musicology is far from being a self-sufficient and self-contained discipline. But an attempt to list all of the peripheral resources would inflate the present work and destroy its focus. There are excellent bibliographies of general reference works currently available. Perhaps the best service to be offered to the young musicologist here is to direct him to Constance M. Winchell's *Guide to Reference Books* (7th ed., 1951, and later supplements) or to Theodore Besterman's *World Bibliography of Bibliographies* (3rd ed., 1955-56). If all else fails, he should be urged to rely on that universal repository of fact and resource, *the reference librarian,* who sits behind a desk in every large library, prepared to guide the inquiring student through the complex paths of information retrieval. But there is a distinct advantage to be gained in approaching the general reference tools from the musician's point of view. Recently Keith E. Mixter has furnished such an approach in his manual on *General Bibliography for Music Research* (1962), published as Number 4 in the Detroit Studies in Music Bibliography (see no. 1131). It is a pleasure to be able to point to that work as a useful complement to this one.

A few further statements should be added to make clear what ground this guide is, and is not, intended to cover. It does not represent the well-rounded library of musical literature; it contains no entries for biography, no local histories, no monographs or studies devoted to most of the subject areas into which the field of music can be subdivided. It is certainly not a basic list of titles which every music library should acquire; but it does provide a list from which the essential materials for a music reference collection can be selected. It can best be described as a bibliography of music bibliographies, its emphasis being on those works which themselves serve as points of departure for further investigations: lists, inventories, alphabetized compilations of facts about music. The one section which falls most conspicuously outside of this pattern of bibliographical emphasis is the section on "Histories and Chronologies." This is the only category in which books are listed for what they contain intrinsically rather than for their function as guides to further information.

In its preliminary forms this book has been put to use in a number of courses in music bibliography throughout the country, and as a result has benefited from the suggestions of several generous-minded critics. I am particularly indebted to Professor Albert T. Luper of the State University of Iowa, and to Professor Otto Albrecht of the University of Pennsylvania for their help in this respect. The form of the annotations owes much to Richard Angell of the Library of Congress, who placed his notes at my disposal. My colleagues in the Music Library of the University of California at Berkeley, Harriet Nicewonger and Minnie Elmer, have made their influence felt on nearly every page in matters that have to do with the selection of titles, the framing of the annotations, and the reading of proof. The work in its present form shows the results of the careful reading made by Frederick Freedman, and the keen editorial eye of Barbara Brown of the Free Press of Glencoe. Their assistance is gratefully acknowledged.

One feature which has been introduced for the first time in the current edition is the citation of book reviews. These are offered as practical aids to the evaluation of the items. No effort has been made to achieve complete coverage: reviews are cited only for the more recent items, and are confined largely to those published in the English-language journals.

The entries are numbered throughout this book, and, for the most part, each title is entered once. There are some instances of duplicate entries, however, when the content of the item calls for its listing in more than one category. Eitner's *Quellen-Lexikon* is a case in point. This title is entered once as a dictionary of biography, and again as a bibliography of early music.

Abbreviations are used sparingly. What they save in space in a work of this kind is rarely commensurate to the inconvenience caused to the user. They are confined to the standard symbols for the dictionaries and journals most frequently cited in reviews: *Grove's* for *Grove's Dictionary of Music and Musicians,* 5th edition; *MGG for Die Musik in Geschichte und Gegenwart; Acta M* for *Acta musicologica; JAMS* for *Journal of the American Musicological Society; MQ* for *The Musical Quarterly;* and *Notes* for *Music Library Association Notes,* 2nd series.

A bibliographer's work is never done. Even as this edition goes to press, I am troubled by the submerged voices of would-be entries which may have been overlooked, and entries which may have been misplaced or misrepresented. Other music bibliographers proceed, unconcerned, with their work, the results of which will eventually call for supplements, or even substantial revisions in our present pattern of organization. But if one were too attentive to such considerations a work of this kind would never reach the point of publication. Now that it has made its appearance, I hope that it will attract collaboration, in the form of corrections, additions, or suggestions for improvement, from all who have occasion to use it.

Vincent Duckles

CONTENTS

MUSIC REFERENCE
AND
RESEARCH MATERIALS

DICTIONARIES AND ENCYCLOPEDIAS

The most comprehensive bibliography of music dictionaries and encyclopedias is found in James B. Coover's Music Lexicography, Denver, 1958 (no. 1126), which offers some 1,335 entries. Other convenient listings appear in the article "Lexika der Musik," by Hans Heinrich Eggebrecht, in MGG, Vol. 7; in A. Hyatt King's survey in Grove's, 5th edition, Vol. 2; and in the Harvard Dictionary of Music. A useful chronological approach is found in a list by Richard Schaal, printed in the Jahrbuch der Musikwelt, 1949, pp. 104-11, and also in Hinrichsen's Music Book, Vol. 7, pp. 594-601, under the title "The Fore-Runners of the Grove-Blom."

The present list includes the most important music dictionaries and encyclopedias in current use, in all modern languages, cited as far as is possible under their latest editions. It also includes a selection of titles of those earlier works available in modern reprints, or which are of continuing value for reference purposes.

GENERAL

As "general" dictionaries and encyclopedias are cited those works in which both terms and biography are treated in the same alphabet. The prototype for such works is Johann Walther's Musikalisches Lexikon, published in 1732 (see no. 43). From this important work two lines of descent may be followed, one leading through a series of concise dictionaries, usually in one volume and intended for quick reference; the other moving in the direction of multi-volume large scale works with extended articles, more properly described as encyclopedias.

1. ABERT, HERMANN J., ed. Illustriertes Musik-Lexikon. Stuttgart, J. Engelhorns Nachf., 1927. 542 p.

A popular general dictionary, based on Riemann and Das neue Musiklexikon. 503 pictures on 72 plates, and numerous short musical examples. Contributing editors: Hermann Abert, Friedrich Blume, Rudolf Gerber, Hans Hoffmann, and Theodor Schwartzkopf.

2. ALGEMENE MUZIEKENCYCLOPEDIE, onder leiding van A. Corbet en Wouter Paap. Redactiesecretaris: J. Robijns. Antwerpen, Zuid-Nederlandse Uitg. ⌐1957-1963⌐ 6 v.

Comprehensive coverage of all aspects of music, including ethnomusicology, popular music, jazz. Brief biographies include performers, musicologists, composers, dancers. Major articles signed by contributors from England, Israeli, U.S., U.S.S.R., etc. Subject bibliographies and discographies, and brief lists of works for composers and musicologists. Valuable for wide biographical range. Illustrated.

3. ALLBORTO, RICCARDO e ALBERTO FERRARI. Dizionario di musica. Milano, Casa Editrice Ceschina ⌐1959⌐ 576 p.

A popular dictionary of terms and biography. Brief biographical entries, mentioning representative works of minor composers, giving full tabulations of works of major composers. Well printed and illustrated, 8 plates in color. No bibliographical references.

4. ARMA, PAUL et YVONNE TIÉNOT. Nouveau dictionnaire de musique. Paris, Éditions Ouvrières ⌐1947⌐ 285 p.

A "pocket" dictionary, comprising some 2,000 biographical entries and 6,000 terms. 365 illustrations and short musical examples. Brief articles and summary listings of composers' works. Table of abbreviations.

5. BLOM, ERIC. Everyman's dictionary of music. Further rev. ed. London, Dent; New York, Dutton, 1958. 687 p.

First pub. in 1946; U.S. ed., 1948; rev. ed., 1954.

A popular, quick-reference book of terms, titles, biographies. Small in size but exceptionally rich in information. Excludes living performers. Summary listings of composers' works.

Review of 1954 ed. by Vincent Duckles in Notes, 13 (1955) p. 70-72.

6. BLUME, FRIEDRICH, ed. Die Musik in Geschichte und Gegenwart. Allgemeine Enzyklopädie der Musik.... Kassel u. Basel, Bärenreiter-Verlag, 1949-

Published in fascicles: No. 97 as of July 1962. Vols. 1-10: A-PRÄF.

A comprehensive music reference work of the highest scholarly merit. German in language, but international in scope and coverage. Articles contributed by specialists throughout the world. Gives complete listings of composers' works and detailed bibliographical references. Many of the articles are full-scale monographs, and all attempt to embody the latest research. Abundant illustrative material.

Reviewed by Willi Apel in JAMS, 3 (1950) p. 142-45; 5 (1952) p. 56-57 and p. 138-39. By Charles Warren Fox in Notes, 7 (1950) p. 466-67; 10 (1953) p. 451-52; 12 (1954) p. 92-93. By Paul Henry Lang in MQ, 36 (1950) p. 141-43; 38 (1952) p. 477-79. By Kurt von Fischer in Die Musikforschung, 6 (1953) p. 260-64; 8 (1955) p. 92-96; 9 (1956) p. 331-36; 10 (1957) p. 423-28; 12 (1959) p. 338-41, the last by Hellmut Federhofer.

Publication of the 5th ed. of Grove's Dictionary in 1954 provided the occasion for some critical comparisons between Grove's and MGG. See Richard S. Hill in Notes, 12 (1954) p. 85-92, and A. Hyatt King, "Grove V and MGG," in The Monthly Musical Record, 85 (1955) p. 115-19, p. 152-57, p. 183-85.

7. BONACCORSI, ALFREDO. Nuovo dizionario musicale
Curci. Milano, Curci ⊏1954⊐ 556 p.

Emphasis on terms, forms, but with essential biographies.
Brief bibliographies for most articles, including references to
modern republications for composers.

Review in Rassegna musicale, 24 (1954) p. 389-91.

8. BORBA, TOMÁS e FERNANDO LOPES GRAÇA.
Dicionário de música, ilustrado. Lisbon Edições Cosmos,
1956. 2 v.

9. BOTTENHEIM, SAM. Prisma encyclopedie der muziek.
Bewerkt en ingeleid door Wouter Paap. ⊏2. druk⊐ Utrecht, Het
Spectrum ⊏1957⊐ 2 v.

10. COEUROY, ANDRÉ. Dictionnaire critique de la musique
ancienne et moderne. Paris, Payot, 1956. 413 p.

Primarily biographical, its chief value is in the section
"Écoles moderne" (p. 92-100): chronological lists by country,
giving brief stylistic characteristics and one or two works for
each composer. Important modern composers are entered in the
main alphabet. Appropriate cross references.

COLLINS ENCYCLOPEDIA OF MUSIC. See no. 44.

11. COOPER, MARTIN, ed. The concise encyclopedia of
music and musicians. New York, Hawthorn Books ⊏1958⊐ 516 p.

English ed.: London, Hutchinson, 1958.

12. CORTE, ANDREA DELLA e G. M. GATTI.
Dizionario di musica. 6. ed. Torino, G. B. Paravia ⊏1959⊐
724 p.

First pub. in 1926. 3rd ed., 1930. 4th ed., 1943.
5th ed., 1956.

Includes personal names, subjects, instruments, cities, covering all countries and periods, but with emphasis on Italian names and topics. Brief biographies list major works, with fair coverage of republications of old music, especially for Italian composers.

13. DICCIONARIO ENCICLOPÉDICO DE LA MÚSICA.
⊏ Dirección general: A. Albert Torrellas ⊐ Barcelona, Central Catalana de Publicaciones ⊏1947⊐ -52. 4 v.

Supersedes Diccionario de la música ilustrado, 1927-29. 2 v.

Contributors include composers and musicologists from Spain, Portugal, and Latin America.

Vol. "Terminología, technología, morfología, instrumentos." Technical terms in all languages, including Greek and Oriental (transliterated). No bibliography or indication of sources of information.

Vols. 2-3: "Biografías, bibliografía, monografías, historia, argumentos de operas." Biographies of composers, performers, musicologists, with emphasis on Spanish and South American musicians. Lists of works for major composers, classified listing for minor figures. Historical articles under names of countries. Extended articles for Spanish provinces, covering folk music, history, composers, institutions, etc. No bibliographical references.

Vol. 4: "Apéndice, por A. Albert Torrellas...."

14. DIZIONARIO RICORDI DELLA MUSICA E DEI MUSICISTI. ⊏ Direttore: Claudio Sartori; redattori: Fausto Broussard, et al. Milano ⊐ Ricordi ⊏1959⊐ 1155 p.

Wide biographical coverage, including living performers, important composers of light music, musicologists. Concise articles, excellent bibliographies and lists of compositions.

Review by Jack A. Westrup in Music and Letters, 41 (1960) p. 80-81. By James B. Coover in Notes, 17 (1960) p. 564-66.

15. DUNSTAN, RALPH. A cyclopaedic dictionary of music.... 4th ed., greatly enl. and rev. London, Philadelphia, Curwen ⌐ 1925 ⌐ 632 p.

First pub. in 1908.

Terms and biography. Very brief entries, numerous short musical illustrations. Intended for amateurs. Suffers from an excess of misleading and useless information. Numerous appendices of vocabulary, pronunciation, music theory, etc. The "Musical Bibliography" (p. 618-31) is chiefly of 19th-century works in English.

16. ENCYCLOPÉDIE DE LA MUSIQUE. ⌐ Publié sous la direction de François Michel en collaboration avec François Lesure et Vladimir Fédorov, et un comité de rédaction composé de Nadia Boulanger, et al. ⌐ Paris, Fasquelle ⌐1958-61⌐ 3 v.

Preceding the dictionary proper is a series of essays (Vol. 1, p. 1-239) devoted to general information about music in society: festivals, concerts, radio, the music press, education in France, copyright laws, institutions and associations. "Livre d'Or," p. 35-76, portraits and facsimile pages from the manuscripts of contemporary composers. Chronological table of music history, p. 203-39.

Much emphasis on ideas and principles rather than on individuals and works. Biographical articles are short. Bibliographical references, many to MGG. Lists of works for major composers. Fuller treatment of subjects. Many signed articles. Excellent illustrative material, musical and pictorial. Especially valuable for its thorough coverage of modern music.

Review by James B. Coover in Notes, 16 (1959) p. 381-83.

17. ENCYCLOPÉDIE DE LA MUSIQUE ET DICTIONNAIRE DU CONSERVATOIRE. Fondateur, Albert Lavignac, Directeur, Lionel de la Laurencie. Paris, C. Delagrave, 1913-31. 2 parts in 11 v.

Originally published in parts.

Part I: "Histoire de la musique." Part II: "Technique, Esthétique, Pédagogie."

The work was designed, in the tradition of the French encyclopedists, as a universal repository of musical knowledge. International in scope, although most of the contributors are French. Many of the studies, particularly in the history part, are full-scale monographs and rank among the most important surveys of their fields. History is treated by country. Some of the important contributors are Maurice Emmanuel, Amédée Gastoué, Oscar Chilesotti, Romain Rolland, Henry Expert, and Rafael Mitjana. Part II deals with music theory, instruction, and aesthetics in all aspects, including acoustics, notation, instrument making, choreography, institutions. Major articles by Charles Koechlin, Paul Rougnon, and Vincent d'Indy. Illustrated; numerous musical examples.

The work lacks an index, and for this reason the detailed tables of contents at the end of each part are most useful as a guide to the contents of the encyclopedia. Partial index, compiled by Robert Bruce, in Music Library Association Notes, ser. 1 (May 1936), not generally available.

18. ENCYCLOPEDIE VAN DE MUZIEK. Hoofdredactio: Louis M. G. Arntzenius ⌐ et al.⌐ Met bijzondere medwerking van J. Kunst ⌐et al.⌐ Amsterdam, Elsevier, 1956-57. 2 v.

Vol. 1: A-H; Vol. 2: I-Z.

19. GROVE, SIR GEORGE, ed. Grove's dictionary of music and musicians. 5th ed., edited by Eric Blom. London, Macmillan; New York, St. Martin's Press, 1954. 9 v.

Supplementary Volume, edited by Eric Blom, associate editor Denis Stevens, 1961. 493 p.

First pub. in 1879-89; 2nd ed., 1904-10, ed. by J. A. Fuller-Maitland; 3rd ed., 1927-28, ed. by H. C. Colles; 4th ed., 1940, ed. by H. C. Colles. A supplementary vol. to the 3rd ed. appeared in 1940, covering the period from 1928 to 1940, with new information pertaining to earlier entries. An American supplement, ed. by W. S. Pratt, pub. in 1920, and again in 1928, containing material on U. S., Canadian, and Spanish American topics.

Grove's Dictionary is the standard and most comprehensive music encyclopedia in English. It includes music history, theory and practice, instruments, terms, and biographies in one alphabet. Signed articles, bibliographies, useful lists of works for composers since Bach.

Although the 5th ed. was completely reset, expanded, and brought up to date, it falls short of MGG as a tool for scholarship; however, it holds an undisputed place as the major music reference work in English.

Review of the 5th ed. by Richard S. Hill in Notes, 12 (1954) p. 85-92; by William Glock in The Score, no. 11 (Mar. 1955) p. 53-56; by Paul Henry Lang in MQ, 41 (1955) p. 215-22; in The Times Literary Supplement, Dec. 3, 1954, p. 778 (anon.). See also A. Hyatt King, "Grove V and MGG," in The Monthly Musical Record, 85 (1955) p. 115-19, p. 152-57, p. 183-85; also corrections and additions in the Musical Times, 96 (1955) p. 591-96, p. 643-51. Review of Supplementary Volume by Vincent Duckles in Notes, 19 (1962) p. 246-47.

20. GURVIN, OLAV og Ø. ANKER, eds. Musikkleksikon. Ny revidert utg. Oslo, Dreyer ⌐1959⌐ 902 columns

First pub. in 1949.

Biography, including jazz musicians, performers, and composers. Title entries for dramatic works, familiar art songs, and folk songs. Terms. Short articles, partial lists of works, occasional bibliographical references. Popular.

21. HUGHES, RUPERT, ed. Music lovers' encyclopedia, containing a pronouncing and defining dictionary of terms, instruments, etc. ... including a key to the pronunciation of sixteen languages, many charts; an explanation of the construction of music for the uninitiated; a pronouncing biographical

dictionary; the stories of the operas; and numerous biographical and critical essays by distinguished authorities. Completely revised and newly edited by Deems Taylor and Russell Kerr. Garden City, N.Y., Garden City Books, ⸤1954⸥ 897 p.

First pub. in 1903 under the title The Musical Guide; subsequent editions in 1913, 1939.

22. JACOBS, ARTHUR. A new dictionary of music. ⸤Harmondsworth, Middlesex⸥ Penguin Books ⸤1958⸥ 416 p.

Hardcover edition with new introduction and corrections, London, Cassell, 1961.

"Another pocket dictionary for the inquiring music-lover, with brief identifications of people (mostly composers and performers), terms, operatic and other specific titles, and all sorts of musical topics. It may be well worth the money, though one wonders whether a pocket music dictionary isn't below the point of diminishing returns from excessive brevity and over-generalization." Quoted from Notes, 16 (1958) p. 68.

23. KELLER, GERARD en P. KRUSEMAN, ed. Geillustreerd muzieklexicon, onder redactie van G. Keller en Philip Kruseman, met medewerking van Sem Dresden, Wouter Hutschenruijter, Willem Landré.... 's-Gravenhage, J. P. Kruseman, 1932. 966 p.

Brief articles, bibliographical references, and lists of important works for composers. Similar to Abert (no. 1) in form and content, but useful in connection with contemporary Dutch names.

24. LAROUSSE DE LA MUSIQUE. ⸤Dictionnaire encyclopédique⸥ en 2 volumes. Publié sous la direction de Norbert Dufourcq, avec la collaboration de Félix Raugel ⸤et⸥ Armand Machabey. Paris, Larousse ⸤1957⸥ 2 v.

A handsome, beautifully illustrated dictionary. Brief but authoritative articles by international contributors. Biographies (composers, performers, musicologists, and choreographers);

title entries (operas, ballets, manuscripts); subjects (terms, places). Some emphasis on ethnomusicology. Bibliographies given in an appendix to each vol. under the same headings as the articles. Only main sources listed.

Special features: Discography and analyses (Vol. 1, p. 596-625; Vol. 2, p. 546-640). Musical examples in analytical section. Two phonorecords, "Illustrations sonores," issued with the encyclopedia in pockets: (1) Les instruments de musique (with Vol. 1); (2) Principaux termes du langage technique (with Vol. 2).

Review by Paul Henry Lang in MQ, 45 (1959) p. 120-23; by James B. Coover in Notes, 16 (1959) p. 381-83.

25. MENDEL, HERMANN. Musikalisches Converstions-Lexikon. Eine Encyklopädie der gesammten musikalischen Wissenschaften. Für Gebildete aller Stände, unter Mitwirkung der Literarischen Commission des Berliner Tonkünstlervereins .... Berlin, L. Heimann; New York, J. Schuberth, 1870-79. 11 v.

2nd edition with supplementary volume, "Ergänzungsband," Berlin, R. Oppenheim, 1880-83. 3rd edition, "Neue wohlfeile Stereotyp-Ausgabe," Leipzig, List & Francke ⌐1890-91⌐

Founded by Mendel, continued (Vols. 7-11) by August Reissmann. One of the major 19th-century general music encyclopedias. Superseded in most respects, but still useful for obscure names and earlier concepts and criticism. Partial lists of works; few bibliographical references.

26. MOORE, JOHN W. Complete encyclopaedia of music, elementary, technical, historical, biographical, vocal, and instrumental. Boston, J. P. Jewett, 1854 ⌐copyright notice, 1852⌐ 1004 p.

Appendix ... Containing Events and Information Occurring Since the Main Work was Issued. Boston, Oliver Ditson, 1875. 45 p.

The first comprehensive American dictionary, containing more than 5,000 terms, 4,000 biographical citations, 200 articles, much of which drawn from Gerber, Choron and Fayolle, Burney, Hawkins, Hogarth, Calcott, Gardiner, Busby, Hamilton, Schilling, and Fétis. Substantial additional material from Dwight's Musical Journal and the New York Musical Times. Especially rich in biographical notices of 18th- and 19th-century musicians, although somewhat weak in early Americana.

27. MOSER, HANS J. Musik Lexikon. Vierte, stark erweiterte Aufl. Hamburg, H. Sikorski, 1954. 2 v.

First pub. 1935, 2nd ed. 1943, 3rd ed. 1951.

Brief, authoritative articles, with special emphasis on bibliographies and lists of early music in new editions. Addressed to German readers, but increasingly international in scope with the later editions... The 4th edition, the first to appear in 2 vols., is extensively revised, with many new articles and with bibliographical additions.

28. MUSIIKIN TIETOKIRJA. Toimituskunta: Toivo Haapanen ⌐et al,⌐ Helsingissa, Kustannusosakeyhtio Otava ⌐1948⌐ 573 p.

Terms, subjects, operas, biographies (including performers, publishers, musicologists, many contemporary composers). Emphasis on Scandinavian musicians. Partial lists of works.

29. MUZIČKA ENCIKLOPEDIJA. ⌐Glavni redaktor: Josip Andreis⌐ Zagreb, Izdanje i naklada leksikografskog zavoda, 1958-

Vol. 1: A-J. 760 p.

Contributors: Yugoslavian musicologists. Major articles signed. Condensed biographical, extended subject articles. Well organized bibliographies and lists of works. Living performers excluded. International coverage, with emphasis on Slavic composers. Excellent in content and appearance.

30. NORLIND, TOBIAS. Allmänt musiklexikon. 2. omarbetade uppl. Stockholm, Wahlström & Widstrand ⌐1927-28⌐ 2 v.

First pub. in parts, 1912-16.

Many biographies, with full lists of compositions, including information as to dates and publishers.

31. PANUM, HORTENSE ⌐og⌐ W. BEHREND. Illustreret musikleksikon. Nyudgave under redaktion af Povl Hamburger, under medvirken af William Behrend, O. M. Sandvik, Jürgen Balzer. Kjøbenhavn, Aschehoug, 1940. 735 p.

First pub. in parts, 1924-26.

Designed for popular use. International in coverage, but with emphasis on Scandinavian names and subjects. Based principally on the 1st ed. of Norlind and the Schytte translations of Riemann.

32. PENA, JOAQUÍN. Diccionario de la música Labor; iniciado por Joaquín Pena, continuado por Higinio Anglés, con la colaboración de Miguel Querol y otros distinguidos musicólogos españoles y extrajanos. Barcelona, Labor, 1954. 2 v.

Begun in 1940 as an adaptation of Riemann, but developed as a new dictionary of music for Spanish-speaking countries. Contributors are Spanish and Spanish-American. Foreign biographies drawn from Riemann, Grove, Baker, Schmidl, etc. Covers bio-bibliography, technique, and history. Designed for professional musicians and for general use.

33. PRATT, WALDO S. The new encyclopedia of music and musicians. New and rev. ed. New York, Macmillan, 1929. 969 p.

First pub. in 1924.

Originally planned as an abridgement of the 2nd ed. of Grove's, but developed as an independent work. Arranged in 3 main alphabets: terms, biography, institutions and organizations. Appendices for bibliography, composers before 1700, and operas and oratorios produced since 1900. Covers primarily the 18th to 20th centuries, with emphasis on living musicians and the American scene. Excellent definitions of musical terms.

34. RIEMANN, HUGO. Musik-Lexikon. 12. völlig neubearbeitete Auflage in drei Bänden. Hrsg. von Wilibald Gurlitt. Mainz, B. Schott's Söhne, 1959-

Vol. 1: Personenteil, A-K, 1969. 986 p. Vol. 2: Personenteil, L-Z, 1961. 976 p.

Gurlitt's edition is the latest in the series based on Riemann's work, first pub. in 1882. The 12th edition is the first in which terms and biography are in separate alphabets: Vols. 1 and 2, "Personenteil"; Vol. 3, "Sachteil." Alfred Einstein was editor of the 9th, 10th, and 11th editions, and added much to the scope and authority of the work.

The Riemann <u>Lexikon</u> is a universal dictionary of music, covering all times and places, and incorporating fully the achievements of German musical scholarship. Superior to Moser in typography and organization, and to Baker in bibliographical coverage. Lists of works are included in the bodies of the articles; modern editions of early works, and bibliographical references, in separate paragraphs.

Riemann has been widely translated, and most of the translators have incorporated new material of national interest. The principal translations are as follows:

<u>Dictionnaire de musique</u>. Traduit d'après le 4me édition par Georges Humbert. Paris, Perrin, 1895-1902. 2me éd., Lausanne, 1913. 3me éd., entièrement refondue et augm. sous la direction de A. Schaeffner, avec la collaboration de M. Pincherle, Y. Rokseth, A. Tessier. Paris, 1931.

<u>Dictionary of Music</u>. New edition, with many additions by the author. Trans. by J. S. Shedlock. London, Augener, 1893. Later eds. in 1902 and 1908.

Muzykal'nyi slovar' ... Moskva, P. Iurgenson, 1901-04.
A Russian trans. from the 5th German edition.

Nordisk musik-lexikon, udarbeidet af H. V. Schytte.
1888-92.

Reviews of the 12th ed. by Vincent Duckles in Notes, 16
(1959) p. 240-42; by Paul Henry Lang in MQ, 45 (1959) p. 563-66;
by Hans H. Eggebrecht in Die Musikforschung, 12 (1959) p. 221-
23; by Charles Van den Borren in Revue belge de musicologie, 14
(1960) p. 137-38.

35. SCHILLING, GUSTAV. Encyclopädie der gesammten
musikalischen Wissenschaften; oder, Universal-Lexikon der
Tonkunst .... Stuttgart, F. H. Köhler, 1835-38. 6 v.

Supplement-Band, hrsg. von G. Schilling, 1842.

A comprehensive work, with emphasis on the subject aspects,
but including numerous biographies displaced or reduced in later
compilations.

36. SCHOLES, PERCY A. The concise Oxford dictionary of
music. London, New York, Oxford Univ. Press, 1952. 655 p.

Primarily a reduction of the Oxford Companion (no. 37).
Includes "some hundreds of short biographical entries for vocal
and instrumental performers and conductors ... and some
hundreds of entries concerning individual compositions." About
10,000 short entries, 3,500 biographical.

Review by Charles Warren Fox in Notes, 9 (1952) p. 605-06.

37. SCHOLES, PERCY A. The Oxford companion to music.
9th ed., completely rev. and reset and with many additions to text
and illustrations. London, New York, Oxford Univ. Press, 1955.
1195 p.

First pub. in 1938.

Intended for the general reader. The <u>Companion</u> is a one-man encyclopedia, unified by the compiler's opinions, tastes, and interests, which are always stimulating but occasionally provincial. Especially strong in articles on the sociology of music, and in a number of special approaches overlooked by most music reference works (e. g. "Misattributed Compositions," "Nicknamed Compositions"). Detailed cross references, but no bibliographies. The bibliographical supplement issued with the 1940 edition has not been reprinted. See no. 375.

Review of the 8th ed. by Charles Warren Fox, in <u>Notes</u>, 8 (1950) p. 177-78; of the 9th ed. by Vincent Duckles, in <u>Notes</u>, 13 (1955) p. 70-72.

38. SOHLMANS MUSIKLEXIKON: Nordiskt och allmänt uppslagsverk för tonkonst, musikliv och dans. Redaktion: Gösta Morin, Carl-Allan Moberg, Einar Sundström. Stockholm, Sohlmanns Förlag ⌐1948-52⌐ 4 v.

Contributors include leading Scandinavian musicologists. Biography, title entries for operas, ballets, etc., subject entries for persons, places, institutions. Good lists of works; bibliographies somewhat uneven. Wide biographical coverage, especially for living performers. Many portraits.

39. SVENSSON, SVEN E. E. Bonniers illustrerade musiklexikon. Under medverkan av Erik Noreen. Stockhohm, A. Bonnier ⌐1946⌐ 1379 p.

Popular, well-illustrated, universal in coverage, but with emphasis on Scandinavian names, especially performers. Bibliographical references.

40. THOMPSON, OSCAR, ed. The international cyclopedia of music and musicians .... 8th ed. rev., edited by Nicolas Slonimsky. New York, Dodd, Mead, 1958. 2397 p.

First pub. in 1939.

The best one-volume general dictionary of music in English. A strong list of contributors, with extended signed articles for major persons and subjects. Large number of title entries.

Particularly valuable for detailed lists of works by major composers, given in tabulated form. Some unevenness in treatment.
Three appendices: 1. plots of some 200 operas, arranged
alphabetically by title; 2. pronouncing guide to names of
composers and titles; 3. bibliography of some 3,500 books on
music, arranged in dictionary order by author and subject.

Review of the 5th ed. by Charles Warren Fox, in Notes, 7
(1950) p. 291-92.

41. TONKONSTEN; Internationellt musiklexikon. Stockholm,
Nordiska Uppslagsböcker ⊏1956-57⊐ 2 v.

Popular, illustrated dictionary giving pronunciations of
foreign names, lists of works and bibliographies for major composers, bibliographical references on important topics. Covers
popular music. Many title entries for operas, ballets, musical
comedy, songs. Signed articles by Scandinavian contributors.

42. TSCHIERPE, RUDOLPH. Kleines Musiklexikon. Mit
systematischen Übersichten und zahlreichen Notenbeispielen. ⊏5.
durchgesehene und ergänzte Aufl.⊐ Hamburg, Hoffmann und
Camps ⊏1955⊐ 412 p.

First pub. in 1946.

An excellent small general dictionary. Brief but inclusive.
Representative works listed for major composers. Bibliographical references, chiefly to German literature. Special tables
illustrating dance forms, theory, and history. An appendix lists
major writers on music, with their fields of specialization; another is a title listing of operas, operettas, oratorios, choral and
orchestral works.

43. WALTHER, JOHANN G. Musikalisches Lexikon, oder
musikalische Bibliothek (1732). Faksimile-Nachdruck, hrsg. von
Richard Schaal. Kassel und Basel, Bärenreiter-Verlag, 1953.
659 p., 22 fold. plates. (Documenta musicologica. Erste
Reihe, 3)

A facsimile edition of the prototype for all general dictionaries of music. Walther's Lexikon (1732) established the pattern
developed in Riemann, Moser, and other modern dictionaries,
and, in itself, constitutes a primary source of information about
late baroque musical knowledge and practice.

44. WESTRUP, JACK A. and F. L. HARRISON. The new
college encyclopedia of music. New York, Norton ⌐1960⌐ 739 p.

Pub. in England, 1959, under the title Collins Encyclopedia
of Music.

A popular "student" dictionary. Detailed summaries of
works for major composers, fields of activity for minor ones.
References to early works republished in standard historical
editions or anthologies. Technical articles with musical illustrations. Title entries for repertory works, instrumental and
vocal. Selective bibliographies, primarily English. British
pronunciations.

Review by James B. Coover in Notes, 17 (1960) p. 564-66.

45. ZENEI LEXIKON, a zenetörténet es zenetudomány
enciklopédiája ... szerkeszttették Szabolcsi Bence es Tóth Aladár.
Budapest, Gyözö Andor, 1930-31. 2 v.

A general music encyclopedia, with major articles, signed by
outstanding musicologists, Hungarian and foreign. Long articles
on national music, forms, music for various instruments.
Biographical articles discuss major works, list others by
category. Short bibliographies.

BIOGRAPHY, INTERNATIONAL

Here are listed dictionaries and encyclopedias, international in
coverage, in which the emphasis is exclusively or mainly on
persons engaged in activities related to music — composers,
performers, scholars, critics, impresarios, etc. The line which
separates biographical dictionaries from volumes of collected

biography is a rather arbitrary one. The distinction is essentially one between works with numerous brief entries, alphabetically arranged, and works which can be described as collections of essays on a fairly limited group of musicians. Works in the latter category have been excluded, and for this reason the user will not find entries for such titles as Donald Brook's Masters of the Keyboard (London, 1947), or his Singers of Today (London, 1949), David Ewen's Dictators of the Baton (New York, 1943), and Madeleine Goss's Modern Music-Makers (New York, 1952).

46. BAKER, THEODORE. Baker's biographical dictionary of musicians. 5th ed. Completely revised by Nicolas Slonimsky. New York, G. Schirmer ⌐1958⌐ 1855 p.

First pub. in 1900. Subsequent eds. in 1919 and 1940.

By far the best biographical dictionary in English. A standard work from its beginning. Through the 3rd ed. early figures were treated briefly, with references to Grove and Eitner. For the 4th ed. these biographies were rewritten as independent articles (by Gustave Reese, Gilbert Chase, and Robert Geiger). The 5th ed. has been greatly enlarged and carefully checked for accuracy. Baker treats musicians in all categories. Long lists of works. Outstanding bibliographical coverage.

Review of the 5th ed. by Brooks Shepard Jr. in Notes, 16 (1959) p. 239-40; by Philip L. Miller in MQ, 45 (1959) p. 255-58.

47. CHORON, ALEXANDRE É. et F. J. M. FAYOLLE. Dictionnaire historique des musiciens, artistes et amateurs, morts ou vivans, qui se sont illustrés en une partie quelconque de la musique et des arts qui y sont relatifs. ... Précédé d'un sommaire de l'histoire de la musique. Paris, Valade, 1810-11. 2 v.

Another printing, 1817.

The first French biographical dictionary of importance. International in scope. Partial lists of works for major composers. A valuable guide to early 19th-century musical opinion.

Translated and expanded in English in A Dictionary of Musicians, 1824 (see no. 49). "Sommaire de l'histoire de la musique," p. xi-xcii.

48. A DICTIONARY OF MODERN MUSIC AND MUSICIANS. Ed. by Arthur Eaglefield-Hull. London, J. M. Dent; New York, E. P. Dutton, 1924. 543 p.

Primarily biographical, although there are entries for terms related to modern music. For the period c. 1880-1920, the best international coverage of any dictionary of its time. Written with the aid of numerous foreign collaborators. Comprehensive lists of works and bibliographies about composers. Includes composers, publishers, musicologists, organizations, new instruments, and terms.

For German translation and expansion, see no. 66.

49. A DICTIONARY OF MUSICIANS, from the earliest ages to the present time, comprising the most important biographical contents of the works of Gerber, Choron and Fayolle, Count Orloff, Dr. Burney, Sir John Hawkins, etc. Together with upwards of a hundred original memoirs of the most eminent living musicians, and a summary of the history of music. London, Sainsbury, 1824. 2 v.

Reprinted in 1827.

Largely a trans. of Choron and Fayolle (no. 47), including the "Summary of the History of Music," with substantial additions of English musicians. The first major biographical dictionary of musicians in English. The tone is popular and anecdotal but furnishes an excellent picture of contemporary taste and opinion. Compiler unknown, although the work has been attributed to the publisher, John Sainsbury.

50. EITNER, ROBERT. Biographisch-bibliographisches Quellen-Lexikon der Musiker und Musikgelehrten der christlichen Zeitrechnung bis zur Mitte des 19. Jahrhunderts .... Leipzig, Breitkopf & Härtel, 1900-04. 10 v.

Reprint, photo-offset, by Musurgia, New York, 1947.

"2. verbesserte Auflage, " Graz, Akademische Druck-u. Verlagsanstalt, 1959-60. This is a reprint of the original work with additional marginal references to the Miscellanea musicae bio-bibliographica, which is reprinted with the "Nachträge" in volume 11. 11 volumes in 6.

Supplemented by Miscellanea musicae bio-bibliographica (no. 63) and by G. Radiciotti's "Aggiunte e correzioni ai dizionari biografici dei musicisti" (no. 68).

Eitner's Quellen-Lexikon is mainly a bibliography of sources, but it does contain biographical information, often useful with respect to obscure names.

Also entered as no. 645.

51. THE ETUDE MUSIC MAGAZINE. Portraits of the world's best-known musicians, an alphabetical collection of notable musical personalities of the world, covering the entire history of music. Compiled and edited by Guy McCoy. Philadelphia, Presser ⌐1946⌐ 251 p.

Portraits and brief identifications of 4, 748 composers, performers, and others, largely reprinted from Etude, 1932-40. Geographical index of American names.

One of the few dictionaries of its kind. Of limited value, since the portraits are reproduced at little more than postage-stamp size.

52. EWEN, DAVID. Composers of today, a comprehensive biographical and critical guide to modern composers of all nations. 2nd ed. New York, H. W. Wilson, 1936. 332 p.

First pub. in 1934.

Brief biographies, critical discussion and classified lists of the principal works for about 200 living composers. Portraits. Lists of recordings.

Superseded by nos. 54 and 117.

53. EWEN, DAVID. Composers of yesterday, a biographical and critical guide to the most important composers of the past. New York, H. W. Wilson, 1937. 488 p.

Biographies, lists of works, bibliographies, lists of recordings, and portraits of about 200 composers from Dunstable to the end of the 19th century. Selected on the basis of current acceptance or importance in music history.

54. EWEN, DAVID. European composers today; a biographical and critical guide. New York, H. W. Wilson, 1954. 200 p.

A companion volume to the previously published American Composers Today (no. 117); together, these two volumes replace Composers of Today (no. 52).

Review by Frank C. Campbell, in Notes, 11 (1954) p. 476.

55. EWEN, DAVID. Living musicians. New York, H. W. Wilson, 1940. 390 p.

First Supplement ..., 1957.

A dictionary of performers, especially American or active in America. Portraits. The supplement contains biographies of 147 musicians who have come into prominence since 1940.

56. FÉTIS, FRANÇOIS J. Biographie universelle des musiciens et bibliographie générale de la musique. 2me éd. Paris, Firmin Didot Fréres, 1866-70. 8 v.

Supplément et complément, pub. sous la direction de M. Arthur Pougin. Paris, 1878-80. 2 v.

First pub. in 1835-44, Fétis' work was a tremendous scholarly achievement for its time. Contains a vast amount of biographical and bibliographical material, complete lists of works, occasionally annotated lists of books about composers. Although outdated and marred by personal bias, it remains a useful starting point for research, since it brings together materials from the earlier stages of musicology.

57. GERBER, ERNST LUDWIG. Historisch-biographisches Lexikon der Tonkünstler, welches Nachrichten von dem Leben und Werken musikalischer Schriftsteller, berühmter Componisten, Sänger, etc. ... enthält. Leipzig, J. G. I. Breitkopf, 1790-92. 2 v.

(See no. 58.)

58. GERBER, ERNST LUDWIG. Neues historisch-biographisches Lexikon der Tonkünstler .... Leipzig, A. Kühnel, 1812-14. 4 v.

Gerber's lexika are early biographical dictionaries of great historical importance. The compiler developed the biographical content of Walther's Lexikon (no. 43) to produce the first full-scale dictionary of musical biography. The 4-vol. edition of 1812-14 does not supersede the earlier 2-vol. work.

59. HUGHES, RUPERT. The biographical dictionary of musicians. Originally compiled by Rupert Hughes, completely revised and newly edited by Deems Taylor and Russell Kerr. Over 8500 entries, together with a pronouncing dictionary of given names and titles and a key to the pronunciation of sixteen languages. New York, Blue Ribbon Books, 1940. 481 p.

A popular reference work. Brief entries with representative works for composers. Useful for abundance of obscure performers entered.

60. THE INTERNATIONAL WHO IS WHO IN MUSIC. Fifth (mid-century) edition. J. T. H. Mize, editor-in-chief. Chicago, Who is who in music ⌐1951⌐ 576 p.

Biographies, with portraits, of persons active in music, including educators, musicologists, private teachers, performers. Not strictly international, since the emphasis is on musicians active or well known in the U.S. Contains a number of supplementary lists and directories, e.g. the principal symphony orchestras in the U.S., Canada, and other countries. Strongly directed toward the commercial aspects of music.

61. INTERNATIONAL WHO'S WHO IN MUSIC AND MUSICAL
GAZETTEER, a contemporary biographical dictionary and a
record of the world's musical activity, edited by Cesar
Saerchinger. New York, Current Literature Pub. Co., 1918.
861 p.

Contains a geographical index and directory of schools and
organizations now only of historical interest, but the biographical
section is still useful for minor figures of the first two decades of
the century. Composers, performers, critics, musicologists,
teachers — their educations, activities, principal works,
addresses.

62. MERSEBURGER, CARL W. Kurzgefasstes
Tonkünstlerlexikon für Musiker und Freunde der Musik.
Begründet von Paul Frank ⌐pseud.⌐ Neu bearbeitet und ergänzt
von Wilhelm Altmann. 14. stark erweiterte Auflage. Regensburg,
G. Bosse, 1936. 730 p.

First pub. in 1860 as P. Frank, Kleines Tonkünstlerlexikon.
Title varies slightly.

Extremely wide coverage but with very brief data. Over
18,000 entries, including composers, librettists, performers,
musicologists. Many minor figures. No lists of works or
bibliographical references. Useful for quick reference.

63. MISCELLANEA MUSICAE BIO-BIBLIOGRAPHICA ...
hrsg. von H. Springer, M. Schneider und W. Wolffheim. 2., um
einen Anhang vermehrte Auflage. New York, Musurgia, 1947.
435 p.

Reprinted in v. 11 of the Akademische Druck-u.
Verlagsanstalt 2. verbesserte Auflage of Eitner's Quellen-
Lexikon, which also contains marginal numerical references to
the Miscellanea.

Originally published by Breitkopf & Härtel in quarterly
issues, 1912/13-1914/16, with an annual index for each of the 3
years covered. Provides corrections and additions to all the
kinds of information in the Quellen-Lexikon (no. 50).

The Musurgia reprint also includes Radiciotti's emendations (no. 68).

64. LES MUSICIENS CÉLÉBRES. ⸢Publié sous la direction de Jean Lacroix.... ⸣ Genève, L. Mazenod ⸢1946⸣ 358 p.

Also pub. in German, under the title Die berühmten Musiker. Genève, 1946.

An "art" publication, chiefly valuable for the fine full-page portraits of musicians it contains. 66 individual biographies and several group articles, chronologically arranged. P. 293-343: brief identifications of other composers.

65. MUSIKENS HVEN-HVAD-HVOR. Udarbejdet af Nelly Backhausen og Axel Kjerulf. København, Politikens Forlag, 1950. 3 v.

Vol. 1: "Musikhistorie." Chronology from antiquity to 1900, with composer index.

Vols. 2-3: Biographies (composers, performers, musicologists) indicating activities and principal works.

Vol. 3, p. 143-414: Title list of 15,000 entries, including operas, repertory works, many popular and musical comedy songs, folksongs. For each, identification, composer, and date if known.

66. DAS NEUE MUSIKLEXIKON, nach dem Dictionary of Modern Music and Musicians, hrsg. von A. Eaglefield-Hull, übersetzt und bearb. von Alfred Einstein. Berlin, M. Hesse, 1926. 729 p.

A German translation of no. 48, with many additions and corrections by Einstein. Most of the information in this revision is incorporated in the 11th edition of Riemann.

67. PRIEBERG, FRED K. Lexikon der neuen Musik. Freiburg & München, K. Alber, 1958. 495 p.

Primarily biographical, but with a few articles on aspects of and trends in contemporary music (film music, radio operas, polytonality, 12-tone music, musique concrète, etc.). Factual rather than critical, covering education, activities, and principal works of 20th-century composers working in modern idioms.

68. RADICIOTTI, GIUSEPPE. "Aggiunte e correzioni ai dizionari biografici dei musicisti." In Sammelbände der Internationalen Musikgesellschaft, 14 (1914) p. 551-67; 15 (1915) p. 566-86

Corrections and additions to Eitner's Quellen-Lexikon (no. 50) with emphasis on Italian composers.

Reprinted with the Miscellanea musicae bio-bibliographica (no. 63) in the Musurgia edition of the Quellen-Lexikon (1947) p. 397-435, and in Vol. 11 of the Akademische Druck-u. Verlagsanstalt, 2. verbesserte Auflage, 1960 (no. 50).

69. SCHMIDL, CARLO. Dizionario universale dei musicisti. Milano, Sonzogno ⌐1928?-29⌐ 2 v.

Supplemento, 1938. 806 p.

Best bio-bibliography in Italian, and best general bio-bibliography for Italian musicians. Emphasis on Italian composers, librettists, and performers, with full articles on well-known persons, brief accounts of minor ones. Dates of first production of dramatic works. Lists of works, including modern republications. A significant feature is articles on Italian literary figures and their relations to music. All forenames are Italianized.

70. YOUNG, PERCY M. Biographical dictionary of composers, with classified list of music for performance and study. New York, Crowell, 1954. 381 p.

Pub. in England under the title A Critical Dictionary of Composers and their Music. London, Dobson, 1954.

Selective list of some 500 composers. Brief critical surveys of each, titles of representative works, and references to further sources of information, usually in English. Intended for the "general student" rather than the specialist.

BIOGRAPHY, NATIONAL

Any dictionary of musical biography may be expected to be strongest in names within its own language group. There are also numerous biographical dictionaries devoted especially to the musicians of individual countries. Only the most important are listed here, with emphasis on recent, currently available publications. Nineteen countries or groups of countries are represented:

Austria, No. 71	Latin America, Nos. 98-100
Belgium, Nos. 72, 73	Poland, Nos. 101, 102
Canada, No. 74	Portugal, Nos. 103-106
England, Nos. 75-78	Russia, Nos. 107-109
France, No. 79	Scandinavia, No. 110
Germany, Nos. 80-87	Spain, No. 111
Holland, Nos. 88-90	Switzerland, Nos. 112-14
Hungary, No. 91	United States, Nos. 115-32
Israel, Nos. 92-95	Yugoslavia, No. 133
Italy, Nos. 96, 97	

Austria

71. STEIRISCHES MUSIKLEXIKON. Im Auftrage des Steirischen Tonkünstlerbundes unter Benützung der "Sammlung Wamlek" bearb. und hrsg. von W. Suppan. Graz, Akademische Druck- und Verlagsanstalt, 1962-

1. Lieferung (1962): A-E.

A biographical dictionary of musicians associated with Graz and other parts of Steirmark. Comprehensive for pre-1800 names; selective for post-1800. Good bibliographical coverage for composers' works and writings on the musicians.

Belgium

72. HEMEL, VICTOR VAN. Voorname Belgische toonkunstenaars uit de 18de, 19de, en 20ste eeuw. Derde bijgewerkte druk. Antwerpen, Cupido-Uitgave ⌐1958⌐ 84 p.

Short biographies of 101 musicians of Belgian descent.

73. VANNES, RENÉ. Dictionnaire des musiciens (compositeurs) ... avec la collaboration de André Souris. Bruxelles, Maison Larcier ⌐1947⌐ 443 p.

Belgian composers from the 15th century to 1830, with comprehensive lists of works published or in manuscript, and references to other sources of information.

Comments by Richard S. Hill in Notes, 6 (1949) p. 607-08.

Canada

74. CANADIAN BROADCASTING CORPORATION. Catalogue of Canadian composers; edited by Helmut Kallmann. Rev. and enl. ed. ⌐Ottawa, 1952?⌐ 254 p.

First published in 1947.

356 brief biographical sketches, giving activities, education, addresses. Listings of works as complete as possible, giving titles, dates of publication, mediums, durations, publishers. Works in manuscript included. List of Canadian publishers and composers' organizations.

England

75. BROWN, JAMES D. and STEPHEN S. STRATTON. British musical biography: a dictionary of musical artists, authors and composers, born in Britain and its colonies. Birmingham, Stratton, 1897. 462 p.

Emphasis on composers living at the time of publication. Great masters treated briefly to afford room for the obscure. Includes a large number of English musicians about whom information cannot be found elsewhere, with excellent bibliographies.

76. PALMER, RUSSELL. British music. London, Skelton Robinson, 1948. 283 p.

"Biographical index of contemporary British musicians and musical organizations," p. 17-255. Portraits.

77. PULVER, JEFFREY. A biographical dictionary of old English music. London, Kegan Paul; New York, Dutton, 1927. 537 p.

English musicians active from about 1200 to the death of Purcell (1695). Cites manuscript sources, contemporary publications, and occasionally modern editions. Somewhat discursive in style, with lists of works scattered through the bodies of the articles, but a useful starting point for the study of early English musicians. See also the author's companion volume covering old English musical terms (no. 189).

78. WHO'S WHO IN MUSIC. Edited by David Simmons. 4th ed. London, Shaw; New York, Hafner, 1962. 331 p.

First published in 1935; 2nd ed., 1937, edited by Sir Landon Ronald; 3rd ed., edited by L. G. Pine, 1949-50.

Primarily devoted to British music and musicians; includes articles on various British musical organizations and many helpful lists (publishers, periodicals, etc.) in the "directory" section. "Overseas section," p. 311-28, is devoted to foreign music publishers, festivals, retailers, wholesalers, manufacturers, agents, orchestras, opera companies. In the 3rd edition the "overseas section" is much more extensive, containing biographical notices of foreign musicians, p. 315-87.

France

79. DICTIONNAIRE DES MUSICIENS FRANCAIS. [Paris] Seghers, 1961. 379 p. (Dictionnaires Seghers, 3)

A pocket, illustrated, dictionary of French musicians. Coverage is selective, particularly as regards contemporary figures. Brief summaries of the major works of composers; no full listings; no bibliographies.

Germany

80. FELLERER, KARL G., ed. Rheinische Musiker. 1.
Folge. Köln, Arno Volk Verlag, 1960. 276 p. (Beiträge zur
rheinischen Musikgeschichte, 43)

2. Folge. Köln, Arno Volk Verlag, 1962. 112 p. (Beiträge
zur rheinischen Musikgeschichte, 53)

The first two of a projected series of volumes giving biographical and bibliographical information on musicians of the
Rhineland. Each volume is alphabetically complete, and a final
index volume will bring all the entries together. The work follows
the pattern established by Mattheson's Grundlage einer Ehren-
Pforte (1740) in that most of the biographies for living musicians
are self-compiled.

The first volume cites 91 musicians, with brief biographical
sketches and full bibliographical information. The second volume
treats 58 names.

81. FEY, HERMANN. Schleswig-Holsteinische Musiker,
von den ältesten Zeiten bis zur Gegenwart; ein Heimatbuch.
Hamburg, C. Holler ⌐1922⌐ 126 p.

Dictionary arrangement. Full bibliographies of compositions,
with authority references.

82. KOSSMALY, KARL und C. H. HERZEL. Schlesisches
Tonkünstler Lexikon, enthaltend die Biographieen schlesischen
Ton künstler, Componisten, Cantoren, Organisten, Tongelehrten,
Textdichter, Orgelbauer, Instrumentenmacher, hrsg. von
Kossmaly & Carlo ⌐pseud.⌐ Breslau, E. Trewendt, 1846-47.
332 p.

Issued in 4 parts, each in a separate alphabet. Long articles,
giving classified lists of compositions, roles for performers,
concert programs.

83. KÜRSCHNERS DEUTSCHER MUSIKER-KALENDER.
2. Ausg. des Deutschen Musiker-Lexikons. Herausgeber:
Hedwig und E. H. Müller von Asow. Berlin, W. de Gruyter,
1954. 1702 col.

First ed., 1929. See no. 87.

Biographies of living German, Austrian, and Swiss musicians
in all categories, and German-born musicians in foreign
countries. Entries give essential biographical information and
detailed lists of works. Excessive abbreviations. Index by date
of birth (1854-1939) and necrology, 1929-54.

84. KÜRSCHNERS BIOGRAPHISCHES THEATER-
HANDBUCH. Schauspiel, Oper, Film, Rundfunk: Deutschland,
Österreich, Schweiz. Hrsg. von Herbert A. Frenzel und Hans
J. Moser. Berlin, W. de Gruyter, 1956. 840 p.

Names, addresses, activities of singers, music directors,
actors, critics, dancers, choreographers, composers, librarians
of theater collections, etc. Entries are for persons living as
of 1956.

85. LEDEBUR, CARL F. H. W. P. J., FREIHERR VON.
Tonkünstler-Lexicon Berlins von den ältesten Zeiten bis auf die
Gegenwart. Berlin, L. Rauh, 1861. 704 p.

Entries for composers, publishers, performers, dilettantes,
born or active in Berlin, with detailed bibliographies of
compositions.

86. LIPOWSKY, FELIX J. Baierisches Musik-Lexikon.
München, J. Giel, 1811. 338 ⌐i.e. 438⌐ p.

An early dictionary of some historical importance of Bavarian
composers and performers. Lists of major compositions.
Occasional title-page transcriptions.

87. MÜLLER, ERICH H., ed. Deutsches Musiker-Lexikon.
Dresden, W. Limpert, 1929. ⌐862⌐ p. 1642 cols.

Preceded Kürschners ..., no. 83.

Living German musicians and foreign musicians active in German concert life: composers, performers, conductors, teachers, scholars. Full lists of works, published and unpublished.

Holland

88. GREGOIR, G. J. Biographie des artistes-musiciens néerlandais des XVIIIe et XIXe siècles, et des artistes étranges résidant ou ayant résidé en Néerlande à la même époque. Anvers, L. Dela Montagne, 1864. 238 p.

Brief biographies of Netherlands musicians. Careers summarized, major works mentioned for composers, but no full listings.

89. LETZER, J. H. Muzikaal Nederland, 1850-1910. Bio-bibliographisch woordenboek ... 2. uitgaaf met aanvullingen en verbeteringen. Utrecht, J. L. Beijers, 1913. 201 p., with 10 p. of additions

Composers, musicologists, performers, etc., active in Holland 1850-1910. Biographies, lists of works, occasionally dates of first performance.

90. STRAETEN, EDMOND VANDER. La musique aux pays-bas avant le XIXe siècle. Documents inédits et annotés. Compositeurs, virtuoses, théoriciens, luthiers; opéras, motets, airs nationaux, académies, maîtrises, livres, portraits, etc. Bruxelles, C. Muquardt, 1867-88. 8 v.

Vols. 2-7 published by G. A. Van Trigt; Vol. 8 by Schott.

Not strictly a biographical dictionary, but an invaluable collection of documents, transcripts of records, biographical and bibliographical notes related to the activities of Flemish musicians (Dutch and Belgian). Vol. 6 is devoted to Flemish musicians in Italy; Vols. 7-8, to Flemish musicians in Spain. Full of information of the greatest interest to students of early European music.

Hungary

91. MOLNÁR, IMRE. A magyar muzsika könyve, szerkesztette Molnár Imre .... Budapets, Merkantil-Nyomda, 1936. 632 p.

Institutions, organizations, and biographical entries for composers, performers, and other musicians.

Israel (and Jewish Musicians in General)

92. GRADENWITZ, PETER. Music and musicians in Israel; a comprehensive guide to modern Israeli music. Tel Aviv, Israeli Music Publications, 1959. 226 p.

Biographies, varying in length, of about 60 composers, grouped by school or tendency. Appendix, p. 133-63, contains an alphabetical listing of composers and their works, but without reference to the biographies. Also given is a list of publishers, and a group of publishers' catalogs.

93. SALESKI, GDAL. Famous musicians of Jewish origin. New York, Bloch, 1949. 716 p.

Informal biographies, classified according to type of activity: composers, conductors, violinists, etc. About 400 entries. Portraits. No bibliographies, but major works are mentioned in the bodies of the articles. p. 680-716: Israeli musicians.

94. STENGEL, THEODORE und HERBERT GERIGK. Lexikon der Juden in der Musik, mit einim Titelverzeichnis jüdischer Werke. Berlin, B. Hahnefeld, 1941. 404 p.

First published in 1940, Berlin. 380 p.

Among the more shameful products of German National Socialism were dictionaries of Jewish musicians compiled to further the purposes of anti-Semitism. This and no. 95 may be mentioned as examples of their kind.

95. GIRSCHNER, OTTO. Repetitorium der Musikgeschichte. Elfte Auflage. Köln, P. J. Tonger, 1941. 380 p.

A question-answer survey of music history.

P. 350-411: "Juden in der Musik," a biographical supplement first introduced in the 9th ed., 1936.

Italy

96. ANGELIS, ALBERTO DE. L'Italia musicale d'oggi. Dizionario dei musicisti: compositori, direttori d'orchestra, concertisti, insegnanti, liutai, cantanti, scrittori musicali, librettisti, editori musicali, ecc. 3. ed. corredate di una appendice. Roma, Ausonia, 1928. 523, 221 p.

Earlier editions: 1918, 1922.

Living Italian musicians, with comprehensive lists of works.

97. DAMERINI, ADELMO. Musicisti toscani; scritti di G. Barblan et al 10-20 settembre 1955, a cura di Adelmo Damerini e Franco Schlitzer. Siena ⌐Ticci⌐ 1955. 81 p.

A publication of the Accademia musicale chigiana.

Latin America

98. MARIZ, VASCO. Dicionário bio-bibliográfico musical (brasileiro e internacional). Pref. de Renato Almeida. Rio de Janeiro, Livraria Kosmos, 1948. 246 p.

Brief biographies of the best-known musical figures since the Renaissance, including performers. Useful for Brazilian musicians. Living persons included.

99. MAYER-SERRA, OTTO. Música y músicos de Latinoamérica. México, Editorial Atlante, 1947. 2 v.

Primarily biographical, although terms, dance forms, instruments are included. Listings of composers' works vary from brief accounts to full tabulations for major composers. Portraits.

100. PAN AMERICAN UNION. MUSIC SECTION. Composers of the Americas, biographical data and catalogs of their works. ⌐Washington, D.C., 1955⌐-

6 vols. to 1962.

Each vol. contains from 4 to 16 names, alphabetically arranged, with brief biographies in English and Spanish, portraits, pages from scores, sometimes autographs. Works are given chronologically within principal mediums, with date of composition, duration, publisher, and recordings if any. Manuscripts included.

Poland

101. CHYBÍNSKI, ADOLF. Słownik muzyków dawnej polski do roku 1800. Kraków ⸤Polskie wydawnictwo muzyczne, 1949⸥ 163 p.

Biographical dictionary of Polish musicians (composers and performers) active in Poland to 1800. Brief articles, mentioning principal works. List of references for each entry. Preface discusses sources of information: Fétis, Eitner, many Polish publications and official records.

102. SOWÍNSKI, WOJCIECH. Les musiciens polonais et slaves, anciens et modernes; dictionnaire biographique .... Précédé d'un résumé de l'histoire de la musique en Pologne .... Paris, A. Le Clerc, 1857. 599 p.

Another edition, in Polish, pub. in 1874.

"Résumé de l'histoire de la musique en Pologne," p. 1-44. "Anciens instruments de musique chez les polonais et les slaves," p. 45-58. Long biographical articles, with full bibliographies for important composers.

Portugal

103. AMORIM, EUGÉNIO. Dicionário biográfico de músicos do norte de Portugal. ⸤Porto⸥ Edições Maranus ⸤1935⸥ 110 p.

Chiefly 19th-century and living composers and performers. Some extended articles, with compositions listed in body of text.

104. MAZZA, JOSÉ. Dicionário biográfico de músicos portugueses, com prefácio e notas de José Augusto Alegria .... ⌐ Lisboa, 1945? ⌐ 103 p.

"Extraido da revista, Ocidente, 1944/45."

A dictionary compiled around 1790 and preserved in a manuscript in the Biblioteca Publica de Évora. Arranged by Christian names; many names of members of religious orders. The dictionary occupies p. 13-40; additional biographical information supplied by the editor from other sources, p. 41-103.

105. VASCONCELLOS, JOAQUIM A. DA FONSECA E. Os musicos portuguezes. Biographia-bibliographia. Porto, Imprensa portugueza, 1870. 2 v.

Long biographical articles, lists and discussions of compositions. Useful for early names, library locations of manuscripts, etc. Discussions of operas include dates and places of first performance. References to authorities.

106. VIEIRA, ERNESTO. Diccionario biographico de musicos portuguezes; historia e bibliographia da musica em Portugal. Lisboa, Moreira & Pinheiro, 1900 ⌐i.e. 1900-04⌐ 2 v.

More inclusive than Vasconcellos (no. 105). Comprehensive lists of works for important composers. Vol. 2 includes supplementary material and a chronological index.

Russia

107. BOELZA, IGOR F. Handbook of Soviet musicians. London, Pilot Press ⌐1944⌐ 101 p.

First printing in 1943.

40 short biographies. Portraits. A separate bibliographical section listing each composer's works. English titles. Dates given when known.

108. SOVETSKIE KOMPOZITORY, kratkiĭ biograficheskiĭ spravochnik. Sostaviteli: G. Bernandt i A. Dolzhanskiĭ. Moskva, Sovetskii Kompozitor, 1957. 696 p.

Short biographical sketches of 1,072 composers, with a full listing of compositions arranged by medium, with dates of first performance for large works. Listings of literary works by the musicians where applicable.

Review by Fred K. Prieberg in Musical America, 78 (July 1958) p. 28-29.

109. VODARSKY-SHIRAEFF, ALEXANDRIA. Russian composers and musicians, a biographical dictionary. New York, H. W. Wilson, 1940. 158 p.

Brief biographies of outstanding figures: composers, performers, teachers, critics. Classified lists of major works, and bibliographical references. Cross references to variant spellings of Russian names.

Scandinavia

110. SUNDELIN, TORSTEN. Norrländskt musikliv. Uppsala, Almqvist & Wiksell, 1946. 358 p.

Spain

111. ALCAHALÍ Y DE MOSQUERA, JOSÉ MARÍA RUIZ DE LIHORI Y PARDINES, BARÓN DE. La música en Valencia. Diccionario biográfico y crítico .... Valencia, Domenech, 1903. 445 p.

Biographies of widely varying length, with summary lists of works for important composers. Under "Anónimos," p. 39-170, the compiler enters into long literary digressions concerning liturgical drama, dance music, military music, etc., with extensive musical examples.

Switzerland

112. REFARDT, EDGAR. Historisch-biographisches Musikerlexikon der Schweiz. Leipzig-Zürich, Hug & Co., 1928. 355 p.

Includes all names connected with Swiss music from the Middle
Ages to the end of the 16th century; musicians and instrument
makers of the 17th and 18th centuries; composers only for the
19th and 20th centuries. Lists of works.

113. SCHUH, WILLI und EDGAR REFARDT. Musikerlexikon
.... Zürich, Atlantis Verlag ⊏1939⊐ 220 p. (Schweizer
Musikbuch, hrsg. von Willi Schuh, II)

Supplements the preceding for contemporary Swiss musicians.
Emphasis is on living musicians, but some important earlier
names are included. Complete lists of works.

114. SWISS COMPOSERS' LEAGUE. 40 contemporary Swiss
composers. Bodensee, Verlag Amriswil, 1956. 222 p.

Brief biographies and critical comment. A few representative works are described and a larger selection listed, with
imprints and instrumentation given. Recordings. Portraits.
Text in English and Spanish.

United States

115. AMERICAN SOCIETY OF COMPOSERS, AUTHORS AND
PUBLISHERS. The ASCAP biographical dictionary of composers,
authors and publishers. Ed. by Daniel I. McNamara. 2nd ed.
New York, Crowell ⊏1952⊐ 636 p.

First pub. in 1948.

"Includes sketches of 2171 writers of lyrics and composers
(1400 of whom are writers and popular musicians) and 402
publishers" (cf. Winchell, 1953). All members and former
members of ASCAP. Major works listed.

116. CALIFORNIA. GOVERNOR'S COMMITTEE TO
ENCOURAGE SELECTION, PERFORMANCE AND PUBLICATION
OF MUSIC OF MERIT BY WESTERN COMPOSERS. A Directory
of contemporary California composers. v. 1-   ⊏ Sacramento,
Calif., Governor's Committee ...⊐ 1961. 33 leaves (typescript)

No more published?

Lists composers alphabetically, with their addresses. Cites published works and commercially available recordings. Committee chairman: Agnes Booe.

117. EWEN, DAVID, comp. American composers today, a biographical and critical guide. New York, H. W. Wilson, 1949. 265 p.

Composers active in the U. S. and Latin America, 1900-46. Principal works listed, and recordings. Bibliographical references to books and periodicals.

Review by Lee Fairley in Notes, 6 (1949) p. 615-16.

See also no. 54.

118. FEATHER, LEONARD. The encyclopedia of jazz. Completely revised, enlarged and brought up to date. New York, Horizon Press, 1960. 537 p.

First published in 1955.

P. 13-90: introductory material, essays on the history, sociology, and structure of jazz. P. 96-473: biographies of jazz musicians, outlining their careers, summarizing their recording activities. Addresses given.

119. GENTRY, LINNELL. A history and encyclopedia of country, western, and gospel music. ⌐ Printed for the author by McQuiddy Press, Nashville, Tenn., 1961 ⌐ 380 p.

A most important reference tool in its own field.

Part II, p. 3-167: anthology of magazine articles on country, western, and gospel music since 1904. Part III, p. 168-75: country music shows since 1924. Part IV, p. 176-351: biographies of country, western, and gospel singers, musicians, and comedians.

120. HISTORICAL RECORDS SURVEY. DISTRICT OF COLUMBIA. Bio-bibliographical index of musicians in the United States of America from colonial times ... sponsored by the Board

of Commissioners of the District of Columbia. 2nd ed.
Washington, D.C., Music Section, Pan American Union, 1956.
439 p.

Reprint of the 1941 edition.

An index to biographical information contained in 66 works
(dictionaries, histories, etc.) on American music, with page
references to the volumes indexed.

121. LAWLESS, RAY McKINLEY. Folksingers and folksongs in America, a handbook of biography, bibliography and
discography. New York, Duell, Sloan and Pearce, 1960. 662 p.

A general book of knowledge for folksong enthusiasts, with
information pertaining to singers, song collecting, sources, and
recordings.

Chaps. 3-8, p. 29-244: brief, informal biographies of
American folk singers.

Review by Rae Korson in Notes, 18 (1960) p. 62.

122. McCARTY, CLIFFORD. Film composers in America;
a checklist of their work. Foreword by Lawrence Morton.
Glendale, Calif., John Valentin [1953] 193 p.

163 names, with film scores listed by date. Index of film
titles; index of orchestrators.

Review by F. W. Sternfeld, in Notes, 11 (1953) p. 105.

Also entered as no. 534.

123. MUSIC AND DANCE IN CALIFORNIA, compiled by
William J. Perlman. Hollywood, Bureau of Musical Research,
1940. 467 p.

Earlier ed., 1933, published under the title Who's Who in
Music and Dance in Southern Calif.

This and the following six titles (nos. 124-29) are a series of
regional reference works covering different sections of the U.S.
Long articles on the development of musical and dance activities.

Biographical sketches of composers, performers, conductors, educators, etc. Portraits. Pronounced emphasis on the commercial aspects of music.

124. MUSIC AND DANCE IN THE CENTRAL STATES. Edited by Richard D. Saunders; compiled by William J. Perlman. Hollywood, Bureau of Musical Research ⌐1952⌐ 173 p.

125. MUSIC AND DANCE IN THE NEW ENGLAND STATES .... Sigmund Spaeth, editor-in-chief; William J. Perlman, director and managing editor. New York, Bureau of Musical Research ⌐1953⌐ 347 p.

126. MUSIC AND DANCE IN NEW YORK STATE. Sigmund Spaeth, editor-in-chief; William J. Perlman, director and associate editor ... 1952 ed. New York, Bureau of Musical Research ⌐1951⌐ 435 p.

127. MUSIC AND DANCE IN PENNSYLVANIA, NEW JERSEY AND DELAWARE. Sigmund Spaeth, editor-in-chief; William J. Perlman, director and managing editor .... New York, Bureau of Musical Research ⌐1954⌐ 339 p.

128. MUSIC AND DANCE IN THE SOUTHEASTERN STATES .... Sigmund Spaeth, editor-in-chief; William J. Perlman, director and managing editor. New York, Bureau of Musical Research ⌐1952 ⌐ 331 p.

129. MUSIC AND DANCE IN TEXAS, OKLAHOMA AND THE SOUTHWEST. Edited by E. Clyde Whitlock and Richard D. Saunders. Hollywood, Bureau of Musical Research ⌐1950⌐ 256 p.

130. NORTH CAROLINA FEDERATION OF MUSIC CLUBS. North Carolina musicians; a selective handbook. Chapel Hill, Univ. of North Carolina Library, 1956. 82 p. (Univ. of North Carolina Library Extension Pubn., v. 21, no. 4)

131. REIS, CLAIRE R. Composers in America; biographical sketches of contemporary composers with a record of their works. Rev. and enl. ed. New York, Macmillan, 1947. 399 p.

First published in 1930 under the title American Composers ....

A survey of music written by American serious composers, 1915 to 1947. Biographies of 332 composers, with a classified listing of their works, manuscripts included (date, publisher, duration). Supplementary list of 125 names without biographical data.

Review by Lee Fairley in Notes, 4 (1947) p. 458-59.

132. WIGGIN, FRANCES (TURGEON). Maine composers and their music; a biographical dictionary .... ⌐Rockland, Maine ⌐ Maine Federation of Music Clubs, 1959. 121 p.

Yugoslavia

133. KOVACEVIC, KRESIMIR. Hrvatski kompozitori i njihova djela. Zagreb, Naprijed, 1960. 553 p.

Biographies of 50 Croation composers, for the most part contemporary, with descriptive accounts of their principal works. Summaries in English. Classified index of works analyzed; general index.

MUSICAL INSTRUMENTS, MAKERS AND PERFORMERS

There is a substantial group of reference books concerned with the construction, performance, and iconography of musical instruments. A great deal of work has been done with respect to the violin, and there is an increasing number of reference tools devoted to keyboard and to wind instruments.

For specific descriptions, prices, and illustrations of individual instruments, particularly those of the string family, the student should not neglect the catalogs of various dealers: Hamma, Herrmann, Hill, Lyon & Healy, Wurlitzer, etc. These are not included in the present listing.

For the iconography of musical instruments, see Buchner (no. 139), Besseler (no. 245), Kinsky (no. 276), and Komma (no. 277).

See also "Bibliographies of Music Literature. Special and Subject: Instruments" (no. 456 ff.) and "Catalogs of Musical Instrument Collections (no. 955 ff).

134. BACHMANN, ALBERTO A. An encyclopedia of the violin. New York, D. Appleton, 1925. 470 p.

Contains a series of alphabets: violin makers in Europe, violin makers in America, European bow makers, American bow makers, string quartets (groups), terms, violinists, music for the violin. Portraits.

135. BACHMANN, ALBERTO A. Les grands violinistes du passé.... Paris, Fischbacher, 1913. 468 p.

Biographies of 40 violinist-composers, varying in length, but with lists of works and a number of full or partial thematic catalogs (i.e. Corelli, Kreutzer, Leclair, Rode, Sarasate, Tartini, Viotti, Vivaldi, etc.).

136. BECHLER, LEO und BERNHARDT RAHM. Die Oboe und die ihr verwandten Instrumente, nebst biographischen Skizzen der bedeutendsten ihrer Meister. Anhang: Musikliteratur für Oboe und englisch Horn, zusammengestellt von Dr. Philipp Losch. Leipzig, C. Merseburger, 1914. 98 p., 32 p. (Anhang)

A history of the oboe and related instruments, with brief biographical sketches of famous players. Supplementary list of works for oboe and English horn, solo and with other instruments.

137. BOALCH, DONALD H. Makers of the harpsichord and clavichord, 1440 to 1840. London, G. Ronald ⌐1956⌐ 169 p.

Lists 820 makers of early keyboard instruments and describes more than 1,000 of their instruments, giving dates, registers, compasses, histories, and present ownership. 32 photo plates.

Review by Frank Hubbard in <u>Notes,</u> 14 (1957) p. 572-73.
Review in <u>The Times Literary Supplement</u>, Dec. 21, 1956.

138. BONE, PHILIP JAMES. The guitar and mandolin:
biographies of celebrated players and composers. ⌐2nd ed.,
enl.⌐ London, New York, Schott, 1954. 388 p.

First pub. in 1914.

Performers and composers, including "standard" composers
who have written for guitar or mandolin. Major works are
mentioned, but there are no complete listings. Portraits.

Review by Richard Capell in <u>Music & Letters</u>, 35 (1954)
p. 254.

139. BUCHNER, ALEXANDER. Musical instruments through
the ages. Trans. by Iris Urwin. London, Spring Books ⌐1956⌐

First pub., with text in Czech, by Artia in Prague. German
edition: <u>Musikinstrumente im Wandel der Zeiten.</u>

Not a dictionary or encyclopedia, but important as a collection
of beautifully reproduced plates, some 323 in number, of musical
instruments and representations of musical performance in
painting, engraving, and sculpture.

140. CLARKE, A. MASON. A biographical dictionary of
fiddlers, including performers on the violoncello and double bass.
London, W. Reeves ⌐1895⌐ 360 p.

Anecdotal accounts.

141. FAIRFIELD, JOHN H. Known violin makers. ⌐New
York, Bradford Press, 1942⌐ 192 p.

Separate listings of European makers from the 16th century,
and American makers. For each, a brief biography, description
of works, and the current price range of the instruments.

142. GORGERAT, GÉRALD. Encyclopédie de la musique
pour instruments à vent. Lausanne, Éditions Rencontre ⌐1955⌐
3 v.

A pretentious work which attempts to cover all information pertaining to the making and performance of wind instruments, and much more that has no particular relevance. Useful fingering charts for all winds. Several special lists:

Vol. 3, p. 243-83: Principal works for wind instruments, solo and ensemble.

Vol. 3, p. 285-340: Dictionary of composers cited in the text. Brief identifications; no page references.

Vol. 3, p. 341-525: Table of French terms, with their equivalents in Italian, German, English, and Spanish.

143. HAMMA, FRIDOLIN. German violin makers; a critical dictionary. Translated by Walter Stewart. London, W. Reeves, 1961. 49 p. 80 pl.

Translated from the 1948 German edition, Meister deutscher Geigenbaukunst. Stuttgart, 1948.

Alphabetical listing of 550 names of important German makers, with plates illustrating their work.

Review by Cynthia L. Adams in Notes, 19 (1961) p. 261-62.

144. HAMMA, FRIDOLIN. Meisterwerke italienischer Geigenbaukunst, ihre Beschreibung und bisher erzielte Preise. Stuttgart, Hamma & Co. ⌐1933⌐ 345 p.

Descriptions of specific instruments, arranged alphabetically by their makers, with biographical information and photographic plates of details.

145. HAUPT, HELGA. "Wiener Instrumentenbauer von 1791 bis 1815, " in Studien zur Musikwissenschaft, Beihefte der Denkmäler der Tonkunst in Oesterreich. Band 24. Graz, 1960. p. 120-84

Alphabetical listing of Viennese instrument makers, in all categories. Gives addresses, dates of activity. Thoroughly documented with primary and secondary source materials.

146. HENLEY, WILLIAM. Universal dictionary of violin and bow makers. [Managing ed., Cyril Woodcock. Brighton, Sussex, Amati Pub. Co., 1959-60] 5 v.

Biographies of varying length. Long accounts of important figures, with descriptions and prices of outstanding instruments. Transcribed labels but no facsimiles. Suffers from a subjective, romantic literary style.

147. HIRT, FRANZ JOSEF. Meisterwerke des Klavierbaus. Geschichte der Saitenklaviers von 1440-bis 1880. Olten, Urs Graf-Verlag, 1955. 521 p.

Beautifully illustrated book, with information about keyboard instruments, their design, construction, makers, etc. Numerous full-page photographic plates, useful sections of biography and bibliography.

148. IRWIN, STEVENS. Dictionary of pipe organ stops. Detailed descriptions of more than 600 stops, together with definitions of many other terms connected with the organ, and an examination of the acoustical properties of many types of pipes and the various divisions of the organ. New York, G. Schirmer [1962] 264 p.

Illustrated. Includes a short bibliography.

149. JACQUOT, ALBERT. Dictionnaire pratique et raisonné des instruments de musique anciens et modernes. 2nd ed. Paris, Fischbacher, 1886. 280 p.

Many names of Eastern instruments included. Some illustrations. Brief definitions. No bibliography.

150. JAHNEL, FRANZ. Die Gitarre und ihr Bau. Technologie von Gitarre, Laute, Mandoline, Sister, Tanbur und Saite. Frankfurt am Main, Verlag Das Musikinstrument, 1963. 250 p.

A compendium of information on the construction of the guitar and other fretted instruments. Bibliography, numerous tables and lists, detailed plans and technical data. A handsomely designed and printed volume, invaluable for the music instrument maker or performer interested in the construction of instruments of this type.

151. JALOVEC, KAREL. The violin makers of Bohemia; including craftsmen of Moravia and Slovakia. London, Anglo-Italian Pubns. ⌐1959⌐ 129 p., 392 plates

Originally published in Czech under the title Cesti houslari. Prague, 1959. German ed., 1959.

Covers the work of some 1,200 Czech violin makers. Photographs of instruments, and a section of makers' labels in facsimile.

152. JALOVEC, KAREL. Italsti houslari. Italian violin makers. Praha, Orbis, 1952. 655 p.

Also a new and rev. ed., London, Anglo-Italian Publications, 1957. 440 p.

Text in Czech and English. Accounts of the makers, with descriptions and dimensions of important instruments. Index by place. Many illustrations, some in color. Facsimiles of labels.

153. LANGWILL, LYNDESAY G. An index of musical wind instrument makers. 2nd and enlarged ed. Edinburgh, 1962. 224 p.

First pub. in 1960.

Alphabetical index of some 3,000 makers of mouth-blown wood-wind and brass instruments, including all forms of bagpipe, ocarinas, etc. Detailed entries for the most important makers. Locations of examples of early instruments in museums and private collections.

P. 131-34: bibliography; p. 135-39: list of instrument collections.

Review by Josef Marx in Notes, 18 (1961) p. 234-36.

154. LÜTGENDORFF, WILLIBALD LEO, FREIHERR VON.
Die Geigen- und Lautenmacher vom Mittelalter bis zur Gegenwart,
nach den besten Quellen bearbeitet ... 4. mit der 3. überein-
stimmende Aufl. Frankfurt am Main, Frankfurter Verlags-
Anstalt, 1922. 2 v.

First pub. in 1904, in 1 vol.

Vol. 1: History of the making of stringed instruments, by
country. Index of manufacturers by city, with dates of birth and
death. Bibliography, p. 403-20. Many illustrations.

Vol. 2: Biographical dictionary of makers of stringed instruments. P. 583-668: facsimiles of trademarks and labels.

155. MICHEL, NORMAN E. Michel's piano atlas. Contains
names of pianos, dates of manufacture, and serial numbers. Pico
Rivera, Calif. ⌐1961⌐

6,580 names of pianos. For some of these, there is no
information other than name; for others, complete lists of serial
numbers.

156. MÖLLER, MAX. The violin-makers of the low
countries (Belgium and Holland). Amsterdam, M. Möller, 1955.
165 p.

A historical survey of violin making in Belgium and Holland.

P. 23-129: photographic plates, chiefly of instruments in
detail. P. 132-53: "Alphabetical Register," brief critical
comments on the makers and their work. Glossary of terms in
English, French, German, and Flemish.

157. MORRIS, W. MEREDITH. British violin makers, a
biographical dictionary of British makers of stringed instruments
and bows, and a critical description of their work. 2nd ed., rev.
and enl. London, R. Scott, 1920. 318 p.

First pub. in 1904.

P. 89-258: alphabetical dictionary of violin and bow makers.
Some labels in facsimile. P. 261-94: "A list of present-day
makers, and a few old makers recently discovered."

158. NIEMANN, WALTER. Klavier-lexikon: Elementarlehre
für Klavierspieler, Anleitung zur Aussprache des italienischen,
Tabelle der Abkürzungen in Wort und Notenschrift, Literaturverzeichnis, ausführliches Fremdwörter-, Sach- und Personal-
lexikon. 4. völlig umgearb. und reich verm. Aufl. ... Leipzig,
C. F. Kahnt, 1918. 365 p.

First pub. in 1912 as Taschen-Lexikon für Klavierspieler.

159. NORLIND, TOBIAS. Systematik der Saiteninstrumente.
Stockholm ⌐ Emil Kihlströms Tryckeri ⌐ 1936-39. 2 v.

At head of title: Musikhistorisches Museum, Stockholm.

Vol. 1: Geschichte der Zither (1936); Vol. 2: Geschichte
des Klaviers (1939).

Detailed classification and description of instruments of the
string family, based on the archive in the Musikhistorisches
Museum in Stockholm where records of some 40,000 instruments
are maintained. Illustrated. Bibliographical references and
locations given for specific instruments in European and American
collections. The work was projected in 4 parts, only 2 of which
were completed.

160. POIDRAS, HENRI. Critical & documentary dictionary
of violin makers old and modern, translated by Arnold Sewell ....
Rouen, Imprimerie de la Vicomté, 1928-30. 2 v.

Originally pub. in French, 1924, with a 2nd ed. in 1930.
There is also a one-vol. English ed., 1928.

Brief biographical notices, with critical comments, arranged
alphabetically under national schools: Italian, French, English,
German, etc. Photographic plates of instruments; facsimiles of
labels.

161. PRAT MARSAL, DOMINGO. Diccionario biográfico, bibliográfico, histórico, crítico de guitarras (instrumentos afines), guitarristas (profesores, compositores, concertistas, lahudistas, amateurs), guitarreros (luthiers), danzas y cantos, terminología. Buenos Aires, Casa Romero y Fernández ⌐1934⌐ 468 p.

The main alphabet contains biographies and lists of compositions.

P. 423-52: dance forms; p. 455-64: terminology.

162. "PROVISIONAL INDEX OF PRESENT-DAY MAKERS OF HISTORICAL MUSICAL INSTRUMENTS (NON-KEYBOARD)." In Galpin Society Journal, 13 (July 1960) p. 70-97

Makers of historical keyboard instruments listed in an appendix, p. 86-87.

A useful guide to sources of modern replicas of historical musical instruments.

163. RODA, JOSEPH. Bows for musical instruments of the violin family. Chicago, W. Lewis & Son, 1959. 335 p.

Brief history and description of the bow, including statistics as to dimensions and weight.

P. 119-325: biographical list of bow makers, with 47 excellent plates of their work.

164. SACHS, CURT. Handbuch der Musikinstrumentenkunde. Leipzig, Breitkopf & Härtel, 1920. 412 p. (Kleine Handbücher der Musikgeschichte nach Gattungen, Bd. 12)

Not precisely a dictionary, but a systematic and historical description of musical instruments classified according to type: idiophones, membranophones, chordaphones, aerophones, etc. Much of the same ground is covered in Sachs' The History of Musical Instruments (New York, Norton, 1940), in which the approach is chronological and by cultural areas.

165. SACHS, CURT. Real-Lexikon der Musikinstrumente, zugleich ein Polyglossar für gesamte Instrumentengebiet; mit 200 Abbildungen. Hildesheim, G. Olms Verlags-buchhandlung, 1962. 442 p.

Unaltered reprint of the original edition, Berlin, 1913.

A technical and historical dictionary of instruments of all periods and countries. Names of instruments and parts of instruments in some 120 languages and dialects, European and Asian. Locations of examples in instrument collections. Illustrations: some bibliographies. This is Sachs' great work in this field, one of the best sources for historical information on musical instruments.

166. STRAETEN, EDMUND S. J. VAN DER. The history of the violin, its ancestors and collateral instruments from the earliest times to the present day; with 48 plates and numerous illustrations in the text. London, Cassell ⌐1933¬ 2 v.

Vol. 1, p. 55-416, and the whole of Vol. 2 consist primarily of biographies of violinists, grouped by period, and under period by country. Biographical index, Vol. 2, p. 443-75. Information on many obscure violinist-composers not elsewhere readily accessible, with lists of works by category.

167. THORNSBY, FREDERICK W., ed. Dictionary of organs and organists. Bournemouth, H. Logan ⌐1912¬ 364 p.

Chiefly concerned with 19th-century British organs and organists.

P. 113-231: "Brief specifications of the principal organs in the British Isles." P. 241-352: "The organist's who's who: Brief biographical notes of the leading British organists."

168. VALDRIGHI, LUIGI FRANCESCO. ... Nomocheliurgografia antica e moderna; ossia, elenco di favvricatori di strumenti armonici con note esplicative e documenti estratti dall'archivio di stato in Modena .... Modena, Coi tipi della Società tipografica, 1884. 327 p.

P. 2-106: an alphabetical listing of 3,516 instrument makers, giving name, nationality, residence, dates of birth and death, name of special instrument, and the school, style, or system. Many of these names are given fuller biographical treatment in the section following, p. 107 to end.

169. VANNES, RENÉ. Dictionnaire universel des luthiers. 2nd éd. revue et augmentée. Bruxelles, Les Amis de la Musique, 1951. 408 ⊏163⊐ p.

Tome second. Tome additif et correctif. Bruxelles, 1959. 198, lxiii p.

First published in 1932, Paris, Fischbacher, under the title Essai d'un dictionnaire universel ....

Most comprehensive of all dictionaries of violin makers. Each volume has its own alphabet of biographical entries. Bibliographical references. Both volumes combined give 3,400 facsimiles of makers' labels. Vol. 2, p. 67-198: index of makers by place of birth or center of activity.

Review by Doris Commander in Violins and Violinists, 12 (Nov. 1951) p. 326; review of Tome second by Albert Van der Linden in Revue belge de musicologie, 14 (1960) p. 144, and by William Lichtenwanger in Notes, 17 (1960) p. 577.

170. VERCHEVAL, HENRI. Dictionnaire du violoniste .... Paris, Fischbacher, 1923. 192 p.

Part I, p. 9-141, includes terms of interest to violinists, history of stringed instruments, etc. Part II, p. 143-92, is a biographical dictionary of violinists, composers, teachers, violin and bow makers, giving dates and nationalities.

171. WÖRTHMÜLLER, WILLI. "Die Nürnberger Trompeten- und Posaunenmacher des 17. und 18. Jahrhunderts." In Mitteilungen des Vereins für Geschichte der Stadt Nürnberg. Bd. 46 (1955) p. 372-480.

Also pub. separately.

A musicological study the major portion of which is a dictionary of 40 Nurmberg brass instrument makers of the baroque period, with a listing of their surviving instruments. Tracing of monograms and other makers' devices. 5 plates.

172. WRIGHT, ROWLAND. Dictionnaire des instruments de musique; étude de lexicologie. London, Battley Bros., 1941. 192 p.

An etymological dictionary of names for musical instruments mentioned in French writings from ancient times to the end of the 19th century. Extremely well documented; precise bibliographical references. One of the few dictionaries of terms to employ a thoroughly etymological approach.

173. ZUTH, JOSEF. Handbuch der Laute und Gitarre. Wien, Verlag der Zeitschrift für die Gitarre, 1926. 297 p.

Terms, and biographies of performers, instrument makers, and composers, giving titles of compositions, publishers, and dates. International coverage for all periods, including many early names. A scholarly work, with supported statements and bibliographical references.

TERMS

Dictionaries of terms have a longer history than any other form of music lexicography. Their prototype is furnished by Johannes Tinctoris' Terminorum musicae diffinitorium (no. 195), a work compiled in the late 15th century. Almost equally significant is Sébastian de Brossard's Dictionnaire de musique, 1701 (no. 179), one of the first in the long line of "modern" dictionaries of music.

A few specialized dictionaries of terms will be found under other headings in this volume. See no. 148 (pipe organ stops); no. 172 (names of musical instruments); no. 199 (liturgical music terms).

174. APEL, WILLI. Harvard dictionary of music. Cambridge, Mass., Harvard Univ. Press, 1944. 824 p.

The standard reference work in English for non-biographical information, designed to provide accurate and pertinent information on all musical topics. Emphasis on historical viewpoint. Good bibliographies; excellent brief historical articles.

175. APEL, WILLI and RALPH T. DANIEL. The Harvard brief dictionary of music. Cambridge, Mass., Harvard Univ. Press, 1960. 341 p.

Paperback edition: New York, Washington Square Press, 1961.

Review by James B. Coover in Notes, 18 (1961) p. 239-40.

176. BAKER, THEODORE. Dictionary of musical terms ... with a supplement containing an English-Italian vocabulary for composers. New York, G. Schirmer, 1923. 257 p.

Useful small manual, with brief definitions of English and foreign words, especially those used in performance. More extended articles on topics such as pitch, notation, instruments. More than 9,000 terms treated.

177. BOBILLIER, MARIE (Michel Brenet, pseud.). Dictionnaire pratique et historique de la musique. Paris, A. Colin, 1926. 487 p.

2nd ed. appeared in 1930.

The standard French dictionary of terms, including terms from Greek and medieval music theory, historical sketches of musical forms. Fairly long articles, excellent small illustrations. No bibliographies.

178. BOBILLIER, MARIE (Michel Brenet, pseud.). Diccionario de la música, histórico y técnico. Tradducion de la última edición francesa, revisada y notablemente ampliada con multitud de artículos nuevos ... por José B. Humbert, J. Ricart Matas & Aurelio Capmany. Barcelona, Iberia, J. Gil [1946] 548 p.

Translation of the 2nd ed. of the preceding, revised and with special emphasis on Spanish terms, Latin and South American terminology and folklore. Profusely illustrated.

179. BROSSARD, SÉBASTIEN DE. Dictionnaire de musique, contenant une explication des termes grecs, latins, italiens & francois, les plus usitez dans la musique. 2nd ed. Paris, Ballard, 1705. 380 p.

Earlier issues appeared in 1701 and 1703. At least two later editions were published in Amsterdam.

Brossard is the prototype for all modern dictionaries of terms. It also contains a listing of more than 900 authors who have written about music. For an early English musical dictionary based on Brossard, see no. 184.

180. CARTER, HENRY H. A dictionary of Middle English musical terms. Bloomington, Indiana, Indiana Univ. Press, 1961. 655 p. (Indiana University humanities series, 45)

Terms are not only defined but quoted in their original contexts with citation of their sources. P. 569-604: bibliography of works quoted; p. 605-49: works consulted but not quoted.

Review by Leonard Ellinwood in Notes, 19 (1961) p. 262-63.

181. DOLZHANSKIĬ, A. Kratkiĭ muzykalnyi slovar. 3rd ed. Moskva, 1959. 517 p.

First published, Leningrad, 1952.

182. ELSEVIER'S DICTIONARY OF CINEMA, SOUND AND MUSIC, in six languages: English/American, French, Spanish, Italian, Dutch and German. Compiled and arranged on an English alphabetical base by W. E. Clason. Amsterdam, New York, Elsevier Publishing Company, 1956. 948 p.

One of a series of polyglot technical dictionaries relating to special fields of science and industry. 3,213 terms, with brief definitions and the equivalent phrases in French, Spanish, Italian, Dutch, and German. Indexes in each of the five languages.

183. GERIGK, HERBERT. Fachwörterbuch der Musik.
⌐Münchberg i. Bayern⌐ B. Hahnefeld ⌐1954⌐ 206 p.

A small, useful dictionary of definitions, in German, of the
most common musical terms, French, Italian, Latin, and some
English.

Reviewed in Die Musikforschung, 8 (1955) p. 245.

184. GRASSINEAU, JAMES. A musical dictionary, being a
collection of terms and characters, as well ancient as modern;
including the historical, theoretical, and practical parts of
music .... London, Printed for J. Wilcox, 1740. 347 p.

Largely an adaptation of Brossard (no. 179), but with some
additions. A later edition, 1769, has an appendix containing
additional terms from Rousseau's Dictionnaire de musique (no.
190).

185. KOCH, HEINRICH CHRISTOPH. Musikalisches
Lexikon, welches die theoretische und praktische Tonkunst,
encyclopädisch bearbeitet, alle alten und neuen Kunstwörter
erklärt, und die alten und neuen Instrumente beschrieben,
enthält .... Frankfurt am Main, A. Hermann dem Jüngern,
1802. 2 v.

One of the first of a long line of German dictionaries of
terms. Particularly important for definitions and concepts
pertaining to late baroque and classic music and instruments.

A revised ed., by Arrey von Dommer, printed in Heidelberg,
1865.

186. LICHTENTHAL, PIETRO. Dizionario e bibliografia
della musica. Milano, A. Fontana, 1826. 4 v.

The first 2 volumes of this work are a dictionary of terms,
the last 2, a bibliography of music literature based on Forkel's
Allgemeine Literatur der Musik (see no. 361). A French edition
of the dictionary of terms, "traduit et augmenté par Dominique
Mondo," appeared in Paris in 1839.
See also no. 365.

187. LIMENTA, FERNANDO. Dizionario lessicografico musicale italiano-tedesco-italiano. Milano, Hoepli, 1940. 391 p.

Designed to provide precise Italian equivalents for German technical terms not adequately treated in most dictionaries.

188. PADELFORD, FREDERICK M. Old English musical terms. Bonn, P. Hanstein, 1899. 112 p. (Bonner Beiträge zur Anglistik, 4)

189. PULVER, JEFFREY. A dictionary of old English music and musical instruments. London, Kagan Paul; New York, E. P. Dutton, 1923. 247 p.

Terms used by Tudor and early Stuart musicians. Fairly long articles, with references to early literary and musical sources for the terms. 10 plates of early English instruments.

190. ROUSSEAU, JEAN J. Dictionnaire de musique. Paris, Duchesne, 1768. 548 ⌐i. e. 556⌐ p. 13 folded plates

Several editions published in Paris and Amsterdam during the 18th century. An English edition, translated by William Waring, published under the title A Complete Dictionary of Music.

Based on articles written by Rousseau for the Diderot and d'Alembert Encyclopedia but not included in that work. Reflects the stimulating and highly personal views of an 18th-century man of letters. Wide influence and considerable historical importance.

191. SINZIG, PEDRO. Dicionário musical. Rio de Janeiro, Kosmos, 1947. 613 p.

A modern Portuguese-language dictionary of terms. Based largely on Apel and Riemann. Bibliographical references.

192. SMITH, W. J. A dictionary of musical terms in four languages. London, Hutchinson, 1961. 195 p.

English terms with equivalents in French, Italian, and German. Pronunciations given in phonetic symbols. No definitions.

193. STAINER, SIR JOHN and W. A. BARRETT. Dictionary of musical terms. New and rev. ed. London, Novello, 1898. 464 p.

Terms in Italian, French, Latin, German, Hebrew, Greek, Russian, Spanish, Arabic, with brief definitions in English.

194. STEPHAN, RUDOLF. Musik. ⸢Frankfurt am Main⸣ Fischer Verlag ⸢1957⸣ 382 p. (Das Fischer Lexikon, Enzyklopädie des Wissens, 5)

General articles cover major topics, with more detailed information approached through an index. Topical bibliographies, p. 355-64. 10 plates. A scholarly summation of musical knowledge for the general reader.

195. TINCTORIS, JOHANNES. ⸢Terminorum musicae diffinitorium⸣ Dictionary of musical terms. Latin-English edition, translated and edited by Carl Parrish, with a bibliographical essay by James B. Coover. New York, Free Press of Glencoe, 1963.

A 15th-century dictionary of musical terms, and one of the first books on music to be printed. 291 definitions of terms, important in understanding 15th-century music theory and practice. The Latin text has been reprinted in Coussemaker's Scriptorum (1867), in Forkel's Allgemeine Literatur der Musik (1792), and with a German translation in Chrysander's Jahrbuch der Musikwissenschaft, I (1863). It appeared in a French translation with introduction and commentary by Armand Machabey (Paris, Richard-Masse, 1951).

196. TOVEY, DONALD F. Musical articles from the Encyclopaedia Britannica. London, New York, Oxford Univ. Press, 1944. 256 p.

Paperback edition: New York, Meridian Books, 1956, as The Forms of Music.

28 articles on the larger aspects of music. Shorter ones (madrigal, sonata, etc.) are briefly historical; others (harmony,

sonata forms, etc.) are comprehensive and analytical. Reprinted from Tovey's contributions to the 11th ed. of the Britannica.

197. VANNES, RENÉ. ... Essai de terminologie musical. Dictionnaire universel comprenant plus de 15,000 termes de musique en italien-espagnol-portugais-français-anglais-allemand-latin et grec .... Thann, "Alsatia," c. 1925. 230 p.

Most extensive manual of its kind, containing 15,000 entries in 8 languages. Includes forms, terms, instruments in current use. Brief definitions given under the original or characteristic language, with equivalents in other languages. No explanatory or historical material.

198. WOTTON, TOM S. A dictionary of foreign musical terms, and handbook of orchestral instruments. Leipzig, Breitkopf & Härtel, 1907. 226 p.

Less comprehensive than Vannes (no. 197). Designed as an aid to score reading, including orchestral terms, instruments, tempo indications, etc. Primarily in French, German, and Italian.

CHURCH MUSIC

This section begins with a listing of several general dictionaries relating to church music. This is followed by a listing of handbooks on the hymnology of various Protestant groups, with citations under the denominations represented. Such handbooks are essentially bibliographies of sacred music, but most of them contain enough biographical and factual information to justify listing them among the encyclopedias and dictionaries of church music.

199. HUGHES, ANSELM. Liturgical terms for music students; a dictionary. Boston, McLaughlin & Reilly ⌐1940¬ 40 p.

Concise definitions of terms likely to occur in the literature of ancient ecclesiastical music of the West. Tables give structure of mass and office. Includes terms from the church calendar, terms referring to notation, texts with explanations of their places in the liturgy.

200. JULIAN, JOHN. A dictionary of hymnology, setting forth the origin and history of Christian hymns of all ages and nations. Rev. ed. with new suppl. London, J. Murray, 1908. 1768 p.

Unaltered reprint in 2 vols. New York, Dover, 1957.

First pub. in 1892.

Entries under authors, titles, and subjects of hymn texts. Brief but adequate biographical notices. Long articles on American, English, Latin hymnody, etc. For individual hymns gives original publication and location in other hymnals. Contains a vast amount of information on musical and literary aspects of Christian hymnody.

201. KORNMÜLLER, UTTO. Lexikon der kirchlichen Tonkunst .... 2. verb. und verm. Aufl. Regensburg, A. Coppenrath, 1891-95. 2 v. in 1

Vol. 1: Dictionary of subjects, terms, instruments connected with Catholic church music, with a subject index of topics discussed in extended articles.

Vol. 2: Biographical dictionary of church musicians. Published works cited for early names, categories of compositions for recent ones.

202. McCUTCHAN, ROBERT G. Hymn tune names, their sources and significance. Nashville, Abingdon Press [1957] 206 p.

Alphabetical listing of tunes, giving their metrical structures and thematic incipits in letter notation. Commentary related to authors, composers, and sources. Numerous cross references. Melodic index. First line index of texts, with author, translator, and tune name.

202A. STUBBINGS, GEORGE W. A dictionary of church music. London, Epworth Press ⊏1949⊐ 127 p.

A practical rather than scholarly reference book for the use of church organists and choir directors. Short explanations of technical terms and concise information on topics related to church music.

203. WEISSENBÄCK, ANDREAS. Sacra musica; Lexikon der katholischen Kirchenmusik. Klosterneuburg, Augustinus Druckerei ⊏1937⊐ 419 p.

Biography, terms, and subjects in one alphabet. Articles on religious organizations and music publishing houses. More comprehensive in coverage than Kornmüller (no. 201), but the articles are briefer.

Congregational

204. COMPANION TO CONGREGATIONAL PRAISE. Edited by K. L. Parry, with notes on the music by Erik Routley. London, Independent Press, 1953. 580 p.

P. 1-336: notes on the words and music for 884 hymns and chants. P. 337-550: biographical notes on hymn writers and composers. Chronological listing of 396 musical sources. Index of tune names, and first line index of hymns.

Episcopal

205. PROTESTANT EPISCOPAL CHURCH IN THE U.S.A. The Hymnal 1940 companion. ⊏3rd ed. rev.⊐ New York, Church Pension Fund, 1956. 741 p.

First pub. in 1949.

Contents: Historical essays on texts and tunes; biographies of authors, composers, translators, and arrangers. List of organ works based on hymn tunes, with publishers. Index of scriptural texts; general index; melodic index; index of tunes; first line index.

206. PROTESTANT EPISCOPAL CHURCH OF ENGLAND. Historical companion to hymns, ancient and modern. Edited by

Maurice Frost. London, Printed for the Proprietors by William Clowes & Sons, 1962. 716 p.

The latest revision of a work compiled in 1909 by W. H. Frere, under the title Historical Edition of Hymns Ancient and Modern; revised in 1950.

P. 1-124: Introduction, with contributions by Egon Wellesz, Ruth Massenger, C. E. Pocknee, and Lowther Clarke, covering the history of hymnody and of the Anglican hymnal. P. 125-478: Texts and commentary for 636 hymns, including the language of the original if translated. Index of first lines, brief biographies of hymn writers, chronological list of authors and translators, alphabetical index of tunes, index of plainsong, notes on the composers with chronology, list of publications and tunes, metrical index.

Evangelical and Reformed

207. HAEUSSLER, ARMIN. The story of our hymns: the handbook to the hymnal of the Evangelical and Reformed Church. St. Louis, Eden Publishing House, 1952. 1088 p.

Commentary on 561 hymns and other liturgical pieces. Biographies of hymn writers and notes on sources. Bibliography. Index of scripture texts, topical index, metrical index, indexes of tune names, composers, arrangers, and sources. First line index.

Lutheran

208. POLACK, William G., comp. The handbook to the Lutheran hymnal. 2nd & rev. ed. St. Louis, Concordia ⌐1942⌐ 681 p.

Texts of and commentary on 660 Lutheran hymns. Bio-graphical and historical notes on the authors and composers. Index of biblical references, table of hymns for feasts and festivals, first line index of hymns and stanzas of hymns, index of tunes, metrical index, topical index, index of authors and translators.

Mennonite

209. HOSTETLER, LESTER, comp. Handbook to the

Mennonite Hymnary. Newton, Kansas, General Conference of the Mennonite Church of North America, Board of Publications, 1949. 425 p.

Commentary on 623 Mennonite hymns and other liturgical pieces. Bibliography. Indexes.

Methodist

210. McCUTCHAN, ROBERT G. Our hymnody, a manual of the Methodist hymnal. 2nd ed. New York, Abingdon Press ⌐1942⌐ 619 p.

First published in 1937.

Commentary on 664 hymns and other liturgical pieces. Hymn calendar, bibliography, and 9 special indexes.

Presbyterian

211. HANDBOOK TO THE HYMNAL. Philadelphia, Presbyterian Board of Christian Education, 1935. 566 p.

Unitarian

212. FOOTE, HENRY W., comp. American Unitarian hymn writers and hymns. Compiled for the Hymn Society of America for publication in the Society's proposed Dictionary of American Hymnology. Cambridge, Mass. ⌐Author⌐ 1959. 270 leaves (typescript)

Contains a historical sketch of American Unitarian hymnody, a catalog of American Unitarian hymn books, alphabetical list of hymn writers, biographical sketches, and first line index of published hymns.

OPERA AND THEATER MUSIC

Dictionaries of opera and theater music are of two principal kinds: (1) they are compilations of facts related to the history or the production of musical dramatic works (The Opera Directory, no. 230, is a good example of a work of this type); or (2) they are listings of operatic works, often chronological or associated with a particular place (e.g., Loewenberg's Annals of Opera, no. 224, or Bauer's Opern und Operetten in Wien, no. 213). Titles in the latter category belong properly in bibliographies of music, but we have entered them here in order to concentrate materials on the musical theater in one section.

Listeners' guides to opera, and collections of opera plots, have been excluded.

One encyclopedia of the theater arts demands mention at this point, although it is not confined to music in its coverage. This is the Enciclopedia dello spettacolo, Roma, 1954 (8 vols. by 1961), an illustrated reference work covering all aspects of the theater, with contributions by outstanding authorities in the field.

213. BAUER, ANTON. Opern und Operetten in Wien; Verzeichnis ihrer Erstaufführhungen in der Zeit von 1629 bis zur Gegenwart. Graz-Köln, Hermann Böhlaus Nachf., 1955. 156 p. (Wiener musikwissenschaftliche Beiträge, 2)

4,856 stage works, listed by title, with an index for composers, an index for authors, and a chronological index.

214. BERNANDT, GRIGORII B. Slovar' oper. Vpervye postavlennykh ili izdannykh v dorevoliutsionnoi Rossii i v SSSR. Moskva, Sovetskii Kompozitor, 1962. 554 p.

A dictionary of operas first performed or first published in Russia during 1736-1959. Entries are alphabetical by title. Information includes genre of the work, composer, first performance, librettist, and literary source, and many details that relate to the production. Indexed by composer, librettist, and author of the original literary source.

215. BURTON, JACK. The blue book of Broadway musicals. Watkins Glen, N.Y., Century House ⌐1952⌐ 320 p.

Lists title, date, composer, author, principals, and musical numbers for more than 1,500 operettas, musical comedies, and reviews, from the 1890's to 1951. Arrangement is by decades, with a general introduction to each period.

216. BURTON, JACK. The blue book of Hollywood musicals; songs from the sound tracks and the stars who sang them since the birth of the talkies a quarter-century ago. Watkins Glen, N. Y., Century House ⊏ 1953 ⊐ 296 p.

"Complementing The Blue Book of Tin Pan Alley (1951) and The Blue Book of Broadway Musicals (1952), this present anthology completes a trilogy on popular music" (introduction).

217. BURTON, JACK. The blue book of Tin Pan Alley, a human interest encyclopedia of American popular music. Vol. 1: 1776-1860-1910. Watkins Glen, N. Y., Century House ⊏1962⊐ 304 p.

First published in 1951, Watkins Glen, Century House. 520 p.

The 1962 publication is the first volume of an expanded new edition which, when completed, will carry the survey through the 1960's. The approach is chronological, with detailed listings of songs by the principal popular composers.

218. CLÉMENT, FÉLIX et P. LAROUSSE. Dictionnaire des opéras (Dictionnaire lyrique) contenant l'analyse et la nomen-clature de tous les óperas-comiques, opérettes et drames lyrique représentés en France et `a l'étranger depuis l'origine de ces genres d'ouvrages jusqu'a nos jours .... Rev. et mis `a jour par Arthur Pougin. Paris, Libraire Larousse ⊏1905⊐ 1203 p.

First published in 1869 under the title Dictionnaire lyrique.

Title entries (frequently under the French form, with refer-ences to other forms) for operas and comic operas presented in France and elsewhere from the beginnings to the present day. For each entry, language of text, number of acts, authors of words and music, place and date of first performance, brief sketch of plot, occasional criticism. Index of composers. A comprehensive work.

219. DASSORI, CARLO. Opere e operisti (dizionario lirico 1541-1902) .... Genova, 1903.

Includes 15,406 operas by 3,628 composers. Author and title lists only: no descriptive and critical matter.

Part I: Alphabetical list of composers, with dates of birth and death, a chronological list under composer of operas, with dates and places of first performance.

Part II: Title list of all operas that have been performed in Italy.

220. EATON, QUAINTANCE. Opera production: a handbook. Minneapolis, University of Minnesota Press, 1961.

Contains useful information on 224 "long" and 148 "short" operas, including timings, difficulty of leading roles, instrumentation, source and cost of sources and parts, photographs of productions, list of performing groups. Various supplementary lists cite further operas, publishers, performing companies.

221. FOG, DAN. The Royal Danish Ballet, 1760-1958, and August Bournonville. A chronological catalogue of the ballets and ballet-divertissements performed at the Royal Theatres of Copenhagen, and a catalogue of August Bournonville's works. Copenhagen, Dan Fog, 1961. 79 p.

Lists 516 ballet works performed by the Royal Danish Ballet, citing the choreographer, composer, and publications of the music if available. Index of titles and of persona. Facsimile plates of music title pages.

222. LESSING, G. E. Handbuch des Opern-Repertoires. ⌐Neubearbeitung⌐ London, New York, Boosey & Hawkes, 1952. 393 p.

An organized compilation of facts related to the performance of 392 operas in the current repertoire, including casts of characters, locales of action, instrumentation, duration of acts, dates of first performance, and publishers of the music. "A work of reference intended for the use of theatrical managers, conductors, dramatists and in libraries" (author's preface).

223. LEWINE, RICHARD and ALFRED SIMON. Encyclopedia of theater music: a comprehensive listing of more than 4,000 songs from Broadway and Hollywood, 1900-1960. New York, Random House, 1961. 248 p.

A guide to the song repertory of the American musical theater.

Part I: Theater songs 1900-24; Part II: Theater songs 1925-60; Part III: Motion picture songs; Part IV: Show chronology 1925-60.

Songs are listed alphabetically by title, with composer, lyricist, show, and year given. Listing of published vocal scores, and index of shows.

224. LOEWENBERG, ALFRED. Annals of opera, 1597-1940, compiled from the original sources; with an introduction by Edward J. Dent. 2nd ed., rev. and corrected. Genève, Societas Bibliographica ⌐1955⌐ 2 v.

First pub. in 1943 by W. Heffer, Cambridge. 879 p.

Chronological list of operas by dates of first performance, including (with a few exceptions) only works known to have been produced. The list is limited to older operas that are extant and modern ones that have obtained interest outside their countries of origin. Each entry includes composer's name, original title of work, English translation for all languages except German, French, and Italian. Name of librettist given, and place and date of first performance.

Vol. 2: Indexes by title, composer, and librettist, and general index for other names, places, and subjects.

A work of distinguished scholarship; essential for the historical study of opera.

Review on 2nd ed., by Edward N. Waters, in Notes, 13 (1956) p. 285-86.

225. MANFERRARI, UMBERTO. Dizionario universale delle opere melodrammatiche. Firenze, Sansoni Antiquariato,

1954-55. 3 v. (Contributi alla Biblioteca bibliografica italica, 4, 8, 10)

Entries under composer, giving title, librettist, place and date of first performance, and first performances in other major opera houses.

226. MOORE, FRANK L. Crowell's handbook of world opera. New York, T. Y. Crowell, 1961.

Contains brief information on individual operas, "people in opera," "characters in the operas," "first lines and titles of famous numbers," chronological list of important operas, glossary of terms used in opera, themes, recordings, and indexes of singers by voice range.

227. MOOSER, ROBERT A. Opéras, intermezzos, ballets, cantates, oratorios jouées en Russie durant le XVIIIe siecle ... Essai d'un répertoire alphabétique et chronologique. 2. éd. Geneva, R. Kister, 1955. 169 p.

First pub. in 1945.

Gives librettist, translators of work, date and place of first performance, language of performance, date of publication of the libretto, etc. Sources of information are well documented. Indexes.

Review in Die Musikforschung, 9 (1956) p. 106.

228. OPERA MANUAL: a handbook of practical operatic information. Edited by Mrs. Charles A. Matz and Marguerite Wickersham. New York, Central Opera Service, 1956.

Contains lists of operas in modern translation; chamber operas, citing voices and instruments needed, sets, duration, source of music. Information on costume and scenery rentals. Bibliography of stagecraft materials; lists of awards for singers; opera activity in the U. S., 1955-56; addresses of publishers, opera groups; unpublished translations, sources of chamber operas.

229. RIEMANN, HUGO. Opern-Handbuch. Repertorium der dramatischmusikalischen Litteratur (Opern, Operetten, Ballette, Melodramen, Pantomimen, Oratorien, dramatische Kantaten, u.s.w.). Leipzig, H. Seemann Nachfolger ⌈n.d.⌉ 862 p.

Originally published by C. A. Koch, Leipzig, 1887.

Intended as an opera supplement to Riemann's Lexikon.

Title articles give genre, number of acts, composer, librettist, first performance. Composer articles give dates, chronological list of operas with names of librettists. Librettist entries give dates and chief activity.

230. ROSS, ANNE. The opera directory. London, John Calder; New York, Sterling Pub. Co. ⌈1961⌉ 566 p.

A source book of current opera facts and figures. Introduction and headings in six languages (English, French, German, Italian, Spanish, Russian). Material organized under 13 headings, the most important of which are: opera singers, conductors, producers and designers, technical staff, theaters and producing organizations, festivals, living composers, works by living composers, librettists, colleges and schools of music, casting index, glossary.

The identical volume is issued with French, German, and English title pages under the imprints of publishers in Paris, Geneva, Berlin, London, and New York. The French title, Annuaire de l'opera 1961-1962, suggests that the work has been projected as a yearbook.

231. SELTSAM, WILLIAM H. Metropolitan opera annals. New York, H. W. Wilson Co., 1947. 751 p.

Chronological listing of Metropolitan Opera performances, with casts, from the initial season (1883-84) through 1946-47. Coverage for each season includes roster, excerpts from press reviews of noteworthy performances. Index by artist, opera. Supplements issued annually in the final issue of each volume of Opera News.

First supplement. 1957. 115 p.

Cumulates the information for 1947-57.

232. TOWERS, JOHN. Dictionary-catalogue of operas and operettas which have been performed on the public stage. Morgentown, W. Va., Acme Pub. Co. ⌈1910⌉ 1045 p.

Title list of 28,015 operas, giving for each composer, his nationality and dates of birth and death. Alternative or translated titles included. Composer index, with titles of operas alphabetically under composer. No information on librettists, no historical or descriptive material.

MISCELLANEOUS

233. BARLOW, HAROLD and S. MORGENSTERN, comps. A dictionary of musical themes. New York, Crown, 1948. 656 p.

Contains 10,000 themes from instrumental works, arranged alphabetically by composer. Indexed by scale degrees in letter notation, with all themes transposed into C major or C minor. Title index.

234. BARLOW, HAROLD and S. MORGENSTERN, comps. A dictionary of vocal themes. New York, Crown, 1950. 547 p.

Contains themes from operas, cantatas, oratorios, art songs, and miscellaneous vocal works, arranged alphabetically by composer. Indexed by scale degrees, with all themes transposed to C major or C minor. Index by title and first line.

Review by Harold Spivacke in Notes, 8 (1951) p. 334-35.

235. BERGER, KENNETH W. Band encyclopedia. ⌈Evansville, Ind., Distributed by Band Associates, 1960⌉ 604 p.

A compendium of information useful to band directors. Includes revisions of the author's earlier publications: Band Bibliography, Band Discography, and Bandmen, a biographical dictionary of band musicians.

Review by Keith Polk in Notes, 18 (1961) p. 424-26; by J. M. Lundahl in Journal of Research in Music Education, 10 (1962) p. 81-82.

236. BURROWS, RAYMOND M. and BESSIE E. REDMOND. Concerto themes. New York, Simon and Schuster ⸤1951⸥ 296 p.

More inclusive than Barlow and Morgenstern (no. 233) for concertos. Arrangement alphabetical by composer. Index by concerto titles, keys, solo instruments. No thematic index.

237. BURROWS, RAYMOND M. and BESSIE C. REDMOND. Symphony themes. New York, Simon and Schuster ⸤1942⸥ 295 p.

238. COBBETT, WALTER W., ed. Cyclopedic survey of chamber music. 2nd ed. London, Oxford Univ. Press, 1963. 3 v.

First published, in 2 volumes, 1929-30.

The second edition is a reissue of the original two volumes, with minor corrections, plus a third volume which brings the work up to date.

Cobbett's Cyclopedia is a biographical and subject dictionary of chamber music, giving full lists of works in this category under composer. Solo works and piano compositions excluded. The main emphasis is critical and analytical. Excellent critical and bibliographical material, with signed articles by outstanding authorities.

The 3rd volume of the 1963 edition is composed of extended articles surveying chamber music since 1929 in Europe, Britain, Russia, and America. The editor, and principal contributor, is Colin Mason. The chapter on "Chamber Music in America" is by Nicolas Slonimsky; on "Soviet Chamber Music" by I. I. Martinov. There is a classified bibliography of literature on chamber music, index of composers discussed in vol. 3; additions and corrections to dates given in the original edition (Slonimsky).

239. GAMMOND, PETER and PETER CLAYTON. Dictionary of popular music. New York, Philosophical Library ⸤1961⸥ 274 p.

A dictionary of names, terms, titles of major popular songs. Listings of works, and recordings, for principal composers of popular music. Pronounced British slant.

240. READ, GARDNER. Thesaurus of orchestral devices. New York, Pitman ⌈1953⌉ 631 p.

"Intended to be a lexicon of instrumentation which will serve the student and/or professional orchestrator in the same manner and to the same degree that Bartlett's Familiar Quotations, Roget's Thesaurus ... aid both the student of literature and the established writer" (preface, p. x). Nomenclature in English, Italian, French, and German, with ranges of instruments, lists of devices with reference to page and measure number of score. List of music publishers and their U.S. agents. Index of nomenclature and terminology.

241. SLONIMSKY, NICOLAS. Thesaurus of scales and melodic patterns. New York, Coleman-Ross, 1947. 243 p.

"A reference book ... for composers in search of new materials." Contains nearly 1,000 scales, both traditional and contrived.

HISTORIES AND CHRONOLOGIES

We have been particularly selective in this area. The titles include only the standard general histories of music in the major European languages, together with some of the more recent outline histories. Excluded are all histories devoted to the music of a particular national group, most early histories (pre-1850) unless, as in the cases of Burney and Hawkins, they are of extraordinary interest and are currently available, and histories of special periods, or forms, except as they occur as part of a comprehensive series. Music histories come and go, and few of those designed for the general reader, or for the music student, may be expected to outlive their time. This will account for the fact that some of the standard occupants of library shelves, such as Dommer, Naumann, Rowbotham, and Rockstro, are missing from this list.

Those who want a comprehensive, chronological listing of music histories will find it in the appendix to Warren Allen's Philosophies of Music History (no. 1118) under the title "Bibliography of Literature concerning the General History of Music in Chronological Order." See also the article "Histories," by S. T. Worsthorne, in Grove's, 5th ed., Vol. 4, pp. 296-306, for both a chronological and a systematic listing.

HISTORIES

242. ABBIATI, FRANCO. Storia della musica. 2nd ed. ⌐ Milano ⌐ Garzanti ⌐1943-46 ⌐ 5 v.

A general history of music for Italian readers. Numerous pictorial and musical illustrations. Each major section followed by an anthology of excerpts from the writings of modern authorities on the period under consideration.

Vol. 1: Roma. Medio Evo. Rinascimento.

Vol. 2: Seicento.

Vol. 3: Settecento.

Vol. 4: Ottocento.

Vol. 5: Novecento.

243. ADLER, GUIDO, ed. Handbuch der Musikgeschichte
.... 2., vollständig durchgesehene und stark ergänzte Aufl.
Berlin-Wilmersdorf, H. Keller, 1930. 2 v.

Unaltered reprint of the 2nd ed., Tutzing, Schneider, 1961.
2 v.

First printed in 1924 in 1 vol. The standard German compendium of music history, representing the fruits of German musicology in its most flourishing and influential period. Major
articles by such scholars as Alfred Einstein, Wilhelm Fischer,
Robert Haas, Friedrich Ludwig, Curt Sachs, Arnold Schering,
Peter Wagner, and Egon Wellesz.

244. AMBROS, AUGUST WILHELM. Geschichte der Musik
.... 3., gänzlich umbearb. Aufl. Leipzig, Leuckart, 1887-1911.

One of the last major one-man histories of music. The
author did not live to carry the 4th vol. past the beginning of the
17th century. Based on original research, the work is particularly important for its coverage of the sources of medieval and
Renaissance music.

Bd. I: Ancient music. 1862. 2nd ed., 1880. 3rd ed., 1887
(B. v. Sakdowsky, ed.).

Bd. II: Music of the Middle Ages. 1864. 2nd ed., 1880
(Otto Kade). 3rd ed., 1891 (Heinrich Reimann).

Bd. III: The Renaissance to Palestrina. 1868. 2nd ed.,
1893 (Otto Kade).

Bd. IV: (not completed by Ambros) Italian music, 1550-
1650). 1878 (Gustav Nottebohm). 2nd ed., 1881. 3rd ed., 1909
(Hugo Leichtentritt).

Bd. V: "Eine Beispielsammlung zu den dritten Bande." 1882 (Otto Kade). 2nd ed., 1887. 3rd ed., 1911.

245. BESSELER, HEINRICH und MAX SCHNEIDER, eds. Musikgeschichte in Bildern. v. 1- Leipzig, Deutscher Verlag für Musik, 1961-

Band II: Musik des Altertums; Lieferung 1: Aegypten ⌐von⌐ Hans Hickmann.

The section on Egypt is the first issue of a multi-volume work projected to cover all phases of music history in pictures. The Kinsky work (no. 276) is taken as a point of departure, but the scope is greatly expanded. Hickmann's volume gives detailed commentary on 121 plates, a chronological table of Egyptian music history (p. 157-71), a bibliography of relevant literature, and an index of names and subjects.

246. BÜCKEN, ERNST, ed. Handbuch der Musikwissenschaft. Wildpark-Potsdam, Akademische Verlagsgesellschaft Athenaion ⌐1927-31⌐ 13 v. in 10

First issued serially in parts.

A series of important monographs on various periods and aspects of music history by the leading German musicologists of the period between World Wars I and II. Well printed and profusely illustrated, including plates in color.

Reprinted by photolithography in black and white. New York, Musurgia, 1949. 13 v. in 9

247. ⌐Vol. 1⌐ Besseler, Heinrich. Die Musik des Mittelalters und der Renaissance ⌐1931⌐ 337 p.

248. ⌐Vol. 2⌐ Blume, Friedrich. Die evangelische Kirchenmusik ⌐1931⌐ 171 p.

249. ⌐Vol. 3⌐ Bücken, Ernst. Geist und Form im musikalischen Kunstwerk ⌐1929⌐ 195 p.

250. ⌐Vol. 4⌐ Bücken, Ernst. Die Musik des 19.
Jahrhunderts bis zur Moderne ⌐1929⌐ 319 p.

251. ⌐Vol. 5⌐ Bücken, Ernst. Die Musik des Rokokos und
der Klassik ⌐1927⌐ 247 p.

252. ⌐Vol. 6⌐ Haas, Robert. Aufführungspraxis der Musik
⌐1931⌐ 298 p.

253. ⌐Vol. 7⌐ Haas, Robert. Die Musik des Barocks
⌐1929⌐ 290 p.

254. ⌐Vol. 8, pt. 1⌐ Heinitz, Wilhelm. Instrumenten-
kunde ⌐1929⌐ 159 p.

255. ⌐Vol. 8, pt. 2⌐ Lachmann, Robert. Die Musik des
aussereuropäischen Natur- und Kulturvölker ⌐1929⌐ 31 p.

256. ⌐Vol. 8, pt. 3⌐ Sachs, Curt. Die Musik der Antike
⌐1928⌐ 32 p.

257. ⌐Vol. 8, pt. 4⌐ Panóff, Peter. Die Altslavische
Volks- und Kirchenmusik ⌐1930 ⌐ 31 p.

258. ⌐Vol. 9⌐ Mersmann, Hans. Die Moderne Musik seit
der Romantik ⌐1928⌐ 225 p.

259. ⌐Vol. 10⌐ Ursprung, Otto. Die katholische Kirchenmusik. ⌐1931⌐ 312 p.

260. BURNEY, CHARLES. A general history of music,
from the earliest times to the present period. With critical and
historical notes by Frank Mercer. London, Foulis; New York,
Harcourt, Brace, 1935. 4 v. in 2

Originally published in London, 1776-89, 4 v. Burney's
history stands with that of John Hawkins at the starting point of
modern historical writing in the music field. Of outstanding

literary value, its present significance is that of a document of 18th-century musical taste and learning.

Reprint by Dover Publications, New York, 1957, 2 v. Republication of first edition projected by Akademische Druck- und Verlagsanstalt, Graz.

261. CANNON, BEEKMAN C., ALVIN H. JOHNSON, and WILLIAM G. WAITE. The art of music, a short history of musical styles and ideas. New York, Crowell ⌐1960⌐ 484 p.

Designed as an introduction to the history of music: little background required. Appendix on "basic principles of music." Index. No bibliography. Brief musical examples in text.

Review by Warner Imig in Journal of Research in Music Education, 9 (1961) p. 172.

262. COLLAER, PAUL et ALBERT VAN DER LINDEN. Atlas historique de la musique ... avec la collaboration de F. van den Bremt. Préf. de Charles van den Borren. Paris, Elsevier ⌐1960⌐ 179 p.

An illustrated survey of music history. 15 full-page maps relating to various aspects of musical culture. More than 700 illustrations. A delight to the eye and a stimulant to the mind.

Review by Robert E. Wolf in MQ, 47 (1961) p. 413-16.

263. COMBARIEU, JULES. Histoire de la musique des origines au début du XXe siècle. Paris, A. Colin, 1946-60. 5 v.

The first three volumes originally published 1913-19.

I. Des origines à la fin du XVIe siècle.

II. Du XVIIe siècle à la mort de Beethoven.

III. De la mort de Beethoven au début du XXe siècle.

IV. L'Aube du XXe siècle, par René Dumesnil (1958).

V. La première moitié du XXe siècle, par René Dumesnil (1960).

264. CONFALONIERI, GIULIO. Storia della musica.
Milano, Nuova accademia editrice ⌐1958⌐ 2 v.

A popular general history. Lavishly printed on glossy paper,
with 34 plates in full color and hundreds of black and white illustrations. No musical examples. Essential bibliography listed, by
chapter, at the end of Vol. 2, where there is also a general index
and an index of illustrations.

265. CORTE, ANDREA DELLA. Antologia della storia della
musica, dalla Grecia antica all'ottocento. 4. ed., rinnovata in
un volume. Torino, G. B. Paravia ⌐1945⌐ 491 p.

First pub. in 1926 in 2 v.

An anthology of writings on music history, chiefly by modern
European scholars, but with a few early documents (i.e., excerpts from Zarlino, Galilei, Caccini, Peri, etc.). Italian text
throughout.

266. CORTE, ANDREA DELLA e G. PANNAIN. Storia
della musica. 2. ed. Torino, Unione Tipografico-Editrice
Torinese, 1944. 3 v.

First pub. in 1935. 2nd ed., 1942. Reprint, 1944.

An illustrated general music history for Italian readers.

I. Dal medioevo al seicento.

II. Il settecento.

III. L'ottocento, il novecento.

267. DUFOURCQ, NORBERT, ed. La musique des origines
à nos jours. Préf. de Claude Delvincourt. Nouv. éd., rev.,
augm. Paris, Larousse, 1954, 591 p.

A reprinting of a work first published in 1946.

A lavishly illustrated compendium of music history and
related fields, the work of 44 scholars, chiefly French, in 5
books, of which the 3rd (p. 83-431) deals with the history of

Western music. Other books concerned with the voice and instruments, ancient and Near-Eastern music, non-European music, musical aesthetics. A series of 17 appendices treat special topics such as notation, music theory, criticism, music libraries and other institutions. 6 colored plates and numerous black and white illustrations.

268. EINSTEIN, ALFRED. A short history of music. 3rd American edition. New York, Knopf, 1947. 438 p.

Originally published in German, 1934.

One of the most perceptive and authoritative concise histories of music. Published in numerous editions and translations. First Amer. ed., 1937; 2nd Amer. ed., 1938; also issued as a paperback, New York, Vintage Books, without musical examples. Most editions incorporate a useful anthology of 39 musical examples, originally published in 1917 as "Beispielsammlung zur älteren Musikgeschichte." A handsome illustrated edition (London, Cassell, 1953) edited by A. Hyatt King unfortunately does not contain the musical supplement.

269. FERGUSON, DONALD N. A history of musical thought. 3rd ed. New York, Appleton-Century-Crofts [1959] 675 p.

First published in 1935; 2nd ed., 1948.

Designed for music history courses at the college level.

270. FINNEY, THEODORE M. A history of music. Rev. ed. New York, Harcourt, Brace, 1947. 720 p.

First published in 1935. A well organized history for students.

271. GROUT, DONALD J. A history of Western music. New York, Norton, 1960. 742 p.

Intended for undergraduate college music students, or for the general reader. "An elementary knowledge of musical terms and of harmony ... has been assumed." Based on a stylistic approach.

Contains numerous musical and pictorial illustrations. An annotated bibliography for further reading, a chronology of musical and historical events, and a glossary of terms not defined within the body of the work.

Review by Albert T. Luper in Notes, 18 (1960) p. 47-48; by Warren Allen in Journal of Research in Music Education, 8 (1960) p. 124-26; and by Alec Harman in Musical Times (Dec. 1962) p. 845-47.

272. GRUBER, ROMAN I. Istoriia muzykal'noi kyl'tury. Moskv. Gosudarstvennoe muzykal'noe izdatel'stvo, 1941-59. 2 v. in 4

General history from antiquity to the beginning of the 17th century, for Russian readers. Vol. 1, pt. 1 deals with Egypt, Mesopotamia, India, China, etc., as well as Greece and Rome. The final chapter of Vol. 2 is concerned with the musical culture of the Western Slavs to the 17th century.

273. HANDSCHIN, JACQUES. Musikgeschichte im Überblick. Luzern, Rüber [1948] 432 p.

A stimulating short history slanted in the direction of medieval and Renaissance music; the first 272 pages are occupied with these areas. Chronological tables, p. 379-85; classified bibliography, p. 396-417.

274. HARMAN, ALEC and WILFRED MELLERS. Man and his music, the story of musical experience in the West. New York, Oxford Univ. Press, 1962. 1172 p.

First pub. in 1957-59, in four separate volumes: Vol. 1, Medieval and early Renaissance music (up to c. 1525); Vol. 2, Late Renaissance and baroque music (c. 1525-c. 1750); Vol. 3, The sonata principle (from c. 1750); Vol. 4, Romanticism and the 20th century.

A history designed for the intelligent layman and stressing the social and cultural backgrounds. P. 1070-99: comparative chronology; p. 1101-24: a list of recommended books and music.

Review of Vol. 2 by J. Merrill Knapp in Notes, 17 (1960)
p. 569-70; of Vols. 3 and 4 by William S. Newman in Notes, 15
(1957) p. 99-101. Review of the composite vol. by Jack A.
Westrup in Music & Letters, 43 (1962) p. 265-66.

275. HAWKINS, SIR JOHN. A general history of the science
and practice of music. London, Payne and Son, 1776. 5 v.

New edition, "with the author's posthumous notes," published by Novello, London, 1853 (the 3rd volume is an "atlas" of
portraits); this edition reprinted by Novello, 1875.

Unabridged republication of the 1853 Novello edition, with a
new introduction by Charles Cudworth, New York, Dover, 1963.
2 v.

A reissue of the same edition has been announced by
Akademische Drucke- und Verlagsanstalt, Graz, 1963.

Hawkins' history appeared in the same year that the first
volume of Charles Burney's history (no. 260) was published. The
two works inevitably invited comparison, largely to Hawkins'
disadvantage. His history, however, has much to recommend it,
particularly in its extensive translations of excerpts from early
theory works, and the inclusion of many examples of early music.

276. KINSKY, GEORG. A history of music in pictures. New
York, Dutton, 1937. 363 p.

Originally pub. in German in 1929; first English ed. 1930;
reprint, New York, Dover, 1951. There is also a French ed.

Pictures include musicians' portraits; music in painting,
drawing, and sculpture; facsimile pages from early music and
theory works; photographs of old instruments. Arranged chronologically from antiquity to the early 20th century. Index to
instruments, place names, and personal names.

277. KOMMA, KARL MICHAEL. Musikgeschichte in
Bildern. Stuttgart, Alfred Kröner, 1961. 332 p.

473 well reproduced illustrations concerned with the history of music from antiquity to the 20th century; detailed commentary on each illustration.

278. KRETZSCHMAR, HERMANN, ed. Kleine Handbücher der Musikgeschichte nach Gattungen. Leipzig, Breitkopf & Härtel, 1905-22. 14 v. in 15

A series of historical monographs dealing with the development of special musical forms or disciplines. Although superseded in many respects, the volumes remain basic studies in the areas with which they are concerned.

279. Vol. 1: Schering, Arnold. Geschichte des Instrumentalkonzerts ... 1905. 226 p. 2. Aufl., 1927.

280. Vol. 2: Leichtentritt, Hugo. Geschichte der Motette. 1908. 453 p.

281. Vol. 3: Schering, Arnold. Geschichte des Oratoriums. 1911. 647 p. Notenanhang, 39 p.

282. Vol. 4: Kretzschmar, Hermann. Geschichte des neuen deutschen Liedes. I. Von Albert bis Zelter. 1911. 354 p.

283. Vol. 5: Schmitz, Eugen. Geschichte der Kantate und des geistlichen Konzerts. I. Geschichte der weltlichen Solokantate. 1914. 327 p. 2. Aufl., 1955.

284. Vol. 6: Kretzschmar, Hermann. Geschichte der Oper. 1919. 286 p.

285. Vol. 7: Kretzschmar, Hermann. Einführung in die Musikgeschichte. 1920. 82 p. (See no. 342.)

286. Vol. 8: Wolf, Johannes. Handbuch der Notationskunde. I: Tonschriften des Altertums und des Mittelalters ....
II: Tonschriften des Neuzeit, Tablaturen, Partitur, Generalbass und Reformversuch. 1913-19. 2 v.

287. Vol. 9: Botstiber, Hugo. Geschichte der Ouverture und der freien Orchesterformen. 1913. 274 p.

288. Vol. 10: Schünemann, Georg. Geschichte des Dirigierens. 1913. 359 p.

289. Vol. 11: Wagner, Peter. Geschichte der Messe. I: Bis 1600. 1913. 548 p.

290. Vol. 12: Sachs, Curt. Handbuch der Musik-instrumentenkunde. 1920. 412 p.

291. Vol. 13: Aber, Adolf. Handbuch der Musikliteratur .... 1922. 696 col. (See no. 349.)

292. Vol. 14: Nef, Karl. Geschichte der Symphonie und Suite. 1921. 344 p.

293. LANG, PAUL H. Music in Western civilization. New York, Norton ⌐1941⌐ 1107 p.

Music in the context of the social, political, and cultural currents of Western civilization. One of the most influential music histories produced in America, it coincided with, and to a large extent contributed to, the general acceptance of music history in American higher education.

Comprehensive bibliography in all languages, one alphabet, p. 1045-65.

German edition, Augsburg, 1947; translations into Spanish, Portuguese, Czech, and Japanese.

294. LANG, PAUL H. and OTTO BETTMANN. A pictorial history of music. New York, Norton, 1960. 242 p.

"Text based on Music in Western Civilization by Paul Henry Lang, " above.

295. MANUEL, ROLAND, ed. Histoire de la musique.
I. Des origines a Jean-Sebastién Bach. ⊏Paris, Gallimard, 1960⊐
(Encyclopédie de la Pléiade, 9) 2238 p.

An important work. The language is French but the approach
is international, comprising contributions by 59 specialists from
different countries. Preliminary chapter on "Elements et
geneses" (128 p.), followed by surveys of the music of non-
European civilizations, of ancient classical and oriental music,
and of the music of the Moslem world (to p. 617). Thereafter
there are chronological and national surveys of the development of
Western music. Chronological tables (p. 1963-2043); glossary of
technical terms (p. 2045-56); indexes of names and of musical
works cited; analytical table of contents.

296. NEF, KARL. An outline of the history of music. Tr.
by Carl Pfatteicher. New York, Columbia Univ. Press ⊏1935⊐
400 p.

Originally pub. as Einführung in die Musikgeschichte, in
1920. An augmented French translation by Yvonne Rokseth
appeared in 1931.

An excellent outline history for use in college or university
music courses. "Brief, yet comprehensive; readable, yet
scholarly" (translator's foreword). Rich in bibliographical
references and musical examples in the text. General bibliography, p. 355-59.

297. THE NORTON HISTORY OF MUSIC SERIES. New York,
Norton, 1940-

A publisher's series consisting of independent works on
different periods in the history of music. It was at one time announced that the volumes would be reissued as a set following
individual publication. In that case some of the titles listed below
may not be included.

The volumes by Reese and Bukofzer are particularly rich in
bibliographical content.

298. Sachs, Curt. The rise of music in the ancient world, East and West. ⊏1943⊐ 324 p.

299. Reese, Gustave. Music in the Middle Ages. ⊏1940⊐ 502 p.

300. Reese, Gustave. Music in the Renaissance. ⊏1954⊐ 1022 p. Rev. ed. ⊏1959⊐

Review by Denis Stevens in Music & Letters, 36 (1955) p. 70-73; review of rev. ed. by E. H. Sparks in Notes, 17 (1960) p. 569.

301. Bukofzer, Manfred. Music in the baroque era; from Monteverdi to Bach. ⊏1947⊐ 489 p.

302. Einstein, Alfred. Music in the romantic era. ⊏1947⊐ 371 p.

303. Salazar, Adolfo. Music in our time; trends in music since the romantic era. Tr. by Isabel Pope. ⊏1946⊐ 367 p.

304. THE NEW OXFORD HISTORY OF MUSIC. London, New York, Oxford Univ. Press, 1954-

Each volume is a composite work made up of contributions by scholars of international repute and edited by a specialist in the field. The set is planned in 10 volumes, plus a volume of chronological tables and general index. There is an accompanying series of recordings issued under the title The History of Music in Sound, with illustrated booklets designed for teaching purposes. All recordings and pamphlets have appeared.

305. Vol. 1: Ancient and oriental music, ed. by Egon Wellesz. 1957. 530 p.

Reviewed by Curt Sachs in Notes, 16 (1957) p. 97-99; by Roy Jesson in MQ, 44 (1958) p. 245-53; by Charles Seeger in Ethnomusicology, 3 (1959) p. 96-97.

306. Vol. 2: Early medieval music up to 1300, ed. by Anselm Hughes. 1954. 434 p.

Review by Charles Warren Fox in MQ, 41 (1955) p. 534-47; by Jeremy Noble in Music & Letters, 36 (1955) p. 65-70.

307. Vol. 3: Ars Nova and the Renaissance (1300-1540), ed. by Anselm Hughes and Gerald Abraham. 1960. 565 p.

Review by Richard H. Hoppin in MQ, 47 (1961) p. 125; by Thurston Dart in Music & Letters, 42 (1961) p. 57-60.

The following vols. are in preparation:

Vol. 4: The age of humanism (1540-1630).

Vol. 5: Opera and church music (1630-1750).

Vol. 6: The growth of instrumental music (1630-1750).

Vol. 7: The symphonic outlook (1745-1790).

Vol. 8: The age of Beethoven (1790-1830).

Vol. 9: Romanticism (1830-1890).

Vol. 10: Modern music (1890-1950).

Vol. 11: Chronological tables and general index.

308. THE OXFORD HISTORY OF MUSIC. ⌐2nd ed.⌐ London, Oxford Univ. Press, 1929-38. 7 v. plus Introductory v.

First printed in 1901-05, in 6 vols. Vols. 4-6 of the 2nd ed. are reprints of the original vols.

309. Introductory vol., ed. by Percy C. Buck. 1929. 239 p.

A symposium by 9 scholars, covering Greek and Hebrew music, notation, musical instruments, theory to 1400, plainsong, folk-song, social aspects of music in the Middle Ages. Chapter bibliographies, p. 223-39.

310. Vols. 1-2: Wooldridge, H. E. The polyphonic period. 2nd ed. rev. by P. C. Buck. 1929-32. 2 v.

311. Vol. 3: Parry, C. Hubert H. The music of the seventeenth century. 1938. 486 p.

312.. Vol. 4: Fuller-Maitland, J. A. The age of Bach and Handel. 2nd ed. 1931. 362 p.

313. Vol. 5: Hadow, W. H. The Viennese period. 1931. 350 p.

314. Vol. 6: Dannreuther, Edward. The romantic period. 1931. 374 p.

315. Vol. 7: Colles, H. C. Symphony and drama, 1850-1900. 1934. 504 p.

316. PINCHERLE, MARC. An illustrated history of music. ⌐Ed. by Georges and Rosamond Bernier⌐ Trans. by Rollo Myers. New York, Reynal ⌐1959⌐ 220 p.

Pub. in France under the title Histoire illustrée de la musique. Paris, Gallimard, 1959.

A magnificently designed volume, with 200 illustrations in black and white and 40 in full color. Traces the history of music from antiquity to modern times. The text is planned as an introduction to music history, but maintains a high standard in accuracy and critical comment. Documentation lacking.

Review by Denis W. Stevens in The Musical Times, 101 (Aug. 1960) p. 493; by Emanuel Winternitz in Notes, 18 (Dec. 1960) p. 48-50; by Jack A. Westrup in Music & Letters, 41 (1960) p. 388.

317. PRUNIÈRES, HENRY. A new history of music; the middle ages to Mozart. Tr. and ed. by Edward Lockspeiser. New York, Macmillan, 1943. 413 p.

Originally pub. in French, Nouvelle histoire de la musique. Paris, 1934-36. 2 v.

Valuable for its emphasis on earlier periods.

318. RIEMANN, HUGO. Handbuch der Musikgeschichte. 2nd ed. ⸤edited by Alfred Einstein⸥ Leipzig, Breitkopf & Härtel, 1920-23. 2 v. in 4

First pub. in 1904-13.

Product of one of the most vigorous and stimulating minds in German musicology, always provocative, frequently misleading. Extensive chapter bibliographies, and sections devoted to brief biographies. Numerous transcriptions of early music, all of which must be viewed in the light of Riemann's unorthodox editorial methods.

319. SACHS, CURT. Our musical heritage, a short history of music. 2nd ed. New York, Prentice-Hall, 1955. 351 p.

First pub. in 1948.

Designed as a textbook for an introductory course in music history. References to essential bibliography and recordings.

320. SALAZAR, ADOLFO. La música en la sociedad europea. ⸤México⸥ El Colegio de México ⸤1942-46⸥ 9 parts in 4 v.

A general history of music for Spanish readers, from antiquity to the end of 19th century.

321. SMIJERS, ALBERT, ed. Algemeene muziek-geschiedenis; geïlustreerd overzicht der Europeesche muziek van de oudheid tot heden. 4. bijgewerkte druk. Utrecht, W. de Haan, 1947. 518 p.

2nd ed., 1940.

A composite history in 8 books, each written by a different Dutch or Flemish scholar under the general editorship of Smijers. Short bibliographies after each book. Plates and numerous musical illustrations in the text.

322. STRUNK, W. OLIVER, ed. Source readings in music history from classical antiquity through the romantic era. New York, Norton, 1950. 919 p.

87 items from the writings of theorists, composers, teachers, critics, and practical musicians, arranged roughly in chronological order under topics. Each item introduced by a few concise and illuminating comments by the editor. The translations are excellent and the editorial work exemplary. An indispensable volume in any library of music history.

Reviewed by Manfred Bukofzer in Notes, 8 (1951) p. 517-18; by Erich Hertzmann in MQ, 37 (1951) p. 430-32; by Leo Schrade in JAMS, 4 (1951) p. 249-51.

323. SUBIRÁ, JOSÉ. Historia de la música. 3. ed., reformada, ampliada, y puesta al dia. Barcelona, Editorial Salvat, 1958. 4 v.

First pub. 1947, 2nd ed., 1951.

Handsomely printed and lavishly illustrated, musically and pictorially. Some emphasis on ethnomusicology. The approach is generally chronological, but with special chapters on the development of notation, 17th-century theory and performance practice.

324. WÖRNER, KARL H. Geschichte der Musik: ein Studien- und Nachschlangebuch. Dritte Auflage. Göttingen, Vanderhoeck und Ruprecht ⌐1961⌐ 486 p.

First pub. in 1954, 2nd ed., 1956.

A well organized outline history, somewhat in the manner of Nef (no. 296). Excellent bibliographical references.

CHRONOLOGIES

325. CHAILLEY, JACQUES. Chronologie musicale en tableaux synoptiques. Paris, Centre de documentation universitaire et S. E. D. E. réunis, 1955. 140 p.

1re partie: De 310-1600.

326. DETHERIDGE, JOSEPH. Chronology of music composers. Birmingham, J. Detheridge, 1936-37. 2 v.

Vol. 1: 820-1810.

Vol. 2: 1810-1913.

More than 2,500 names of important composers, arranged chronologically by date of birth. Brief comments on activity, fields of composition, nationality. Alphabetical index of names. Numerous inaccuracies and misleading statements, but valuable as the most comprehensive work of its kind.

327. MATTFELD, JULIUS. Variety music cavalcade, 1620-1961: a chronology of vocal and instrumental music popular in the United States .... With an introduction by Abel Green. Revised edition. Englewood Cliffs, N. Y., Prentice-Hall, 1962. 713 p.

First published as Variety Music Cavalcade, 1620-1950. 1952. 637 p.

Originally appeared in a modified form as Variety Radio Directory 1938-39, supplemented in weekly issues of Variety.

Lists popular music chronologically, with a brief account of the parallel social and historical events occurring each year. Index lists all musical works by title, with date of first publication.

Review by Irving Lowens in Notes, 20 (1963) p. 233-34.

Also entered as no. 536.

328. MIES, PAUL and N. SCHNEIDER. Musik im Umkreis der Kulturgeschichte. Ein Tabellenwerk aus der Geschichte der Musik, Literatur, bildenden Künste, Philosophie und Politik Europas. Köln, P. J. Tonger ⌐1953⌐ 2 v.

Vol. 1: chronological tables of musical periods and events;

Vol. 2: parallel tables of history, philosophy, literature, art and architecture.

329. SCHERING, ARNOLD. Tabellen zur Musikgeschichte, ein Hilfsbuch beim Studium der Musikgeschichte. Fünfte Auflage bis zur Gegenwart ergänzt von Hans Joachim Moser. Wiesbaden, Breitkopf & Härtel, 1962. 175 p.

First pub. in 1914; 3rd ed., 1921; 4th ed., 1934.

Chronological tables outlining the important events in music history from antiquity to 1962, including birth and death dates of musicians, the principal events in their lives, significant publications and performances, and dates marking the activity of important music centers and stylistic developments. Parallel historical and cultural events are given. The 4th edition contains a 30-page supplement giving a detailed listing of the contents of the major Denkmäler and Gesamtausgaben published by Breitkopf & Härtel. The 5th edition has an index of names and subjects.

330. SLONIMSKY, NICOLAS. Music since 1900. 3rd ed., rev. and enl. New York, Coleman-Ross, 1949. 759 p.

First pub. in 1937, New York, Norton, 2nd ed., 1938.

Contains a "Tabular View of Stylistic Trends in Music, 1900-1948," p. xxix-lxiii; "Descriptive Chronology, 1900-1948," p. 3-626; "Letters and Documents," p. 629-711. There is an index to the descriptive chronology, p. 713-59.

The earlier editions contained a "Concise Biographical Dictionary of 20th Century Musicians," omitted in the 3rd ed.

The chronology records significant events in the development of contemporary music: dates of composition and first

performance, the founding of institutions and societies, births
and deaths of contemporary musicians. International in scope,
but an increased emphasis on American music for the decade
from 1937 to 1948. Quotes many of the major documents in the
history of contemporary music.

GUIDES TO SYSTEMATIC AND HISTORICAL MUSICOLOGY

In this section are a group of works designed to introduce the
student to the methods and materials of musical research. They
vary widely in pattern and approach, some concerned with the
content, others with the methodology of the discipline. Some
emphasize the historical aspects of research, others the systematic. The present list is not intended to be exhaustive. A full
century has passed since the term "Musikwissenschaft" was
introduced by Friedrich Chrysander (Jahrbücher für Musikwissenschaft, 1863), and ever since that time musicologists have been
attempting to define their field, to plot its structure and its
relationships to other areas in the humanities. For a general
discussion of the history of musical scholarship, and a comprehensive bibliography on the subject, see the article "Musikwissenschaft," by Walter Wiora and Hans Albrecht, in MGG, Vol. 9,
col. 1192-1220. For a recent consideration of the underlying
concepts and scope of the field, see "Musicology Reconsidered, "
by Lloyd Hibberd, in Acta M, 31 (1959) p. 25-31.

331. ALLEN, WARREN D. Philosophies of music history.
New York, American Book Co. ⌐1939⌐ 382 p.

One of the few discussions, in English, of musical historiography.

This work is cited elsewhere (no. 1118) for its chronological
bibliography of music histories.

332. ADLER, GUIDO. Methode der Musikgeschichte.
Leipzig, Breitkopf & Härtel, 1919. 222 p.

This, together with the author's Der Stil in der Musik (1911,
2nd ed. , 1929), is a basic and pioneer study of the content and
method of historical musicology. Contains a bibliographical
supplement, "Verzeichnis von bibliographischen Hilfswerken für

musikhistorische Arbeiten, " now outdated but of interest as a listing of music reference resources prior to World War I.

333. BROECKX, JAN L. Methode van de muziek-geschiedenis, met een inleiding door Prof. Dr. Fl. Van der Mueren. Antwerpen, Metropolis, 1959. 368 p.

A comprehensive survey of the methods and content of historical musicology. The three major divisions of the work are concerned with (1) basic concepts (Algemene beginselen), (2) working procedures (Arbeidregels), and (3) terminology. Numerous bibliographical references in the text and a bibliographical appendix, p. 329-39.

334. CHAILLEY, JACQUES, ed. Précis de musicologie. Paris, Presses Universitaires de France, 1958. 431 p.

A syllabus published under the auspices of the Institute of Musicology of the University of Paris. Contributions by 25 French musicologists covering varied aspects of musical research. The emphasis is historical. Main approach is chronological, but with special chapters devoted to music bibliography, ethnomusicology, instruments, dance, philosophy and aesthetics, etc. Bibliography stressed throughout.

335. FELLERER, KARL G. Einführung in die Musikwissenschaft. 2. neubearb. und erweiterte Aufl. Münchberg, B. Hahnefeld ⊏ 1956 ⊐ 190 p.

First pub. in 1942.

Historical musicology plays a comparatively minor role in this survey of the content of musical knowledge. Emphasis is on systematic areas: acoustics, aesthetics, psychology, sociology, and pedagogy. Extensive bibliographies for each chapter.

Reviewed by Glen Haydon in Notes, 11 (Dec. 1953) p. 111-12; in Die Musikforschung, 8 (1955) p. 96-97.

336. GARRETT, ALLEN M. An introduction to research in music. Washington, Catholic University of America Press, 1958. 169 p.

An attempt to survey the content and methods of musicology in a course intended for first-year graduate students in music. The approach is superficial and misleading.

Reviewed by Donald J. Grout in Notes, 16 (March 1959) p. 246-47.

337. GLEASON, HAROLD. Music literature outlines. Ser. 1-5. Rochester, N. Y., Levis Music Stores, 1949-55.

Ser. 1: Music in the Middle Ages and Renaissance. 2nd ed.

Ser. 2: Music in the baroque.

Ser. 3: American music from 1620-1920.

Ser. 4: Contemporary music. (mimeographed)

Ser. 5: Chamber music from Haydn to Ravel.

Historical outlines with copious bibliographical references, including recordings. The organization of Series 1 and 2 follows closely that of the works by Reese and Bukofzer in the Norton History of Music series.

338. HAYDON, GLEN. Introduction to musicology; a survey of the fields, systematic & historical, of musical knowledge & research. New York, Prentice-Hall, 1941. 329 p.

Unaltered reprint by Univ. of North Carolina Press, Chapel Hill, 1959.

Systematic musicology (acoustics, psychology, aesthetics, theory, and pedagogy) occupies the first 243 pages of this work. Historical musicology treated in p. 247-99. Each section has its special bibliography, with a general bibliography in p. 301-13.

339. HUSMANN, HEINRICH. Einführung in die Musikwissenschaft. Heidelberg, Quelle & Meyer ⸤1958⸥ 268 p.

An introduction to systematic musicology. Much attention given to acoustical and psychological aspects of the materials. The approach embraces all musical phenomena in all cultures. Extensive bibliography organized by chapter headings, p. 235-55.

Reviewed by Werner Korte in Die Musikforschung, 13 (1960) p. 340-42.

340. IRVINE, DEMAR B. Methods of research in music. Part I: Methods. Seattle, Washington, 1945. 69 p. (typescript)

A syllabus for music research students at the college level. Emphasis on methodology, with chapters covering "the field," "the problem," "the sources," "the facts," "the report." No bibliography.

341. IRVINE, DEMAR B. Writing about music; a style book for reports and theses. ⊏Seattle, Univ. of Washington Press, 1956⊐ 74 p.

A guide for the preparation of the research report in music, with detailed instructions regarding the preparation of the manuscript, documentation, use of illustrations, and abbreviations.

342. KRETZSCHMAR, HERMANN. Einführung in die Musikgeschichte. Leipzig, Breitkopf & Härtel, 1920. 82 p. (Kleine Handbücher der Musikgeschichte, 7)

A brief narrative account of the content of and sources for the historical study of music. Relevant literature is mentioned in context. Chapter I traces the development of music historiography through the 19th century. Also cited as No. 284.

343. MORGAN, HAZEL B. Music research handbook, for: music education, music theory, music history, music literature, musicology ... in collaboration with Clifton A. Burmeister. Evanston, Ill., The Instrumentalist, 1962. 110 p.

A compendium of devices and methods intended to assist
students in writing "research" papers. What is implied by
"research" rarely extends beyond the requirements for a student's
term report.

344. MOSER, HANS JOACHIM. Lehrbuch der Musikgeschichte. 10. durchgesehene und verm. Aufl. Berlin-
Halensee, Deutscher Musikliteratur-Verlag ⌐1950⌐ 434 p.

First pub. in 2 vols. in 1936.

An outline history with bibliographical supplements to each
section.

345. RIEMANN, HUGO. Grundriss der Musikwissenschaft.
4. Aufl., durchgesehen von Johannes Wolf. Leipzig, Quelle &
Meyer, 1928. 160 p. (Wissenschaft und Bildung, 34)

346. SCHIEDERMAIR, LUDWIG. Einführung in das Studium
der Musikgeschichte; Leitsätze, Quellen, Übersichten und
Ratschläge. 4. umbearb. und erweiterte Aufl. Bonn, F.
Dümmlers Verlag, 1947. 167 p.

First pub. in 1918.

Brief surveys, with bibliographies, of the major historical
periods. Concluding chapters deal with methodology, institutions,
advice to students, and career possibilities, all pertaining to the
German scene. A useful appendix lists major Gesamtausgaben
and the contents of several publishers' series devoted to early
music.

347. SPIESS, LINCOLN B. Historical musicology, a
reference manual for research in music ... with articles by Ernst
C. Krohn, Lloyd Hibberd, Luther A. Dittmer, Tsang-Houei Shu,
Tatsuo Minagawa, Zdenek Nováček. Brooklyn, The Institute of
Mediaeval Music ⌐1963⌐ 294 p. (Musicological studies, 4)

"A text and reference book of musical research, includes
lists of suggested topics for class and seminar reports, term
papers, and dissertations; with a copious bibliography, index of

publishers, etc. " (quoted from publisher's prospectus). The bibliography consists of 1,980 numbered items, in all categories, distributed throughout the text.

348. WESTRUP, SIR JACK. An introduction to musical history. London, Hutchinson University Library ⊏1955⊐ 174 p.

A small, practical introduction to the study of music history. "This is not a history of music. It is simply an attempt to outline some of the problems which historians and students have to face, and to give some idea of the conditions in which music has come into existence" (author's preface). Although intended as a lay-man's guide, this little book is one of the few clear treatments of music historiography in English.

Review by Allen P. Britton in Journal of Research in Music Education, 3 (1955) p. 154.

BIBLIOGRAPHIES OF MUSIC LITERATURE

The term "music literature" as applied here refers to writings on music as opposed to musical scores. Such writings may appear in the form of periodical articles or monographs; they may be cited in complete, self-contained bibliographical works, or in serial publications, and they can be organized in terms of a variety of subject fields. Nearly every dissertation or research study will have its bibliography of relevant literature, and most of the authoritative dictionaries or encyclopedias have subject bibliographies appended to their articles. It would be impossible to cite them all, but the titles selected are numerous enough to form a substantial section of the present book. Following is an outline of the subdivisions employed:

> Bibliographies of Music Literature
> General
> Current or Annual
> Lists of Music Periodicals
> Special and Subject
>> Contemporary Music
>> Dissertations
>> Ethnomusicology
>> Instruments
>> Jazz
>> Medieval and Renaissance Music
>> Music Education
>> National Music
>> Opera and Theater Music
>> Primary Sources
>> Sacred Music

See also under "Catalogs of Music Libraries and Collections." Most of the published catalogs provide separate sections for their holdings of books on music.

GENERAL

349. ABER, ADOLF. Handbuch der Musikliteratur in systematisch-chronologischer Anordnung. Leipzig, Breitkopf & Härtel, 1922. 696 col. (Kleine Handbücher der Musikgeschichte, 13)

A classified bibliography for students of music history. International coverage, although strongest in German materials. Entries from at least 13 important musicological journals are included. Subject and author indexes.

Also listed as part of the Kretzschmar series, no. 291.

350. ADLUNG, JACOB. Anleitung zu der musikalischen Gelahrtheit, 1758. Faksimile-Nachdruck hersg. von H. J. Moser. Kassel, Bärenreiter, 1953. 814 p. (Documents Musicologica, Erste Reihe: Druckschriften-Faksimiles, IV)

2nd ed., rev. by J. A. Hiller, appeared in 1783.

Chronologically one of the first important critical bibliographies of music literature. The author proposed to list all works on musical subjects necessary to "educated music lovers and particularly to lovers of keyboard music" as well as to builders of organs and other instruments.

See the brief but valuable description of this work in Gustave Reese's Fourscore Classics of Music Literature (no. 513) (New York, Liberal Arts Press, 1957), p. 74-75.

351. AZHDERIAN, HELEN WENTWORTH. Reference works in music and music literature in five libraries of Los Angeles County. Los Angeles, Pub. for the Southern Calif. Chapter of the Music Library Association, by the Univ. of Southern Calif., 1953. 313 p.

A Partial Supplement of Holdings in the USC Library, January 1952-June 1962. Prepared by Joan M. Meggett. (July 1962) 13 p. (hexagraph reproduction) Supplements entries for:

Editions, Historical

   General (2233-2520), p. 116-32.

   Individual Composers (2521-2593), p. 133-37.

Liturgical Music, Hymnology and Psalmody (3746-4036), p. 198-212.

A bibliography of musicological literature, approx. 4,500 items. International coverage. Full bibliographical citations. Classified listing with author index. The libraries represented are: Henry E. Huntington Library, William Andrews Clark Memorial Library, Los Angeles Public Library, and the libraries of the University of Southern California and the University of California at Los Angeles.

Reviewed by Otto Albrecht in <u>Notes</u>, 11 (1954) p. 468-69; and by Vincent Duckles in <u>JAMS</u>, 7 (1954) p. 242-43.

352. BECKER, CARL F. Systematisch-chronologische Darstellung der musikalischen Literatur von den frühesten bis auf die neueste Zeit .... Leipzig, R. Friese, 1836. 570 col. and 34 p.

<u>Nachtrag</u>, 1839.

A classified bibliography of many now obscure works. It fills the gap, chronologically, between Forkel (no. 361) and Lichtenthal (no. 365) and Eitner's Bücherverzeichniss ..., 1885 (no. 360). Includes newspaper and periodical articles. Gives place of publication, date, pagination, with brief annotations. 33-page index by subject, author, etc.

353. BELKNAP, SARA Y. Guide to the musical arts. New York, Scarecrow Press, 1957. (not paginated)

Indexes 11 English-language and 2 foreign music and theater journals for the period 1953-56. Two major sections: I. Articles; II. Illustrations. The <u>Guide</u> has serious short-comings as a reference tool: unnumbered pages, confused entries, much space devoted to ephemera. Its chief value lies in the section on illustrations.

See also the author's Guide to the Performing Arts,
No. 380.

354. BLECHSCHMIDT, RENATE. "Bibliographie der
Schriften über Musik aus der Deutschen Demokratischen Republik,
1945-1959." In Beiträge zur Musikwissenschaft, Jahrg. 1 (1959)
Heft 3 p. 51-75; Jahrg. 2 (1960) Heft 1 p. 50-68; Heft 2 p. 64-78

Classified list covering the writings on music produced in
East Germany for the 5-year period.

355. BLOM, ERIC. A general index to modern musical
literature in the English language, including periodicals for the
years 1915-26. London, Philadelphia, Curwen [1927] 159 p.

Entries for books by author, for parts of books by catchword
subject, in one alphabet.

356. BRIQUET, MARIE. La musique dans les congrès
internationaux (1835-1939). Paris, Heugel, 1961. 124 p.
(Publications de la Société Française de Musicologie, 2èm sér.
Tome X)

A bibliographical survey of the contributions on music made
at international congresses from 1835 to 1939. Classified listing
of 164 congress reports with the papers on music itemized.
Indexed by place of meeting, by chronology, by author, and by
subject.

357. CARL GREGOR, DUKE OF MECKLENBURG.
Bibliographie einiger Grenzgebiete der Musikwissenschaft. Baden-
Baden, Librairie Heitz, 1962. 200 p. (Bibliotheca bibliographica
Aureliana, 6)

A bibliography devoted to subject matter in areas peripheral
to the traditional emphasis of historical musicology. Includes
books and periodical articles on aesthetics, psychology, and
sociology of music, relations between music and the other arts,
the musical interests of poets, writers, philosophers, etc.

3,519 entries, alphabetical by author, with indexes of subjects and of persons as subjects.

358. DARRELL, ROBERT D. Schirmer's guide to books on music and musicians; a practical bibliography. New York, G. Schirmer [1951] 402 p.

A bibliography of then (1951) currently available books in English. Detailed subject classification, numerous annotations. Full bibliographical information, including publishers' 1951 prices.

Appendix I (p. 346-77): selected books in French, German, Italian, and Spanish. Appendix II (p. 378-84): juvenile literature. Key to publishers, chiefly American, p. 385-95.

Reviewed by Raymond Kendall in Notes, 9 (1951) p. 119-20; by Richard S. Angell in JAMS, 5 (1952) p. 60-61.

359. DEUTSCHE STAATSBIBLIOTHEK (Berlin). Neuer-werbungen ausländischer Musikliteratur 1954-55. Berlin, Deutsche Staatsbibliothek, 1956. 90 p. (Bibliographische Mitteilungen, 12)

A classified list of books on music, non-German publications, acquired by the Deutsche Staatsbibliothek (East Berlin) in 1954-55. Most of the titles were published during the preceding 10 years; a few are earlier.

360. EITNER, ROBERT. Bücherverzeichnis der Musik-literatur aus dem Jahren 1839 bis 1846 im Anschluss an Becker und Büchting .... Leipzig, Breitkopf & Härtel, 1885. 89 p. (Beilage zu Monatshefte für Musikgeschichte)

Intended to bridge the gap between Becker's Nachtrag (no. 352) and the listings in the Deutschen Buchhandel ersch. Bücher und Zeitschriften, published by Büchting from 1847-66.

361. FORKEL, JOHANN N. Allgemeine Litteratur der Musik, oder Anleitung zur Kenntniss musikalischer Bücher, welche von den ältesten bis auf die neusten Zeiten bey den

Greichen, Römern und den meisten neuern europäischen Nationen
sind geschreiben worden. Leipzig, Schwikert, 1792. 540 p.

The first important comprehensive bibliography of music
literature. A classified listing of some 3,000 works on all aspects
of musical knowledge, with brief biographical notices of their
authors and descriptive annotations. Complete tables of contents
are given for the most important works.

Forkel's classification has served as the model for many
subsequent bibliographies (See Scott Goldthwaite, "Classification
Problems, Bibliographies of Literature about Music," in Library
Quarterly ⌐Oct. 1948⌐ p. 255 ff.).

A reprint of the 1792 edition is projected for 1963, by Georg
Olms, Hildesheim. Forkel's work was expanded and translated
by Lichtenthal in 1826. See nos. 186 and 365.

362. KAHL, WILLI und WILHELM-MARTIN LUTHER.
Repertorium der Musikwissenschaft. Musikschrifttum, Denkmäler
und Gesamtausgaben in Auswahl (1800-1950) mit Besitzvermerken
deutscher Bibliotheken und musikwissenschaftlicher Institute.
Kassel, Bärenreiter, 1953. 271 p.

A comprehensive bibliography of music literature, broadly
classified, including useful lists of Festschriften, conference
reports, and critical editions. Prepared as a union list of
musicological holdings in postwar German libraries. Some 2,795
items. Indexed by persons, subjects, and geographical locations.

Reviewed by Otto E. Albrecht in Notes, 11 (1954) p. 468-69;
by Vincent Duckles in JAMS, 7 (1954) p. 242-45.

363. KROHN, ERNST C. The history of music: an index to
a selected group of musicological publications. St. Louis,
Washington University, 1952. 463 p. (Washington University
Library Studies, 3) Reissue, Baton Music Co., St. Louis, 1958.

A classified index of articles on music history in 39 of the
leading musicological publications — chiefly German and English
periodicals. General arrangement is chronological, with subdivisions by subject. Includes book reviews.

Reviewed by Richard Appel in <u>Notes</u>, 10 (1952) p. 105-06; by Scott Goldthwaite in <u>JAMS</u>, 6 (1953) p. 250-51; by Wolfgang Schmieder in <u>Die Musikforschung</u>, 6 (1953) p. 278-80.

364. LEGUY, JEAN. Catalogue bibliographique des livres de langue française sur la musique .... Paris, E. Ploix, 1954. 59 p.

<u>Fascicule complémentaire au catalogue général de 1954</u>, et <u>supplément 1954-59</u>. Paris, 1959. 43 p.

Classified listing of French books on music in print, or available through E. Ploix-Musique. Primarily a dealer's catalog, but a useful source of bibliographical information. Gives author, title, place of publication, pagination, size, and price. No publishers given.

365. LICHTENTHAL, PIETRO. Dizionario e bibliografia della musica. Milano, A. Fontana, 1826. 4 v.

Vols. 3-4 are a translation of Forkel's <u>Allgemeine Litteratur der Musik</u> (no. 361) with additions to 1826. Vols. 1-2 are a dictionary of musical terms, cited as no. 186.

366. McCOLVIN, LIONEL R. and H. REEVES. "Musical literature." In their <u>Music Libraries</u> . London, Grafton, 1937-38. 2 v.

Vol. 1, p. 55-214: Classified list of 2,146 titles, about 90 per cent of which are English. Somewhat uneven, overdeveloped in topics of particular British interest, but in general one of the best lists of music literature in English. Strong in biography.

367. MATERIAŁY DO BIBLIOGRAFII MUZYKI POLSKIEJ. ⌐Redaktor serii: Tadeusz Strumiłło Kraków⌐ v. 1- Polskie Wydawnictwo Muzyczne ⌐1954⌐ -

Tom III: Bibliografia Polskiego piśmiennictwa muzycznego, opracowal Kornel Michałowski, 1955. 280 p.

A classified bibliography of books on music in Polish. Lists of theses and dissertations, 1917-54. Index.

For other vols. of this set, see no. 558.

368. MATTHEW, JAMES E. The literature of music.
London, E. Stock, 1896. 281 p.

Essays on the literature of music, in historical sequence to
the 18th century, thereafter by topics: histories, biographies,
dictionaries, sacred music, opera, instruments, music as a
science, bibliography. Narrative style. Useful survey of the
earlier literature.

369. THE MUSICAL QUARTERLY. Cumulative index,
1915 thru 1959 ⌐v. 1-45⌐ Compiled by Herbert K. Goodkind.
New York, Goodkind Indexes ⌐1960⌐ 204 p.

Cumulative Index Supplement, 1960 thru 1962. New York,
1963.

The main volume indexes by author and subject in separate
alphabets, the supplement in one alphabet. Indexes book reviews,
"Current Chronicle, " as well as articles.

370. MUSIC & LETTERS. Index to volumes 1-40, 1920-59.
London, Oxford Univ. Press ⌐1962⌐ 140 p.

An index largely compiled by Eric Blom before his death in
1957 and completed by Jack A. Westrup. In two major sections:
(1) articles (filed by author and subject in one alphabet); (2) reviews (similarly treated). Reviews of music not indexed.

371. LA RASSEGNA MUSICALE. Indice generale delle
annate 1928-1952 ⌐v. 1-22⌐. Torino, Roggero & Tortia
⌐1953?⌐ 174 p.

An index, compiled by Riccardo Allorto, of articles, musical
performances reviewed, book reviews, record reviews, and
musical subjects.

372. REFARDT, EDGAR. Verzeichnis der Aufsätze zur
Musik in den nichtmusikalischen Zeitschriften der Universitäts-
bibliothek Basel. Leipzig, Breitkopf & Härtel, 1925. 105 p.

A classified list of writings on music in over 500 non-musical newspapers and periodicals, arranged alphabetically by author. One of the few efforts to compile a bibliography of musical literature in journals outside of the music field.

373. RIVISTA MUSICALE ITALIANA. Indici dei volumi I a XX (1894-1913). Compiled by Luigi Parigi. Torino, Fratelli Bocca, 1917. 256 p.

Indici dei volumi XXI a XXXV (1914-28). Compiled by A. Salvatori and G. Concina. Torino, 1931. 195 p.

Both index articles, works reviewed, and subjects. The second volume contains a retrospective index of musical examples.

374. ROYAL MUSICAL ASSOCIATION. Index to papers read before the members ... 1874 to 1944. Leeds, Printed by Whitehead & Miller for The Royal Musical Association, 1948. 56 p.

A subject and an author index to the first 70 volumes of the Proceedings of the Association. The subject index was compiled by Alfred Loewenberg, the author index by Rupert Erlebach.

375. SCHOLES, PERCY A. A list of books about music in the English language, prepared as an appendix to The Oxford Companion to Music. London, New York, Oxford Univ. Press, 1940. 64 p.

A subject list which derives chiefly from the compiler's own library. Bibliographical information uneven, frequently lacking place of publication. There is an informal preface, occasional annotations.

Issued as a supplement to the 2nd ed. of the Oxford Companion (no. 37).

376. USPENSKAĨA, S. L. Literatura o muzyke, 1948-1953. Moskva, Izdatel'stvo Vsesoĩuznoĩ knizhnoĩ palaty, 1955. 343 p.

Classified list of books and periodical articles in Russian, 1948-53. Name index, list of periodicals (including non-musical periodicals and newspapers).

Two further vols. in this series have appeared: 1958, covering the years 1954-56, and 1959, covering 1957. The latest is: Uspenskaîa S. , & B. Yagolim, Sovetskaya literatura o muzyke; bibliograficheskii ukazatel za 1957 god. Moskva, Sovetskii Kompozitor, 1959. 191 p. 1,967 numbered entries. (See Notes, 18 ⸤1960⸣ p. 82.)

CURRENT OR ANNUAL

The only way to keep abreast of publication in the field of music literature is to consult a variety of current listings. Many of these treat special subject areas. Periodicals which carry regular listings of music literature are cited in the section following by title, with annotations directing attention to the relevant sections. Several of the current bibliographies of music (scores) also concern themselves with music literature; see no. 551 ff.

377. ACTA MUSICOLOGICA. v. 1- Internationale Gesellschaft für Musikwissenschaft, 1928-

"Index novorum librorum, " a department appearing in most issues of this journal, is one of the best sources of bibliographical information for the period between 1930 and 1950. Gives a classified listing of books on music in all languages. Department discontinued after 1952.

378. AFRICAN MUSIC. Journal of the African music society. v. 1- Roodepoort, Transvaal, Union of South Africa, 1954-

Each annual issue has a section of "books and pamphlets received, " as well as reviews of current publications in ethnomusicology.

379. AMERICAN BIBLIOGRAPHIC SERVICE. Quarterly check-list of musicology. An international index of current books, monographs, brochures & separates. v. 1 Darien, Connecticut, American Bibliographic Service, 1959-

An unclassified numbered listing of current writings on music. Full bibliographical information, including prices.

Indexed by authors, editors, and translators in the last issue of each volume.

380. BELKNAP, SARA Y. The guide to the performing arts, 1957. v. 1-   New York, Scarecrow Press, 1960-

An annual periodical index to the performing arts. Began as a supplement to the Guide to the Musical Arts (no. 353). Contains a "general" section and a "television arts" section. References to performers, performing groups, as well as general subject headings. As of 1963, 5 volumes of this guide have appeared, covering the years 1957-61.

381. BIBLIOGRAPHIE DES MUSIKSCHRIFTTUMS. Jahrgang, 1936-   Leipzig, Frankfurt a/M, F. Hofmeister, 1936- (Heraus-gegeben im Auftrage des Instituts für Musikforschung, Berlin)

Editors: 1936-37, Kurt Taut; 1938-39, Georg Karstädt, (1940-49, suspended publication); 1950-   Wolfgang Schmieder.

A bibliography of books and an index to periodical articles in all European languages. A large number of non-musical journals included. Classified by broad subjects, with an index of names (author and subject) and places. Emphasis on "serious" music.

This bibliography follows in a direct line of descent from the listings in Peters Jahrbuch (no. 388).

Review of Jahrgang 1950-51 by Richard Schaal in Die Musikforschung, 8 (1955) p. 371-72; by Richard S. Hill in Notes, 11 (1954) p. 555-57; by Scott Goldthwaite in JAMS, 8 (1955) p. 55-57. Review of Jahrgang 1952-53 by Richard Schaal in Die Musikforschung, 10 (1957) p. 440.

382. A BIBLIOGRAPHY OF PERIODICAL LITERATURE IN MUSICOLOGY .... Nos. 1-2 (1938/39-1939/40). Washington, D.C., American Council of Learned Societies, 1940-43. 2 v.

Indexes approximately 240 periodicals, all European languages, musical and non-musical, from Oct. 1938 through

Sept. 1940. Signed abstracts or annotations for most of the articles. Broadly classified listings.

First volume contains a list of graduate theses accepted in American colleges, universities, and conservatories, Oct. 1, 1938 - Sept. 1, 1939.

Vol. 1 compiled by D. H. Daugherty; Vol. 2 added compilers, Leonard Ellinwood and Richard S. Hill.

383. BULGARSKI MUZIKALEN KNIGOPIS: trimesechen bibliografski biuletin za novoizliazla literatura po muzika i noti. Sofiia, 1958-

Issued by Bulgarski Bibliografski Institut "Elin Pelin."

Quarterly. Classified list of books and periodical articles on music and publications in musical notation issued in Bulgaria. Cumulative index, the October-December issue, containing index for the entire year.

384. DEUTSCHE MUSIKBIBLIOGRAPHIE. Jahrgang 1-Leipzig, F. Hofmeister, 1829-

Title varies: 1829-1942, Hofmeisters musikalisch-literarischer Monatsbericht.

Brief lists of German, Swiss, and Austrian publications of music and music literature. Alphabetical by author, giving date and place of publication, pagination, and price. Indexed by publisher. A monthly publication useful chiefly for its listings of music. Entries are cumulated in Hofmeister's Jahres-verzeichnis .... (no. 390).

Also cited as no. 554.

385. ETHNOMUSICOLOGY. JOURNAL OF THE SOCIETY FOR ETHNOMUSICOLOGY. v. 1- Middletown, Conn., Wesleyan Univ. Press, 1953-

Title varies: 1953-57, Ethno-Musicology Newsletter.

"Current Bibliography" section in each issue lists books and periodical articles related to the field. Organized by geographical areas and topics. The journal also publishes from time to time special bibliographies devoted to the work of leading ethno-musicologists.

386. FONTES ARTIS MUSICAE. Review of the International Association of Music Libraries. v. 1-   Paris, International Association of Music Libraries, 1954-

Each issue contains a "Liste internationale sélective" of music publications classified by country. Music literature appears under the sub-heading "Ouvrages sur la musique et ouvrages didactiques. "

387. HOFMEISTERS HANDBUCH DER MUSIKLITERATUR. Bd. 1-   Leipzig, F. Hofmeister, 1844-

Cumulation of Jahresverzeichnis der deutschen Musikalien und Musikschriften (no. 390).

Preceded by a similar work by Anton Meysel, Leipzig, 1817, listing music and music literature through 1815, with 10 supplements (2-8 by F. Hofmeister; 9-10 by C. F. Whistling) to 1827. Carl Friedrich Whistling issued a revised edition in 1828, with 3 supplements (1829; 1834 by F. Hofmeister; and 1839 by F. Hofmeister).

Title varies: Vols. 1-3 (up to 1844), C. F. Whistling's Handbuch der musikalischen Literatur; Vols. 4-6 (1844-1867), Handbuch der musikalischen Literatur; Vols. 4-18 (1844-1933) also called Ergänzungsband 1-15. Publication interrupted in Vol. 19 (1943) covering the years 1934-40, through the letter "L" in the alphabet.

The Handbuch is of greatest importance for its music (score) listings, but each volume contains an Anhang devoted to "Bücher und Schriften über Musik. " The long life of this series, plus the leading position occupied by German music publishing during the period covered, make it one of the major music reference tools.

388. JAHRBUCH DER MUSIKBIBLIOTHEK PETERS. v. 1-47. Leipzig, C. F. Peters, 1895-1940?

Most issues contain a section, "Verzeichnis der in allen Kulturländern erschienenen Bücher und Schriften über Musik, " edited at various times by Rudolf Schwartz, George Karstädt, and Kurt Taut. Does not include periodical literature.

This section, expanded to include periodicals, has been continued as the Bibliographie des Musikschrifttums, published separately (no. 381).

389. JAHRBUCH FÜR LITURGIK UND HYMNOLOGIE. Bd. 1- Kassel, Johannes Stauda-Verlag, 1955-

Each volume has an extensive "Literaturbericht, " classified, frequently annotated, covering all aspects of liturgics and hymnology.

390. JAHRESVERZEICHNIS DER DEUTSCHEN MUSIKALIEN UND MUSIKSCHRIFTEN. Jahrgang 1- Leipzig, F. Hofmeister, 1852-

An annual listing cumulated in Hofmeisters Handbuch der Musikliteratur (no. 387).

Title varies: Vols. 1-77 (1852-1928), Verzeichnis der im Jahre ... erschienen Musikalien; Vols. 78-91 (1929-42), Hofmeisters Jahresverzeichnis.

Also cited as no. 556.

391. JOURNAL OF THE INTERNATIONAL FOLK MUSIC COUNCIL. v. 1- Pub. with the assistance of the International Music Council under the auspices of UNESCO, 1949-

Each volume of this yearly publication contains a section, "Publications Received, " which gives a brief authoritative review of a wide range of publications in the field, including periodicals, recordings, and important articles.

392. JOURNAL OF MUSIC THEORY. v. 1- New Haven, Conn., Yale School of Music, 1957-

Each issue contains a "Bibliography of Current Periodical

Literature" covering articles related to music theory; articles chiefly in English, but a selection from other languages.

393. THE MUSIC INDEX; the key to current music periodical literature. v. 1, no. 1- Detroit, Information Service, Inc., Jan. 1949-

Currently indexes approximately 185 periodicals by subject and author. Pub. in 12 monthly numbers, with an annual cumulation. Reviews are indexed under "Book Reviews."

Music index subject heading list, annual, published separately.

1954 annual cumulation reviewed by Richard Appel in Notes, 14 (1957) p. 364-65; 1955 and 1956 cumulations by James B. Coover in Notes, 16 (1958) p. 45-46. Review by Richard Schaal in Die Musikforschung, 10 (1957) p. 442-43.

394. MUSIC LIBRARY ASSOCIATION NOTES, a magazine devoted to music and its literature. 2nd Ser. 1- The Music Library Association, 1948-

"Book Reviews," a department compiled and edited by William Lichtenwanger and supplemented by a list of current publications on music, is the most comprehensive listing of current music literature available. Since Dec. 1950 the list has been international in scope; classified by language.

395. MUSIC TEACHERS NATIONAL ASSOCIATION. COMMITTEE ON LITERATURE ABOUT MUSIC. "Report." 1906- In its Proceedings (annual) 1906-

Classified lists of books on music in English, giving author, title, publisher, pagination, and price. Includes some translations, new editions, and reprints.

Excellent listings of material in English, carefully selected, some annotations. Listed by author and subject.

396. MUSICA DISCIPLINA. A yearbook of the history of music. v. 1- American Institute of Musicology, 1946-

Title varies: Vol. 1, <u>Journal of Renaissance and Baroque Music</u>.

Most of the volumes contain a bibliography of books, periodical articles, and editions related to early music; also doctoral dissertations. Compiled since 1958 by Wolfgang Schmieder.

397. "MUSICAL LITERATURE." In <u>The British Catalogue of Music</u>. London, Council of the British <u>National Bibliography</u>, 1957-

An annual listing, broadly classified, of all books about music published in Great Britain. "Musical Literature" appears first in the classified section. Scores occupy the greater part of the volumes. Indexed by author and title.

See also no. 551.

398. THE MUSICAL QUARTERLY. v. 1- New York, G. Schirmer, 1915-

The "Quarterly Book-List" in each issue is a selection of books of musicological interest in all languages. Less comprehensive than the current listings in <u>Notes</u> (no. 394). Compilers, successively, since 1936: Edward N. Waters, Lee Fairley, Frank C. Campbell, Donald W. Krummel, Carroll D. Wade, and Fred Blum.

399. NATIONAL ASSOCIATION OF SCHOOLS OF MUSIC. A list of books on music. Cincinnati, 1935. 57 p.

<u>Supplements</u> 1-10, 1936-57.

Primarily an annotated listing of books in English, with smaller selections of foreign musical literature, critical editions, contemporary American scores. Prices given through the 8th supplement. A cumulative index of the original list and first seven supplements was printed in 1952.

400. SVENSK TIDSKRIFT FÖR MUSIKFORSKNING. v. 1- Stockholm, 1919-

Since 1927 has maintained an annual listing of "Svensk musikhistorisk bibliografi, " compiled since 1946 by Åke Davidsson. Broadly classified. Indexes Swedish periodicals.

401. VIERTELJAHRSSCHRIFT FÜR MUSIKWISSENSCHAFT. Ed. by Friedrich Chrysander and Philipp Spitta. v. 1-10. Leipzig, 1885-94.

Each volume contains a "Musikalische Bibliographie, " compiled by F. Ascherson, which usually includes a listing of scholarly music books, critical editions, and the contents of current scholarly periodicals in all European languages.

402. ZEITSCHRIFT DER INTERNATIONALEN MUSIK-GESELLSCHAFT. v. 1-15. Leipzig, 1899/1900-1913/14.

Most volumes contain a department called "Eine ständige Übersicht über alle für die Musikforschung und ihre Nachbargebiete bemerkenswerten Abhandlungen und Aufsätze, die in Musik- und anderen Zeitschriften veröffentlicht werden. "

Indexes approximately 84 periodicals, chiefly musical, in many languages. Vols. 1-11, by author only; Vols. 12-15, by subject with "see" references from the author.

403. ZEITSCHRIFT FÜR MUSIKWISSENSCHAFT. v. 1-17. Leipzig, 1918-35.

Indexes once a year the periodical literature on music in some 200 journals, in many languages. 1914-18 covered retrospectively in the 1918 index, thus articulating with no. 402.

LISTS OF MUSIC PERIODICALS

Probably the most comprehensive list of music periodicals is found in the article "Periodicals, Musical, " compiled by A. Hyatt King for the 5th edition of Grove's (see no. 420). The best chronological survey is still offered by Freystätter (no. 412), but this has been supplemented and expanded in certain respects by the recent historical study by Rohlfs (no. 422).

404 - APEL, WILLI. "Periodicals, Musical." In his Harvard Dictionary of Music. Cambridge, Harvard Univ. Press, 1944. p. 567-68

A selected list of historical music periodicals, current and recent periodicals classified according to countries, and musicological periodicals.

405. BLUM, FRED. "East German music journals: a checklist," In Notes, 19 (1962) p. 399-410

Lists 100 periodicals in alphabetical order (including secondary titles, former titles, and succeeding titles) as well as providing a critical description of a variety of East German music serials.

406. CAMPBELL, FRANK C. A critical annotated bibliography of periodicals. Memo no. 33 (July 1962) of The American Choral Foundation, Inc. ⸤ New York, American Choral Foundation, 1962 ⸥ 14 p.

Evaluates 44 periodicals that treat choral music and materials, giving pertinent details (address, price, emphasis of the periodical, etc.).

407. CLOUGH, F. F. and G. J. CUMING. "Phonographic periodicals, a survey of some issued outside the United States." In Notes, 15 (Sept. 1958) p. 537-58

A critical description of some 30 foreign periodicals devoted to recordings, with additional comments on record coverage in general periodicals.

408. COOVER, JAMES B. "A bibliography of East European music periodicals." In Fontes artis musicae (1956) p. 219-26; (1957) p. 97-102; (1958) p. 44-45, 93-99; (1959) p. 27-28; (1960) p. 16-21, p. 69-70; (1961) p. 75-90; (1962) p. 78-80

"This bibliography is an attempt at a comprehensive and authoritative listing of all music periodicals which have been and which are being published in the countries of Bulgaria,

Czechoslovakia, Estonia, Finland, Hungary, Latvia, Lithuania, Poland, Rumania, the USSR and Yugoslavia" (compiler's introduction).

409. "EUROPÄISCH MUSIKZEITSCHRIFTEN 1945-1948." In Jahrbuch der Musikwelt. Bayreuth, J. Steeger, 1949. p. 111-23

Organized by country. Information brief and inconsistent, with German periodicals given most complete coverage; Russian, Czech, and others very incomplete.

410. FAIRLEY, LEE. "A check-list of recent Latin American music periodicals." In Notes, 2 (1945) p. 120-23

Lists 23 periodicals from the collections of the Library of Congress and the Pan American Union, with brief comments on the general nature of each. Covers publications established between 1940 and 1945.

411. FREDERICKS, JESSICA M. ⌐et al.⌐ "Music magazines of Britain and the U.S." In Notes, 6 (1949) p. 239-63, 457-59; 7 (1950) p. 372-76

Lists 200 periodicals, arranged alphabetically by title, with a subject and type index. Brief descriptions of nature and contents.

412. FREYSTÄTTER, WILHELM. Die musikalischen Zeitschriften seit ihrer Entstehung bis zur Gegenwart. Chronologisches Verzeichniss der periodischen Schriften über Musik. München, T. Riedel, 1884. 139 p.

Based on E. Gregoir's Recherches historiques concernant les journaux de musique, Antwerp, 1872.

A chronological listing, from 1722 to 1884, with extensive annotations as to content, editors, contributors, etc. Chiefly useful as a source of information on early periodicals.

413. HEYER, ANNA HARRIET. "Periodicals." In her Check-List of Publications of Music. Ann Arbor, Univ. of Michigan, 1944. p. 1-10

A list of 30 important music periodicals in English, French, German, and Italian, with their locations in major U.S. libraries.

414. MALM, WILLIAM P. "A bibliography of Japanese magazines and music." In Ethnomusicology, 3 (1959) p. 76-80

Annotated bibliography of 25 Japanese periodicals related to music and the dance. Place, publisher, date of first issue and price given.

415. "MUSIC ⌈SECTION⌉ " In Ulrich's Periodicals Directory; A Classified Guide to a Selected List of Current Periodicals, Foreign and Domestic. 9th ed. ... New York, R. R. Bowker Co., 1959. p. 526-31

See also earlier editions.

Lists 123 periodicals, about half of which are not included in The Music Index (no. 419). Gives full title, first year, frequency, price, publisher and address. Also indicates the presence of illustrations, reviews, abstracts, or bibliographies, and where each journal is indexed.

416. MUSIC LIBRARY ASSOCIATION (NORTHERN CALIF. CHAPTER) RESOURCES COMMITTEE. A Union list of music periodicals (published 1949-61) in the libraries of Northern California. Ed. by C. R. Nicewonger. ⌈Pub. for the Resources Committee, Northern Calif. Chapter, Music Library Association, 1962⌉ 71 p. (typescript)

Covers the holdings of 24 Northern California libraries.

417. "PERIODICALS AND OTHER SERIAL PUBLICATIONS." In Reference Works in Music and Music Literature in Five Libraries of Los Angeles County. Ed., Helen W. Azhderian. Los Angeles, 1953. p. 213-39

Lists 217 English language publications, and 118 foreign, with locations in libraries in the Los Angeles area.

418. "PERIODICALS AND TRADE PUBLICATIONS." In The Musician's Guide; the Directory of the World of Music, 1957 Edition. New York, Music Information Service, Inc., 1957. p. 640-55

Basic information on 178 American and 153 foreign periodicals, some of which have ceased publication.

419. "PERIODICALS INDEXED." In The Music Index 1960 Annual Cumulation. Detroit, Information Service, Inc., 1963.

A listing of more than 185 titles of periodicals currently covered by the Index. Addresses and subscription prices given. In its first year (1949) the Music Index treated only 81 titles. Since that time there has been a constant increase in periodicals indexed.

420. "PERIODICALS, MUSICAL." In Grove's .... 5th ed. v. 6, p. 638-65. Compiled by A. Hyatt King.

A list of over 1,000 music periodicals from all parts of the world, arranged by countries alphabetically, in chronological order of the first date of appearance.

See also the corrections and additions to the above list in the Supplementary Volume (1961) p. 344-47.

421. RIEDEL, A. Répertoire des periodiques musicaux belges. Bruxelles, Commission belge de bibliographie, 1954. 48 p. (Bibliographia belgica, 8)

330 items, of which the first 130 are music serials; the remainder are periodicals in the usual sense.

422. ROHLFS, ECKART. Die deutschsprachigen Musikperiodica, 1945-57. Regensburg, G. Bosse, 1961. 108, 115 p. (Forschungsbeiträge zur Musikwissenschaft, 11)

A source book of information about music periodicals, their history, bibliographical coverage, distribution, and subject emphasis. Not confined to German journals. The systematic bibliographic Anhang, p. 5-64, lists 589 periodicals in 12 different categories. Indexed by chronology, place, title.

Reviewed by Fred Blum in Notes, 19 (1961) p. 77-78.

423. "UNITED STATES MUSIC PERIODICALS." In The Music Magazine / Musical Courier: The Annual Directory of the Concert World 1963. Compiled and edited by Max D. Jones. Evanston, Summy-Birchard Co., 1963. p. 100-02

A listing of 153 American music periodicals. A list of 224 "Foreign Music Periodicals" is found on p. 154-57.

424. "VERZEICHNIS DER ZEITSCHRIFTEN UND JAHR-BÜCHER." In Hofmeisters Jahresverzeichnis, v. 100. Leipzig, F. Hofmeister, 1953. p. 334-39

Lists more than 100 German and Austrian periodicals and yearbooks available in 1951.

See also earlier editions.

425. "ZEITSCHRIFTEN." In Repertorium der Musikwissenschaft. Bearb. von Willi Kahl und Wilhelm-Martin Luther. Kassel und Basel, Bärenreiter, 1953. p. 23-39

Lists 187 music periodicals, in all European languages, with their locations in German libraries. Selected for musicological importance.

SPECIAL AND SUBJECT: CONTEMPORARY MUSIC

426. BASART, ANN PHILLIPS. Serial music, a classified bibliography of writings on twelve-tone and electronic music. Berkeley and Los Angeles, University of Calif. Press, 1961. 151 p. (Univ. of Calif. Bibliographic Guides)

A classified bibliography of 823 items, treating the literature of 12-tone music, electronic music, the Viennese school (Schönberg, Berg, and Webern), and 20 other contemporary composers using serial techniques. Author and subject indexes.

Review by Dika Newlin in Notes, 19 (1961) p. 256-57; by

James B. Coover in Journal of Music Theory, 6 (1962) p. 316-17.

427. DELIÈGE, CELESTIN. "Bibliographie" ⌐of serial and experimental music⌐ . In Revue belge de musicologie, 13 (1959) p. 132-48

Broadly classified bibliography, with an introduction surveying the literature of the field.

428. EDMUNDS, JOHN and GORDON BOELZNER. Some twentieth century American composers, a selective bibliography ... With an introductory essay by Peter Yates. v. 1- New York, The New York Public Library, 1959-

v. 1, 57 p. v. 2, (1960), 55 p. , with an introductory essay by Nicolas Slonimsky.

"This bibliography has been made with the purpose of bringing together in a single body separately published writings by and about a representative group of twentieth-century American composers ... conservative, moderate, dodecaphonic, and experimental (electronic and non-electronic)" (editor's preface). Volume 1 includes bibliographies for 15 composers; volume 2, for 17, with two appendices: composers cited in one of 21 standard reference works, and composers not cited in these works but who are under 35 and merit some attention.

Both volumes are "reprinted with additions" from the Bulletin of The New York Public Library (July-August 1959; July 1960).

SPECIAL AND SUBJECT: DISSERTATIONS

Doctoral dissertations, along with articles in scholarly periodicals, represent the growing edge of research activity in any field. We are currently well supplied with bibliographies of doctoral studies in music for the United States (no. 429) and for Germany (no. 436), but studies produced in other countries are less easy to locate. Included here are only those reference tools concerned exclusively with studies in music. There are a number of comprehensive national bibliographies of dissertations from which music titles can be extracted. For these, the user should consult

Winchell's Guide to Reference Books, 7th ed. (1951) and its
Supplements. See also Keith Mixter's General Bibliography for
Music Research (no. 1131).

429. DOCTORAL DISSERTATIONS IN MUSICOLOGY. 3rd
ed. Compiled by Helen Hewitt. Philadelphia, American Musicological Society, 1961. 113 p.

First published, 1952, in photo-offset from typed copy.

2nd edition, 1958, published jointly with the Music Teachers
National Association.

Supplements to the 1952 list appeared in the May-June issue
of the American Music Teacher (1953-56) and in JAMS, 7 (1954)
p. 131-40; 8 (1955) p. 116-22; 9 (1956) p. 202-09. Supplements to
the 2nd edition appeared in the American Music Teacher, 8 (1959)
p. 10 ff., and in JAMS, 11 (1958) p. 217-26. Supplement to the
3rd edition in JAMS, 15 (1962) p. 330-46.

The 1952 publication is still useful in its own right because it
contains material deleted from the later compilations (studies
tangential to musicology—in fields such as acoustics, psychology,
and history, or pursued in departments other than music).

The 3rd edition gives 829 entries for dissertations completed
or in progress, grouped by historical periods, with additional
classifications for non-historical studies. Indexed by author and
subject. Serial numbers identify those studies available for
purchase on microfilm or microcards.

430. "IM JAHRE ... ANGENOMMENE MUSIKWISSEN-
SCHAFTLICHE DISSERTATIONEN." In Die Musikforschung,
v. 1-   1948-

A listing, annually or at more frequent intervals, of doctoral
dissertations in music completed in German, Austrian, and Swiss
institutions of higher learning.

431. MERRIAM, ALAN P. "An annotated bibliography of
theses and dissertations in ethnomusicology and folk music accepted at American universities." In Ethnomusicology, 4 (1960)
p. 21-35

Supplement I, by Frank J. Gillis. In Ethnomusicology, 6 (1962) p. 191-214.

The Merriam list gives 180 items, including both Master's and Doctor's studies. The Gillis list cites 197 items, without duplicating the original list, and expands the coverage to studies completed in foreign universities. It also provides a subject index and an index of institutions.

432. MUSIC EDUCATORS NATIONAL CONFERENCE. COMMITTEE ON RESEARCH IN MUSIC EDUCATION. Bibliography of research in music education, 1932-1944. Comp. by Arnold M. Small ⌐et al.⌐ . ⌐Iowa City⌐ State University of Iowa Press, 1944. 55 p.

Theses and dissertations organized by state and school.

433. MUSIC EDUCATORS NATIONAL CONFERENCE. THE MUSIC EDUCATION RESEARCH COUNCIL. Bibliography of research studies in music education, 1932-1948. Comp. by William S. Larson. Chicago, Music Educators National Conference, 1949. 119 p.

This second edition of the preceding item contains more than 1,600 titles. A 4-page supplement with nearly 350 additional titles is provided as an insert.

Review by George Henderson in Notes, 7 (1949) p. 121.

434. MUSIC EDUCATORS NATIONAL CONFERENCE. COMMITTEE ON BIBLIOGRAPHY OF RESEARCH PROJECTS AND THESES. Bibliography of research studies in music education, 1949-56. Comp. by William S. Larson. In Journal of Research in Music Education, 5:2 (1957) 225 p.

Continuation of the above.

Lists all completed research studies in music education "which make a contribution to the teaching of music." Arranged alphabetically by state, university, and author. Gives degree awarded and date. Topical index.

435. NORTHWESTERN UNIVERSITY (EVANSTON, ILL.)
SCHOOL OF MUSIC. Bibliography of research, School of Music,
Northwestern University: theses, projects, dissertations. Ed.
by Hazel B. Morgan. Evanston, Illinois, 1958. 47 p.

436. SCHAAL, RICHARD. Verzeichnis deutschsprachiger
musikwissenschaftlicher Dissertationen, 1861-1960. Kassel,
Bärenreiter, 1963. 167 p. (Musikwissenschaftliche Arbeiten,
hrsg. von der Gesellschaft für Musikforschung, 19)

An alphabetical listing, by author, of 2,819 music dissertations in the German language. Publication data given if the
work is in print. Subject index.

437. "VERZEICHNIS DER IM BERICHTSJAHR ... BEI
DER DEUTSCHEN BÜCHEREI ZU LEIPZIG REGISTRIERTEN
MUSIKWISSENSCHAFTLICHEN DISSERTATIONEN UND
HABILITATIONSSCHRIFTEN." ⌐ Comp. by Ortrun Landmann⌐
In Deutsches Jahrbuch der Musikwissenschaft. Leipzig,
Peters, 1957-

Continues a bibliography of dissertations originally published
in the Peters Jahrbuch. See no. 388.

438. "VERZEICHNIS DER MUSIKWISSENSCHAFTLICHEN
DISSERTATIONEN IN DEUTSCHLAND, 1885-1948." ⌐ Comp. by
Richard Schaal⌐ In Jahrbuch der Musikwelt. Bayreuth, J.
Steeger, 1949. p. 58-103

A subject listing of German music dissertations. Minimum
entries.

SPECIAL AND SUBJECT: ETHNOMUSICOLOGY

The field of ethnomusicology has attracted a great deal of interest
and research activity in recent years. It developed as a discipline
along scientific lines as "comparative musicology" in the first
decades of the present century. It now supports its own journal,
Ethnomusicology (see no. 385), and several specialized research
organizations: The African Music Society, The International Folk

Music Council, etc. No attempt has been made to list the many useful bibliographies appended to monographs, dissertations, and important periodical articles in this field. The selection has been confined, with a few exceptions, to the major self-contained bibliographies of folk and primitive music.

See also under "Bibliographies of Music Literature. Current or Annual, " nos. 378, 385, 391; under "Bibliographies of Music Literature. Special and Subject: Dissertations, " no. 431; and under "Discographies, " nos. 1090-98.

439. BOSE, FRITZ. Musikalische Völkerkunde. Freiburg, Atlantis-Verlag, 1953. 197 p. (Atlantis-Musikbücherei)

"Bibliographie, " p. 144-63. 393 items.

440. DENSMORE, FRANCES. "The study of Indian music in the nineteenth century. " In American Anthropologist, 29 (1927) p. 77-86

A survey of early studies in the field of American Indian music; generally valuable, although it contains some errors.

441. EMSHEIMER, ERNST. "Musikethnographische Bibliographie der nichtslavischen Völker in Russland. " In Acta M, 15 (1943) p. 34-63

A bibliography of 433 items concerned with the music of the non-Slavic peoples of Russia. Classified according to ethnic group. German translations for Slavic titles. Some editions of folk music cited, but chiefly concerned with periodical articles and monographs. Full bibliographical information.

442. HAYWOOD, CHARLES. A bibliography of North American folklore and folksong. Second rev. ed. New York, Dover Publications, 1961. 2 v.

First pub. in 1 vol. by Greenberg, New York, 1951.

Vol. 1, 748 p., is concerned with the non-Indian Americans north of Mexico; Vol. 2, p. 749-1159, with the American Indians north of Mexico. Subdivisions in Vol. 1 include general bibliography, regional bibliography, ethnic and occupational bibliography. Vol. 2 is subdivided by cultural areas. Entries for folklore and for folk music are separated under each heading; recordings included. General index. End papers are maps of regional and cultural areas.

Review of the first ed. by Duncan Emrich in Notes, 8 (1951) p. 700-01.

443. HENRY, MELLINGER EDWARD. A bibliography for the study of American folk songs, with many titles of folk songs (and titles that have to do with folk songs) from other lands. London, Mitre Press, 1937. 142 p.

Studies and collections of music are interfiled in one alphabet. The emphasis is on the English-Scottish ballad and its derivatives.

444. HERZOG, GEORGE. Research in primitive and folk music in the U.S., a survey. Washington, D.C., Amer. Council of Learned Societies, 1936. 97 p.

Surveys U.S. resources for the study of primitive and folk music as of 1936. Record archives are described and their holdings tabulated; collections of primitive musical instruments listed. Bibliographies given for each of the main sections.

445. KUNST, JAAP. Ethnomusicology, a study of its nature, its problems, methods and representative personalities, to which is added a bibliography. 3rd, enl. ed. The Hague, Nijhoff, 1959. 303 p.

First pub. in 1950 under the title Musicologica; the 2nd ed., 1955, contains a selective bibliography.

Bibliography, p. 79-215: Lists 4,552 items, most of them with location symbols referring to libraries in Western Europe. Items which contain extensive bibliographies within themselves are marked with an asterisk. Portraits of musicologists.

Ethnomusicology ... Supplement to the 3rd Edition. The Hague, Nijhoff, 1960. 45 p.

Adds some 500 bibliographical items; new record listings through 1958. Additional portraits.

Review of the 3rd ed. by Bruno Nettl in Notes, 16 (Sept. 1959) p. 560–61; of the Supplement, by William Lichtenwanger in Notes, 19 (1961) p. 79.

446. KURATH, GERTRUDE P. "Tantsy narodov SSSR— bibliografia. Folk dances of the USSR—Bibliography." In Ethnomusicology, 3 (1959) p. 142–50

Compiled with the aid of I. I. Potehkin, Estelle Titiev, and Robert H. Whitman. Alphabetical by author. All entries transliterated, with English translations given.

LAWLESS, RAY McKINLEY. Folksingers and folksongs in America .... See no. 121.

447. LAWS, GEORGE M. Native American balladry; a descriptive study and a bibliographical syllabus. Philadelphia, American Folklore Society, 1950. 276 p. (Publications of the American Folklore Society. Bibliographical Series, v. 1)

Special bibliographies of primitive and folk music.

448. LEAGUE OF NATIONS. INTERNATIONAL INSTITUTE OF INTELLECTUAL COOPERATION. Musique et chanson populaires. Paris, Institut International de Coopération Intellectuelle, 1934. 257 p.

A reference book intended to establish an international listing of the museums, archives, libraries, and other institutions, public and private, concerned with research or collecting in the field of popular music, with a description of their facilities. Contributions by leading specialists arranged alphabetically by country. Most of the contributions contain bibliographies of studies and editions, and a list of names and addresses of specialists.

449. LEAGUE OF NATIONS. INTERNATIONAL INSTITUTE OF INTELLECTUAL COOPERATION. Folklore musical;

répertoire international des collections et centres de documentation avec notices sur l'état actuel des recherches dans les différents pays et références bibliographiques. Paris, Département d'Art, d'Archéologie et d'Ethnologie, Institut International de Coopération Intellectuelle ⌐1939⌐ 332 p.

Organization similar to the preceding item. Special section devoted to the international phonorecord archives in Berlin, Paris, and Vienna. P. 309-32: supplement of additions and corrections to the 1934 volume, above.

450. LOMAX, ALAN and S. R. COWELL. American folk song and folklore, a regional bibliography. New York, Progressive Education Association, 1942. 59 p.

451. MERRIAM, ALAN P. "An annotated bibliography of African and African-derived music since 1936." In Africa, 21 (1951) p. 319-30

452. NETTL, BRUNO. Reference materials in ethnomusicology. Detroit, Information Service, Inc., 1961. 46 p. (Detroit studies in music bibliography, 1)

A narrative and critical discussion of the leading reference materials in the field, organized in terms of the structure of the discipline. P. 37-46: a list of publications cited, with full bibliographical information.

453. NETTL, BRUNO. Theory and method in ethnomusicology. New York, The Free Press of Glencoe, 1964

Chapter 2 is a history of the field which focuses on bibliography. In addition, each chapter is followed by a list of publications cited.

454. VARLEY, DOUGLAS H. African native music, an annotated bibliography. London, The Royal Empire Soc., 1936. 116 p.

Two sections of general bibliography followed by local bibliographies relating to 30 African countries. Special section on "African Survivals in the New World." List of museums containing collections of African instruments. Author index. Brief but informative annotations.

455. WATERMAN, RICHARD ⊏ et al.⊐ "Bibliography of Asiatic musics." In <u>Notes</u>, 5:1-8:2 (Dec. 1947-Mar. 1951) 181 p. in all

A classified bibliography, published serially. 3,488 books, monographs, articles, sections of larger works, texts, transcriptions and recordings, arranged geographically and ethnologically. All European languages, including Russian and Romanized Turkish.

SPECIAL AND SUBJECT: INSTRUMENTS

456. GRAAF, G. A. C. DE. Literature on the organ, principally in Dutch libraries. Amsterdam ⊏1957⊐ 71 p.

A list of over 1,250 titles of books, brochures, and reprints concerning the use, the history, and the building of organs. Does not include books on organ playing.

457. HERON-ALLEN, EDWARD. De fidiculis bibliographia: being an attempt towards a bibliography of the violin .... London, Griffith, Farran & Co., 1890-94. 2 v.

Classified bibliography of literature on the violin in all its aspects. Full bibliographical data and copious annotations. The work was issued in parts, printed on recto only, and concludes with four supplements.

458. HUTSCHENRUYTER, WILLEM. Bijdrage tot de bibliographie der muziekliteratuur. Een, zooveel mogelijk aangevulde samenvatting der boek- en tijdschrift-oversichten, die sedert 1885 zijn opgenomen in het "Vierteljahrschrift für Musikwissenschaft," het "Zeitschrift der Internationalen Musikgesellschaft," het "Zeitschrift für Musikwissenschaft" en het "Jahrbuch der Musikbibliothek Peters." ⊏ v. 1 ⊐ Instrumentale Muziek, mechanische muziek, electrische muziek, klokken.

Zeist, 1941- 513 p. (typescript)

Incomplete. A projected comprehensive bibliography of music literature that progressed only so far as to include instrumental music, electrical music, and bells.

459. MILLER, DAYTON C. Catalog of books and literary material relating to the flute and other musical instruments, with annotations. Cleveland, Priv. pr., 1935. 120 p.

"Includes books and pamphlets, short magazine articles, newspaper clippings, concert programs, maker's catalogues and price-lists, index of poetical quotations, patent specifications, novels, etc. " "So far as possible all works treating of any of the wind instruments are included. " Unclassified. Brief annotations.

The literary portion of one of the largest collections ever assembled on the flute and related materials. Now in the Music Division of the Library of Congress.

For the catalog of this collection see no. 997.

460. SCHLESINGER, KATHLEEN. A bibliography of musical instruments and archaeology .... London, W. Reeves, 1912. 100 p.

Only the first 20 pages devoted to works on musical instruments and the orchestra. Short sections on catalogs of instrument collections, and general works on music. The greater part of the volume is devoted to classical and medieval antiquities.

461. TORRI, LUIGI. La costruzione ed i costruttori degli istrumenti ad arco. Bibliografia liutistica storico-tecnica. 2a edizione .... Padova, G. Zanibon ⌐1920⌐ 43 p.

Brief critical and descriptive annotations. Alphabetically arranged, with a subject index.

SPECIAL AND SUBJECT: JAZZ

462. MERRIAM, ALAN P. A bibliography of jazz. With the assistance of Robert J. Brenford. Philadelphia, American

Folklore Society, 1954. 145 p. (Publications of the American Folklore Society. Bibliographical series, 4)

3,324 numbered entries, arranged alphabetically by author, with subject emphasis indicated by a code system. List of 113 jazz periodicals. Subject index.

Review by Marshall W. Stearns in Notes, 12 (1955) p. 436-37.

463. REISNER, ROBERT GEORGE. The literature of jazz; a selective bibliography. With an introduction by Marshall W. Stearns. New York, The New York Public Library, 1959. 63 p.

A preliminary edition appeared in the Bulletin of The New York Public Library, March-May, 1954.

Classified as to books on the subject, background books, a selective list of magazine references, magazines devoted wholly or principally to jazz.

Review by William Lichtenwanger in Notes, 16 (1959) p. 398.

SPECIAL AND SUBJECT: MEDIEVAL AND RENAISSANCE MUSIC

464. REESE, GUSTAVE. "Bibliography." In his Music in the Middle Ages. New York, Norton, 1940. p. 425-63

A listing of books, periodical articles, facsimiles, and editions. Somewhat difficult to use because the material is organized under chapter headings, but one of the most comprehensive bibliographies available for students of medieval music.

465. REESE, GUSTAVE. "Bibliography." In his Music in the Renaissance. New York, Norton, 1954. p. 884-946

A comprehensive bibliography of monographs, editions, and periodical articles related to Renaissance music. Unclassified, alphabetical arrangement.

466. SMITH, CARLETON SPRAGUE and WILLIAM DINNEEN. "Recent work on music in the Renaissance." In Modern Philology, 42:1 (Aug. 1944) p. 41-58

A bibliographical article in narrative style citing and evaluating research and editorial activity in Renaissance music from about 1900 to the date of publication.

467. SUÑOL, GREGÓRIO MARÍA. "Bibliographie générale." In his Introduction a la paléographie musicale Grégorienne. Paris, Desclés, 1935. p. 511-65

This bibliography first appeared in 1925 as part of the original Spanish edition of the author's work on Gregorian paleography.

317 items on medieval music with emphasis on plainchant. Listed in order of publication and broadly classified.

SPECIAL AND SUBJECT: MUSIC EDUCATION

468. INTERNATIONAL SOCIETY FOR MUSIC EDUCATION. International listing of teaching aids in music education. Edited by Egon Kraus. Cologne, International Society for Music Education (Distributing agent: Möseler Verlag, Wolfenbüttel), 1959. 52 p.

A classified bibliography of materials concerned with instruction in music published since 1945.

Review by Theodore Normann in Journal of Research in Music Education, 8 (1960) p. 55-56.

469. MODISETT, KATHERINE C. "Bibliography of sources, 1930-1952, relating to the teaching of choral music in secondary schools." In Journal of Research in Music Education, 3 (1955) p. 51-60

A classified bibliography of 236 items, with a brief introductory survey of the field and its problems.

470. MUSIC EDUCATORS NATIONAL CONFERENCE. COMMITTEE ON BIBLIOGRAPHY. "Music education materials, a selected bibliography." Published as v. 7, no. 1, of the Journal of Research in Music Education (1959). 146 p.

A classified listing of materials. Major groupings are:

elementary music education; junior high school; choral materials; instructional materials for . . . instrumental music; music appreciation guides and reference materials; music theory texts and workbooks; audio-visual aids; teacher training.

471. MUSIC EDUCATORS NATIONAL CONFERENCE. CURRICULUM COMMITTEE. Music education source book ⌐number one⌐ . Ed. by Hazel N. Morgan. Chicago, Music Educators National Conference, 1951. 268 p.

First printed in 1947.

Various sections contain brief bibliographies; the 1951 printing has an appendix of revisions and additions. Much of the bibliographical material in the first four printings is now somewhat out of date.

472. MUSIC EDUCATORS NATIONAL CONFERENCE. MUSIC IN AMERICAN EDUCATION COMMITTEES. Music in American education. Music education source book, number two. Ed. by Hazel N. Morgan. Chicago, Music Educators National Conference, 1955. 365 p.

Brief bibliographies to various chapters and sub-chapters, concerned with aspects of American public school music.

473. MUSIC EDUCATORS NATIONAL CONFERENCE. Selected bibliography, music education materials. ⌐Prepared for the U.S. Department of State by a special committee of the MENC⌐ Chicago, Music Educators National Conference ⌐1952⌐ 64 p.

Contains five bibliographies, classified, partially annotated: music education materials for elementary schools; collections for junior high; collections for senior high; instrumental music materials; textbooks on music education. Emphasizes school music performance materials.

SPECIAL AND SUBJECT: NATIONAL MUSIC

The first fourteen entries in this section call attention to a series of articles which have appeared in Acta musicologica, Journal of the International Musicological Society, since 1957. These articles survey the bibliographical and research activities in music in various countries since the end of World War II. Most of them cite major scholarly publications, dissertations, and important music reference works.

Austria

474. WESSELY, OTHMAR. "Die österreichische Musikforschung nach dem zweiten Weltkrieg, " in Acta M, 29 (1957) p. 111-19

Belgium

475. CLERCX-LEJEUNE, SUZANNE. "La musicologie en Belgique depuis 1945, " in Acta M, 30 (1958) p. 199-214; with a supplement in v. 31 (1959) p. 130-32

Finland

476. RINGBOM, NILS-ERIC. "Die Musikforschung in Finnland seit 1940, " in Acta M, 31 (1959) p. 17-24

France

477. LESURE, FRANÇOIS. "La musicologie française depuis 1945, " in Acta M, 30 (1958) p. 3-17

Germany

478. HECKMANN, HARALD. "Musikwissenschaftliche Unternehmungen in Deutschland seit 1945, " in Acta M, 29 (1957) p. 111-19

Holland

479. REESER, EDUARD. "Musikwissenschaft in Holland, " in Acta M, 32 (1960) p. 160-74

Israeli

480. GERSON-KIWI, EDITH. "Musicology in Israel, " in Acta M, 30 (1958) p. 17-26

Italy

481. ALLORTO, RICCARDO e CLAUDIO SARTORI. "La musicologia Italiana dal 1945 a oggi, " in Acta M, 31 (1959) p. 9-17

Latin America

482. DEVOTO, DANIEL. "Musicología Latinoamericana, " in Acta M, 31 (1959) p. 91-109

Portugal

483. KASTNER, MACARIO SANTIAGO. "Veinte años de musicología en Portugal (1940-1960), " in Acta M, 32 (1960) p. 1-11

Scandinavia

484. ROSENBERG, HERBERT. "Musikwissenschaftliche Bestrebungen in Dänemark, Norwegen und Schweden in den letzten ca. 15 Jahren, " in Acta M, 30 (1958) p. 118-37

Switzerland

485. SCHANZLIN, HANS PETER. "Musikwissenschaft in der Schweiz, " in Acta M, 30 (1958) p. 214-24

United States

486. GOLDTHWAITE, SCOTT. "The growth and influence of musicology in the United States, " in Acta M, 33 (1961) p. 72-79; with a "Codetta: some details of musicology in the United States, " by Jan Larue, p. 79-83

Yugoslavia

487. CVETKO, DRAGOTIN. "Les formes et les résultats des efforts musicologiques yougoslaves, " in Acta M, 31 (1959) p. 50-62

488. CHASE, GILBERT. Guide to Latin American music. Washington, D.C. The Library of Congress, Music Division, 1945. 274 p.

General bibliography of 301 items, followed by listings related to individual Latin American countries; 2,699 items in all. Each section has an informative introduction, and there are numerous descriptive and critical annotations. Index of authors, and of names and subjects.

2nd ed., 1962, under the title A Guide to the Music of Latin America. 411 p.

489. CORREIA DE AZEVEDO, LUÍS H. [et al.] Bibliografia musical brasileira (1820-1950). Rio de Janeiro, 1952. 252 p. (Ministerio da Educação e Saúde, Instituto Nacional do Livro, Col. BI, Bibliografia 9)

1,639 titles under 13 subject sections. Includes writings by Brazilian authors on non-Brazilian music. Publications containing music only are omitted.

Review by A. Hyatt King in Music & Letters, 35 (Jan. 1954) p. 67-68; by Charles Seeger in Notes, 11 (1954) p. 551-52.

490. DAVIDSSON, ÅKE. Bibliografi över Svensk Musik-litteratur, 1800-1945. Uppsala, 1948. 215 p.

A classified bibliography of general works, general music histories, histories of music in Sweden, works on musicians of all nationalities, and theoretical works. Restricted to works by Swedish authors except for subjects connected with Swedish music. 5,432 items in all. Index.

491. HISTORICAL RECORDS SURVEY. DISTRICT OF COLUMBIA. Bio-bibliographical index of musicians in the U.S.A. from Colonial times. Washington, D.C., Library of Congress. Music Division, 1941. 439 p. (Pan Amer. Union Music Division. Music ser. 2)

Reprinted in 1956.

"Indexes biographical material in about 65 books giving biographies of musicians in the U.S. Names are given in as complete form as possible, followed by dates of birth and death when ascertainable, and references to works in which biographical material is to be found" (preface).

P. 421-39: a list of special studies, biographies, and autobiographies pertaining to the persons whose names appear in the Index.

492. KINSCELLA, HAZEL GERTRUDE. "Americana index to The Musical Quarterly, 1915-1957." Pub. as v. 6:2 (1958) of the Journal of Research in Music Education. 144 p.

493. LISSA, ZOFIA. "Die Musikwissenschaft in Volkspolen (1945-1956)." In Die Musikforschung, 10 (1957) p. 531-47

Translated from the Polish by Werner Kaupert.

In narrative style with many titles quoted. Discusses the state and organization of Polish musicology since World War II.

494. MICHAŁOWSKI, KORNEL. Bibliografia polskeigo piśmiennictwa muzycznego. Cracow, Polskie Wydawnictwo Muzyczne, 1955. 280 p. (Materialy do bibłiografii muzyki polskiej, 3)

A classified bibliography of some 2,000 items of Polish music literature. Includes a list of music theses completed in Polish universities, 1917-54.

495. "MUSIC ⸢SECTION⸤ ." In Handbook of Latin American Studies, a Guide to the Material Published in 1935-1948. nos. 1-14 .... Cambridge, Mass., Harvard Univ. Press, 1936-51. 14 v.

496. NEF, KARL. Schriften über Musik und Volksgesang. Bern, K. J. Wyss, 1908. 151 p. (Bibliographie der schweizerischen Landeskunde, Faszikel V 6 d)

A classified bibliography of literature on Swiss music history and practice. Index of names.

497. POTÚČEK, JURAJ. Súpis slovenských hudobnín, a

literatúry o hudobníkoch. Bratislava, Nakadatel'stvo slovenskej akadémie vied a umeni, 1952. 435 p.

List of musicians, briefly identified, active in Slovakia to 1949, or mentioned in Slovak periodical literature. Bibliographies of works with Slovak texts, 1881 to 1949. Chronological index, classified index, name index.

498. POTÚČEK, JURAJ. Súpis slovenských hudobnoteoretických prác (knižné publikácie, studie, clánky, kritigy a referáty). Bratislava, Vydavatel'stvo slovenskej akadémie vied, 1955. 469 p.

Bibliography of music and books on music published in Czechoslovakia: classified bibliography of literary and theoretical works, including periodical articles, p. 15-216. List of theoretical works in chronological order, 1519-1853, p. 219-25. Biographical section, including under composer's name both publications of music and biographical or critical articles, p. 223-380. Classified list of music published 1950-52, p. 383-403. Chronological index of music, 1830-1953.

General index.

499. RAJECZKY, B. "Musikforschung in Ungarn 1936-1960 (Bibliographischer Bericht). " In Studia musicologica, 1 (1961) p. 225-49

A brief survey of recent Hungarian musical scholarship, with a classified bibliography of music literature. Hungarian titles are given with German translations. Sections on folkmusic, Hungarian music history, general music history, collective works.

500. ROCHA DA SILVA GUIMARÃES, BERTINO D. Primeiro esboco duma bibliografia musical portuguesa, com uma breve notícia histórica de música no nosso país. Porto, 1947. 174 p.

P. 15-36: brief history of Portuguese music.

The bibliography includes works on music by Portuguese authors, works on music in Portugal by native or foreign authors, old Portuguese pedagogical works, special bibliographies (sacred music, villancicos, opera, etc.), and music periodicals.

501. SCHAAL, RICHARD. Das Schrifttum zur musikalischen Lokalgeschichts Forschung. Kassel, Bärenreiter, 1947. 62 p.

A bibliography of works about music in various European cities and provinces, arranged alphabetically by location. Includes articles from a few leading periodicals. Very brief citations.

502. SENDREY, ALFRED. Bibliography of Jewish music. New York, Columbia Univ. Press, 1951. 404 p.

A classified bibliography of 5,854 items concerned with works about Jewish music and musicians, Jewish music in relation to other fields of knowledge, ethnological aspects, etc. Includes periodical articles.

Part II of this work entered as no. 546.

Review by Milton Feist in MQ, 37 (1951) p. 432-35; by Ernst C. Krohn in JAMS, 7 (Summer 1954) p. 150-52.

503. VYBORNY, ZDENEK. "Czech music literature since World War II," in Notes, 16 (1959) p. 539-46

Trans. from the German by William Lichtenwanger.

A classified bibliography, each section preceded by a brief descriptive statement. Titles given in Czech with English translations.

504. WOODFILL, WALTER L. "Bibliography." In his Musicians in English Society. Princeton, N. J., Princeton Univ. Press, 1953. p. 315-61

A substantial listing of the primary and secondary sources for the study of English music in the late 16th and early 17th centuries.

P. 320-36: "Works published before 1701." P. 347-61: "Works written and printed after 1700."

The Woodfill bibliography is cited as a particularly good example of the kind of information to be expected in histories of national music, or monographs related to the music of a local school or development.

SPECIAL AND SUBJECT: OPERA AND THEATER MUSIC

505. BAKER, BLANCH M. "Music." In Theater and Allied Arts, A Guide to Books Dealing with the History, Criticism, and Technique of the Drama and Theater and Related Arts and Crafts. New York, H. W. Wilson, 1952. p. 428-41

Broadly classified and selected list. Items are annotated. Few have more than an indirect bearing on theater music.

506. BUSTICO, GUIDO. Bibliografia delle storie e cronistorie dei teatri italiani. Milano, Bollettino bibliografico musicale, 1929. 82 p.

Sub-title: "Il teatro musicale italiano."

Part I (p. 19-27) is a general bibliography of the Italian musical theater. Part II (p. 31-83) is a bibliography of the musical theater in specific Italian cities, arranged alphabetically by place. Includes periodical articles. Some brief descriptive annotations.

507. GROUT, DONALD J. "Bibliographies, lexicons, guides, histories and other works dealing with opera in general" (p. 539-46). "Works dealing with particular operas, composers, schools, regions or periods" (p. 547-661). In his A Short History of Opera. New York, Columbia Univ. Press, 1947.

One of the most comprehensive bibliographies of literature on opera. Includes both books and articles in leading European and American periodicals. Arranged alphabetically by author.

SPECIAL AND SUBJECT: PRIMARY SOURCES (EARLY MUSIC LITERATURE)

The bibliographies in this category are concerned with writings on music which appeared before 1800. For further listings of early music literature, one should consult the general bibliographies compiled before 1840, such as Becker (no. 352), Forkel (no. 361), and Lichtenthal (no. 365). See also the narrative bibliography by James E. Matthew (no. 368) and the catalogs of libraries with noteworthy holdings in early music theory, such as the U.S. Library of Congress (no. 943), the Paul Hirsch Library (no. 784), and the library of the late Alfred Cortot (no. 747).

508. BUKOFZER, MANFRED F. "Check-list of baroque books on music." In his Music in the Baroque Era. New York, Norton, 1947. p. 417-31

Theory treatises, instruction books, histories written between c. 1590 and 1770. Modern facsimiles and reprints indicated. Arranged alphabetically by author.

509. COOVER, JAMES B. "Music theory in translation: a bibliography." In Journal of Music Theory, 3 (1959) p. 70-95

Includes only English translations. An alphabetical listing by author of works from antiquity to the present day.

510. DAVIDSSON, ÅKE. Bibliographie der musiktheoretischen Drucke des 16. Jahrhunderts. Baden-Baden, Heitz, 1962. 99 p. (Bibliotheca bibliographica aureliana, 9)

A bibliography of 16th-century music theory works; more than 600 titles, arranged alphabetically by author, with bibliographical references. Index of persons (printers, editors, etc.); bibliography, p. 85-88. 25 facsimile plates.

Future volumes projected to cover the 17th and 18th centuries.

Review by Fred Blum in Notes, 20 (1963) p. 234.

511. DAVIDSSON, ÅKE. Catalogue critique et descriptif des ouvrages théoriques sur la musique imprimés au XVIe et au XVIIe siècles et conservés dans les bibliothèques suédoises. Upsala ⌐ Almquist & Wiksells⌐ 1953. 83 p.

A union catalog of early works on music theory in Swedish libraries. 108 items fully described, with locations and references to relevant literature. P. 77-83: bibliography of works cited.

512. FARMER, HENRY G. The sources of Arabian music: an annotated bibliography of Arabic manuscripts which deal with the theory, practice, and history of Arabian music. Bearsden, Scotland, Issued privately by the author, 1940. 97 p.

Arranged chronologically by century from the 9th to the 17th centuries. Preceded by a brief general discussion of the sources of Arabian music. Author index.

513. REESE, GUSTAVE. Fourscore classics of music literature; a guide to selected original sources on theory and other writings on music not available in English, with descriptive sketches and bibliographical references. New York, The Liberal Arts Press, 1957. 91 p.

80 works presented in chronological order, with illuminating descriptions and comments. This bibliography, sponsored by the American Council of Learned Societies, was intended to stimulate new English editions and translations of important early theory works. Index of titles.

514. RILEY, MAURICE. "A tentative bibliography of early wind instrument tutors. " In Journal of Research in Music Education, 6 (1958) p. 3-24

Listing is chronological under the various instruments: flute, oboe, clarinet, bassoon, horn, trumpet, trombone, tuba, and related instruments. Annotated.

515. SMITS VAN WAESBERGHE, JOSEPH, ed. The theory of music from the Carolingian era up to 1400. v. 1-   Edited by Joseph Smits van Waesberghe with the collaboration of Peter Fischer and Christian Maas. Descriptive catalogue of manuscripts. München, G. Henle Verlag ⌐1961⌐ 155 p. (International Inventory of Musical Sources)

"Offers a description of all manuscripts, in which are preserved Latin treatises — however small — dealing with the theory of music which was in use from the Carolingian era to 1400" (preface). Index of libraries; index of authors, and of incipits of anonymous treatises.

Review by James B. Coover in Journal of Music Theory, 6 (1962) p. 314-15.

SPECIAL AND SUBJECT: SACRED MUSIC

Bibliographies of writings on sacred music are surprisingly few in number. Additional references will be found in the various handbooks on hymnology (nos. 204-212). See also the current listings in the Jahrbuch für Liturgik und Hymnologie (no. 389) and Gregório Suñol's bibliography of works related to Gregorian chant (no. 467).

516. BUSZIN, WALTER ⌈et al.⌉ A bibliography on music and the church. Prepared for the Commission on Music, Dept. of Worship and the Arts, National Council of Churches of Christ in the U.S.A. New York, National Council of Churches of Christ, 1958. 16 p.

BIBLIOGRAPHIES OF MUSIC

In this category are listed bibliographies of musical scores as distinct from writings about music. As a group this section lends itself to fewer subdivisions than the preceding "Bibliographies of Music Literature," the major approaches being that of the performer in search of music appropriate to his particular instrument or ensemble, and that of the student of early music.

Not included here are the numerous listings of the works of individual composers, including the thematic catalogs. One of the best approaches to information of this kind is through the biographical dictionaries such as Baker (no. 46) and Riemann (no. 34) or such comprehensive encyclopedias as MGG (no. 6). For thematic catalogs, except for the most recent, a useful guide is found in the Music Library Association's Check List of Thematic Catalogues (no. 1142).

The catalogs of individual music publishing firms are also excluded, except where their coverage extends beyond the output of a single business house.

GENERAL

Here are included those bibliographies in which the intent of the compiler is to cover a large or heterogeneous body of musical materials (performance being one of several possible interests), or music confined to a particular national group: Belgian, Swedish, Finnish, etc.

517. AMERICAN SOCIETY OF COMPOSERS, AUTHORS AND PUBLISHERS. ASCAP symphonic catalog, 1959. New York, The American Society of Composers, Authors and Publishers, ⌐1960⌐ 375 p.

An alphabetical listing, by composers and arrangers, of symphonic literature controlled by ASCAP. Entries give instrumentation, duration, and publisher.

For a parallel volume issued by Broadcast Music, Inc., see no. 521.

518. ARONOWSKY, SALOMON. Performing times of orchestral works. Foreword by Percival R. Kirby. London, E. Benn, 1959. 802 p.

Covers both standard and minor composers of all countries and periods, with some emphasis on British names. Arrangements listed under both composer and arranger. Operas, orchestral versions of single songs, and opera excerpts appear frequently. No precise indication of edition or publisher, but lists of publishers and publishers' organizations are given (p. xiii-xxix). A more lavish and expensive publication than seems warranted by the contents.

Review by Howard Mitchell in Notes, 17 (1960) p. 237-39.

519. BERKOWITZ, FRIDA P. Popular titles and subtitles of musical compositions. New York, Scarecrow Press, Inc., 1962. 182 p.

An alphabetical listing of 502 works, by title, with brief accounts of the origins of the popular titles. Bibliography; composer index.

For works covering similar material, see nos. 525 and 537.

520. BOLL, ANDRÉ. Répertoire analytique de la musique française des origines à nos jours. Paris, Horizons de France [1948] 299 p.

Part 1: a list of composers of the French school, with dates, arranged alphabetically within chronological historical periods.

Part 2: a classified list of published French secular music, alphabetical by composer; followed by a similar listing of sacred music. Publishers indicated. Indexed by works and by composers.

521. BROADCAST MUSIC, INC. Symphonic catalogue. New

York, Broadcast Music, Inc. ⌐1963⌐ 132 p.

An alphabetical listing, by composer, of symphonic works the performing rights of which are controlled by Broadcast Music, Inc. Entries give instrumentation, duration, and publisher.

For a parallel volume issued by The American Society of Composers, Authors and Publishers, see no. 517.

522. BRYANT, E. T. Music librarianship; a practical guide. London, James Clarke; New York, Hafner ⌐1959⌐ 503 p.

Part II, p. 289-487, is a series of lists of recommended musical scores for libraries, classified under instrumental music, vocal music, miniature score. Detailed annotations. Also entered as no. 1122.

523. CENTRE BELGE DE DOCUMENTATION MUSICALE. Catalogus van werken van Belgische componisten. Bruxelles, Centre Belge de Documentation Musicale, 1953-57. 20 numbers.

A useful series of paper-bound catalogs (11 in French, 9 in Flemish) averaging 20 pages each, devoted to contemporary Belgian composers and their works.

524. CHIPMAN, JOHN H. Index to top-hit tunes (1900-1950) ... with a foreword by Arthur Fiedler. Boston, Bruce Humphries, 1962. 249 p.

An alphabetical index, by title, of the most popular American songs of the first half of the 20th century. Gives key, composer and author, publisher and original publication date; source in film or musical comedy. Chronological index; short bibliography.

525. CUDWORTH, CHARLES. "Ye olde spuriosity shoppe, or, Put it in the Anhang." In Notes, 12 (1954-55) p. 25-40, 533-53

A lively discussion of the problems of plagiarism, hoaxes, misattribution, and the use of pseudonyms in the music field. The article contains three useful supplements: (1) spuriosities proper, listed under their supposed composers; (2) nicknamed and falsely titled compositions: (3) pseudonyms, altered forms of names, and nicknames.

For works covering similar material, see nos. 519 and 537.

526. CUSHING, HELEN G. Children's song index, an index to more than 22,000 songs in 189 collections comprising 222 volumes. New York, H. W. Wilson, 1936. 798 p.

A dictionary catalog of children's song literature. Main entry is by song title, with subordinate entries under composer, author of the words, and subject. References from first line to title. Foreign titles given in the original language. There is a preliminary "catalog of collections indexed," p. xv-xxxiii, and a "directory of publishers" at the end of the volume.

527. DEDINSKY, IZABELLA K. Zeneművek, 1936-40. Budapest, Kiadja az országos széchényi könyvtár, 1944. 286 p. (Az 1936-40. Évkör magyar szakkönyvészete)

Classified bibliography of music published in Hungary, 1936-40. Includes both popular and serious music.

528. DEUTSCHER MUSIKVERLEGER-VERBAND. Der Bonner Katalog. Verzeichnis der urheberrechtlich geschützten musikalischen Werke mit reversgebundenem Aufführungsmaterial. Bonn, Musikhandel-Verlagsgesellschaft M. B. H. ⌐1959⌐ 326 p.

A listing, alphabetical by composer, of musical works protected by international copyright under the Bern Convention. Also includes copyright editions of works by early composers. Type of work indicated by symbol; duration and publisher given. P. vii-x: Names and addresses of publishers.

An excellent source of information on published contemporary works.

529. "DOCUMENTS DU DEMI-SIÈCLE: Tableau chronologique des principales oeuvres musicales de 1900 à 1950, établi par genre et par année. Numéro spécial." La revue musicale, no. 216 (1952) 154 p.

A list, year by year, of the important musical works of the first half of the 20th century, together with miscellaneous information relating to music for each year. Catalogs of six publishers, with significant works issued by them between 1900 and 1950: Heugel, Costallat, Amphion, Ricordi, Choudens, Ouvrières. Minimum bibliographical information.

530. FÖRENINGEN SVENSKA TONSÄTTARE. Nyare svenska orkesterverk samt instrumental- och vokalverk med orkester. Katalog. Swedish orchestral works (20th century) including instrumental soli and vocal works with orchestra. Stockholm, 1956. 109 p.

Supplement, 1959. 15 p.

Earlier lists published in 1937 and 1944. Title varies: Nyare svenska orkester- och vokalverk, katalog.

Classified listings of works under composers' names in alphabetical order. Information given includes publishers, instrumentation, timings.

531. FOSTER, MYLES B. Anthems and anthem composers, an essay upon the development of the anthem from the time of the Reformation to the end of the 19th century; with a complete list of anthems (in alphabetical order) belonging to each of the four centuries.... London, Novello, 1901. 225 p.

532. FULD, JAMES H. American popular music (reference book) 1875-1950. Philadelphia, Musical Americana, 1955. 94 p.

Supplement ... 1956. 9 p.

A bibliography of some 250 selected American popular songs. Detailed information as to first printing, copyright date, description of cover. 20 plates of song covers. An interesting attempt to approach American popular song with the methods of descriptive bibliography.

533. HOFMEISTER, FRIEDRICH. Verzeichnis der in Deutschland seit 1868 erschienenen Werke russischer

Komponisten. ⌐Leipzig, Druck der Buchdruckerei Frankenstein, 1949?⌐ 253 p.

Alphabetical listing of composers, with their works in order of opus number. Detailed bibliographical information, including price, but lacking in date of publication.

534. McCARTY, CLIFFORD. Film composers in America; a checklist of their work. Foreword by Lawrence Morton. Glendale, Calif., John Valentin ⌐1953⌐ 193 p.

163 names, with film scores listed by date. Index of film titles; index of orchestrators.

Review by F. W. Sternfeld in Notes, 11 (1953) p. 105.

Also entered as no. 122.

535. McCOLVIN, LIONEL R. and H. REEVES. "Music: a comprehensive classified list." In their Music Libraries. London, Grafton, 1937-38. v. 2, p. 1-209

A guide to selection for music librarians. A classified list containing for the most part music in print at the time of compilation. Emphasis on British publishers, though some foreign material is included. Suggests basic stock for libraries of different kinds.

536. MATTFELD, JULIUS. Variety music cavalcade, 1620-1961; a chronology of vocal and instrumental music popular in the United States .... Revised edition. Englewood Cliffs, N. J., Prentice-Hall, 1962. 713 p.

First published as Variety Music Cavalcade, 1620-1950. 1952. 637 p.

Originally appeared in a modified form as Variety Radio Directory, 1938-39, supplemented in weekly issues of Variety.

A chronological bibliography of American popular music, with references to parallel social and historical events for each year. Index of musical works by title, with date of first publication.

Review by Irving Lowens in <u>Notes</u>, 20 (1963) p. 233-34.

Also entered as no. 327.

537. MIES, PAUL. Volkstümliche Namen musikalischer
Werke. Bonn, Musikhandel-Verlags ⊏1960⊐ 32 p.

Popular titles for musical compositions listed under
composers, with an alphabetical index of titles.

See also no. 519 and 525 for works with similar content.

538. THE MUSIC TRADER'S GUIDE TO WORKS BY
TWENTIETH CENTURY BRITISH COMPOSERS, together with the
names of their publishers; comprising instrumental works, songs,
text books and manuals up to and including June 1955. Compiled
by L. D. Gibbin. London, Boosey & Hawkes ⊏1956⊐ 132 p.

Works listed alphabetically by title under composers' names.
Brief entries for works by 76 composers. Supplementary listing
of "other British composers and their principal publishers. "

539. NATIONAL JEWISH WELFARE BOARD. BIBLIOG-
RAPHY COMMITTEE. Bibliography of Jewish instrumental
music. New York, National Jewish Music Council ⊏1948⊐ 16 p.

<u>Addenda</u> ⊏1950⊐ 7 leaves.

A selective list of the "best and most interesting works that
are easily available, either in published form or through rental. "
Classified according to various combinations of instruments.
Publishers indicated.

540. NATIONAL JEWISH WELFARE BOARD. BIBLIOG-
RAPHY COMMITTEE. Bibliography of Jewish vocal music.
New York, National Jewish Music Council ⊏c. 1948⊐ 36 p.

<u>Addenda</u> ⊏1950?⊐ 16 leaves.

A selective list of available Jewish vocal music, "in good
taste, and ... suited for programming. " Classified by genre.
Language or languages of text, and publishers indicated.

541. NORDISKA MUSIKFÖRLAGET. Swedish orchestral works. Annotated catalogue. ⸤Commentary by Edvin Kallstenius⸥ Stockholm, Nordiska Musikförlaget ⸤1948⸥ 85 p.

"This catalogue is intended as a guide to conductors, members of programme-committees and other music lovers who wish to learn something about Swedish composition" (foreword). Descriptions of selected works by 25 contemporary Swedish composers. Portraits and brief biographical sketches.

542. PAN AMERICAN UNION. MUSIC SECTION. Latin American orchestral music available in the United States. Washington, Pan American Union ⸤1956⸥ 76 p.

Supersedes a shorter list of similar character issued in 1955.

Part I: a classified list of Latin American music available at publishing houses and from other agencies. Part II (p. 25-79): Latin American music in the Edwin A. Fleisher Collection in the Free Library of Philadelphia.

543. REDDICK, WILLIAM. The standard musical repertoire, with accurate timings. Garden City, N. Y., Doubleday & Co., 1947. 192 p.

A classified list of overtures, orchestral works, works for piano and for violin, songs, and choral numbers, with timings, to the nearest 5 seconds, of familiar recordings. Designed primarily for program directors of radio stations.

544. SÄVELTÄJÄIN TEKIJÄNOIKEUSTOIMISTO TEOSTO. Catalogue of Finnish orchestral and vocal compositions. Helsinki, Teosto (Composers' copyright bureau) ⸤1951⸥ 88 p.

Lists works for 57 Finnish composers, giving title, instrumentation, duration, publisher. Brief biographical sketches. English translations of Finnish titles.

545. SEARS, MINNIE E. Song index; an index to more than 12,000 songs in 177 song collections .... New York, H. W. Wilson Co., 1926. 650 p.

Supplement; an index to more than 7,000 songs in 104 collections .... 1934. 366 p.

Contains titles, first lines, authors' names, and composers' names in one alphabet. Each song is indexed fully under title, with added entry under composer and author and cross references from first line and variant or translated titles. Classified and alphabetical listings of song collections indexed.

546. SENDREY, ALFRED. Bibliography of Jewish music. New York, Columbia Univ. Press, 1951. 404 p.

Part II (p. 209-339): a classified list of about 4,000 pieces of Jewish music, alphabetical by composer within classification, giving scoring, author and language of text, etc. Publisher and year indicated for published works; some manuscripts also included.

The first section of this work is entered as no. 502.

547. THOMPSON, LEILA (FERN). Partial list of Latin American music obtainable in the U.S., and Supplement. 3rd ed., rev. & enl. Washington, D. C., Pan American Union, Division of Music & Visual Arts, 1948. 56 p.; 17 p. (mimeographed)

The 1st and 2nd editions were prepared by Gilbert Chase, 1941 and 1942.

"Concerned with concert music to the exclusion of popular and folk music." Classified by genre and country. Scoring, language of text, and publisher indicated. Indexed by country and composer.

548. UNIVERSAL-HANDBUCH DER MUSIKLITERATUR aller Zeiten und Völker. Als Nachschlagewerk und Studienquelle der Welt-Musikliteratur .... Wien, Pazdirek & Co. ⌐1904-10?⌐ 14 v.

A list of music in print and available in the trade at time of publication. Primarily useful for 19th-century material and in establishing the existence of and dates of editions. Arrangement under composer by opus number when possible, otherwise by title.

549. UPTON, RAYMOND. Index of miniature scores:
British availability. London, D. Jackson, 1956. 120 p.

Works listed alphabetically by composer.

Review by Betty Buyck in Notes, 14 (1957) p. 367.

550. WAS WIR SINGEN. KATALOG DES IN DER
DEUTSCHEN DEMOKRATISCHEN REPUBLIK ERSCHIENENEN
WELTLICHEN LIED- UND CHORMATERIALS. Band I: 1945-
1958 Auswahl. Herausgegeben vom Zentralhaus für Volkskunst.
Leipzig, Friedrich Hofmeister ⌐ 1959⌐ 255 p.

Title listing of 6,396 entries, supplemented by lists of
collections and of cantatas and oratorios under composer.
Indexed by subtitles or working titles, by voice combination and
affective theme, and by national character. Further indexes by
writer of text and composer.

CURRENT

The current music bibliographies listed below restrict their
entries to music only. For a full coverage one should be
acquainted with the various national bibliographies in which music
appears in company with entries from other fields. An excellent
introduction to the use of these major bibliographical tools is
found in an article by Donald W. Krummel and James B. Coover,
"Current National Bibliographies, Their Music Coverage," in
Notes, 17 (1960) p. 375-88. (no. 1137)

See also the current listings and reviews in such periodicals
as Notes, Fontes artis musicae, Acta and Music Review.

551. THE BRITISH CATALOGUE OF MUSIC. 1-   London,
The Council of the British National Bibliography, 1957-

Published quarterly, the last issue each year being a
cumulated annual volume. Organized in two parts: a classified
section and an alphabetical section. There is also a section

devoted to musical literature. List of music publishers, with their British agents specified.

Also cited, in part, as no. 397. The classification scheme used in this catalog has been published separately; see no. 1121.

552. BRÜNN. UNIVERSITA. KNIHOVNA. Prírustky hudebnin v cesko. Slovenských knihovnäch. Spracoval Zdeněk Zouhar. Praha, Statní Pedagogicke Nakladatelstvi, 1953-

Joint accession list of ten principal music libraries in Czechoslovakia, containing two or three thousand items per year. Classified by medium, without index.

553. DANSK MUSIKFORTEGNELSE. Udgivet af Dansk Musikhandlerforening. v. 1- København, 1931- (8 v. through 1959)

An index to music issued by Danish music publishers. Arranged alphabetically with composers and titles interfiled. Each volume covers three years of publication, except for the 1960 issue, which covers 1955-59.

554. DEUTSCHE MUSIKBIBLIOGRAPHIE. Jahrgang 1-Leipzig, F. Hofmeister, 1829-

See no. 384 for full annotation.

555. HOFMEISTERS HANDBUCH DER MUSIKLITERATUR. Bd. 1- Leipzig, F. Hofmeister, 1844-

See no. 387 for full annotation.

556. JAHRESVERZEICHNIS DER DEUTSCHEN MUSIKALIEN UND MUSIKSCHRIFTEN. Jahrgang 1- Leipzig, F. Hofmeister, 1852-

See no. 390 for full annotation.

557. LETOPIS' MUZYKAL'NOĬ LITERATURY; organ gosudarstvennoĭ bibliografiĭ SSSR. Izdaetsîa s 1931 goda;

vykhodit 4 raza v god. Moskva, Izdatel'stvo vsesoiuznoi knizhnoi palaty, 1931.

Quarterly. Organization and content varies slightly. In 1960, a classified list of publications in musical notation. Includes literary works with musical supplements or extensive musical illustrations, and music issued in periodicals. Index by composer for each issue, and separate lists of books, magazines, newspapers containing music. Annual index of vocal works by title and first line; and by language of text. Entries give full bibliographical information, including complete contents, price, size of edition.

558. MATERIAŁY DO BIBLIOGRAFII MUZYKI POLSKIEJ.
⌐ Redaktor serii: Tadeusz Strumiłło. Kraków⌐ v. 1- Polskie Wydawnictwo Muzyczne ⌐1954⌐-

Tom I: Opery polskie, opracował Kornel Michałowski. 1954. 277 p. Polish operas and foreign operas with Polish settings or subjects, listed by title, giving composer, librettist, date and place of first performance. Composer, librettist, and chronological indexes.

Tom II: Piesni solowe S. Moniuszki, katalog tematyczny, opracował Erwin Nowaczyk. 1954. 332 p. Thematic catalog of 304 songs by Moniuszki, giving authors of texts, lists of editions, etc.

Tom III: Bibliografia Polskiego pismiennictwa muzycznego, opracował Kornel Michałowski. 1955. 280 p. Classified bibliography of books on music in Polish. List of theses and dissertations, 1917-54. Index.

Tom IV: Polska muzyka kameralna, katalog, w oprac. T. Strumiłły i Z. Szweykowskiego. ⌐ in preparation?⌐

Tom V: Polska muzyka symfoniczna, katalog w oprac. T. Strumiłły i Z. Szweykowskiego. ⌐ in preparation?⌐

559. U.S. COPYRIGHT OFFICE. Catalog of copyright entries. Music. Third series, v. 1- 1947- Washington, D.C., Copyright Office, The Library of Congress, 1947-

From 1891 to 1906, the quarterly copyright index was issued by the Treasury department, and musical compositions were included as part of the general series. In a new series, from 1906 to 1946, a music catalog was published separately. In 1946 it was subdivided into separate sections: Published music, Unpublished music, and Renewal registrations, with main entries by composer and a classified index. This arrangement was maintained until Vol. 11 of the Third Series (1958), when the listings were grouped under "Current Registrations" and "Renewal Registrations, " with the main entry under title and a name index for composers.

560. U.S. LIBRARY OF CONGRESS. Library of Congress catalog, music and phonorecords, a cumulative list of works represented by Library of Congress printed cards. Washington, The Library of Congress, 1954-

Current music accessions, printed or recorded, of the Library of Congress and of libraries participating in its cooperative cataloging program. Includes purchased current or retrospective materials and a selection of recent copyright deposits. Entries are reproduced from the library's printed cards. Name and subject index. Semi-annual, with annual cumulation.

MUSIC FOR PERFORMANCE

A summary classification of the items within this section:

Band: no. 574.

Chamber Ensemble: nos. 563-67, 569, 584, 590, 601.

Orchestra: nos. 570, 575, 587, 594, 605.

Organ: nos. 595, 604, 607, 613.

Piano: nos. 571, 580, 582, 593, 599, 602, 603, 609.

Stringed instruments:

Violin: nos. 573, 577, 578, 584, 591, 610.

Viola: nos. 572, 573, 584, 591.

Cello: nos. 578, 584, 597, 614.

Bass: no. 583.

Voice, Solo: nos. 576, 588.

Voice, Choral: nos. 589, 592, 600, 606, 612.

Wind Instruments:

Ensemble: nos. 585, 586, 590.

Clarinet: nos. 579, 596, 598, 611.

Flute: nos. 581, 596.

Recorder: nos. 561, 615.

561. ALKER, HUGO. Blockflöten-Bibliographie. Aufführungspraxis — Literatur — Spielgut. Wien, Universitätsbibliothek, 1960-61. 2 v. (Biblos-Schriften, 27-28)

A source book of bibliographical information for performers on the recorder. Each volume contains a bibliography of writings on the instrument and its performance, including early accounts, a bibliography of instruction manuals, and a classified listing of modern editions of recorder music. Supplementary essays on history and performance practice. Facsimile plates from early recorder methods.

562. ALKER, HUGO. Literatur für alte Tasteninstrumente. Versuch einer Bibliographie für die Praxis. Wien, H. Geyer, 1962. 82 p.

The main division is between music for harpsichord and music for organ (without pedals). Brief entries, with publisher and editor given. Collections entered by title and filed in the same alphabet with composers. Emphasizes music currently available in practical editions.

563. ALTMANN, WILHELM. Handbuch für Klavierquartettspieler ... Mit 237 Notenbeispielen .... Wolfenbüttel, Verlag für Musikalische Kultur & Wissenschaft, 1937. 147 p.

Notenbeispiele ... in pocket at end of Handbuch.

A companion to a selective list of piano quarters, arranged chronologically by birthdates of composers. German works curtailed in an effort toward international coverage. Brief descriptive and critical commentaries. Index of composers.

564. ALTMANN, WILHELM. Handbuch für Klavier-quintettspieler ... Mit 343 Notenbeispielen. Wolfenbüttel, Verlag für Musikalische Kultur & Wissenschaft, 1936. 178 p.

Notenbeispiele ... in pocket at end of Handbuch.

Similar to the above, with emphasis on piano quintets.

565. ALTMANN, WILHELM. Handbuch für Klavier-triospieler; Wegweiser durch die Trios für Klavier, Violine und Violoncell. Mit fast 400 Notenbeispielen. Wolfenbüttel, Verlag für Musikalische Kultur & Wissenschaft, 1934. 237 p.

566. ALTMANN, WILHELM. Handbuch für Streich-quartettspieler .... Berlin, M. Hesse, 1928-31. 4 v.

Vols. 1-2: string quartets; Vol. 3: string trios, quintets, sextets, octets; addenda to quartets; Vol. 4: works for strings and winds.

A companion to string literature, giving brief descriptions and analyses of works in the standard repertory, as well as of lesser known works. Arrangement within each category is chronological.

567. ALTMANN, WILHELM. Kammermusik-Katalog; ein Verzeichnis von seit 1841 veröffentlichten Kammermusikwerken. 6. bis August 1944 ergänzte Auflage. Leipzig, F. Hofmeister, 1945. 400 p.

Succeeded by Richter (see no. 601).

Chamber music published since 1841, as separate works or in collections or series. Classified by medium, with composer indexes. Entries give publisher and date of first and succeeding editions. International coverage.

568. ALTMANN, WILHELM. Katalog der seit 1861 in den
Händel gekommenen theatralischen Musik ... ein musikbiblio-
graphischer Versuch. Wolfenbüttel, Verlag für Musikalische
Kultur & Wissenschaft, 1935.

Incomplete: published in parts through the letter L.

Operas, ballets, and incidental music since 1861, arranged
by composer with references from librettist, etc. Entries list
scores and piano-vocal scores, give publisher, date, and
language of text; date and place of first performance. Does not
include American and English publishers.

569. ALTMANN, WILHELM. Kleiner Führer durch die
Streichquartette für Haus und Schule .... Berlin/Halensee,
Deutscher Musikliteratur-Verlag ⌐c. 1950⌐ 166 p.

An abridgement of the author's Handbuch für Streich-
quartettspieler (no. 566) concentrating on the classical literature
with curtailment of the post-Brahms works.

570. ALTMANN, WILHELM. Orchester-Literatur-Katalog;
Verzeichnis von seit 1850 erschienenen Orchester-Werken ....
Leipzig, F. E. C. Leuckart, 1926-36. 2 v.

Orchestral music published since 1850, listing scores,
miniature scores, parts, and arrangements. Vol. 2 gives, in
addition, instrumentation and duration, and contains a composer
index to both volumes. Thematic quotations given for works
whose serial numbers are often confused, e.g. Haydn's
symphonies, Händel's concertos, etc.

571. ALTMANN, WILHELM. Verzeichnis von Werken für
Klavier vier- und sechshändig sowie für zwei und mehr Klaviere.
Leipzig, F. Hofmeister, 1943. 133 p.

Classified catalog of works for piano, 4 and 6 hands, and for
2 or more pianos, with and without other instruments. Includes
both original works and arrangements. Alphabetical by composer

within classifications. Index.

572. ALTMANN, WILHELM & W. BORISSOWSKY. Literaturverzeichnis für Bratsche und Viola d'amore. Wolfenbüttel, Verlag für Musikalische Kultur & Wissenschaft, 1937. 148 p.

A classified catalog, including solo works, duos, and other combinations in which the viola has the leading role. Lists works in manuscript, and all known editions of published works, with dates. Includes transcriptions as well as original works.

573. BAUDET-MAGET, A. Guide du violiniste; oeuvres choisies pour violon, ainsi que pour alto et musique de chambre, classées d'après leur degré de difficulté. Lausanne, Paris, etc., Foetisch Frères ⌈n. d.⌉ 295 p.

Selective list of violin, viola, and string ensemble music from mid-17th century to the present. Classified according to genre and degree of difficulty.

574. BERGER, KENNETH. Band music guide. Ed. by Kenneth Berger and the staff of The Instrumentalist Co. 2nd edition. Evanston, Ill., The Instrumentalist Co., 1960. 390 p. First pub. c. 1956.

Title entries only. Of limited value.

575. BUSCHKÖTTER, WILHELM. Handbuch der internationalen Konzertliteratur. Berlin, Walter de Gruyter & Co., 1961. 374 p.

Compiled as the successor to Theodor Müller-Reuter's Lexikon der deutschen Konzertliteratur (no. 594). Alphabetical arrangement by composer, with works listed chronologically under each composer. Information includes performance time, instrumentation, date of composition, performance, publisher.

576. COFFIN, BERTON. The singer's repertoire. 2nd ed. New York, Scarecrow Press, 1960. 4 v.

First published in one volume, 1956.

Classified catalog of solo songs, each volume devoted to a particular voice range; information on subject, accompaniment, publisher.

Review by Arnold Caswell in Journal of Research in Music Education, 9 (1961) p. 76.

577. FARISH, MARGARET K. Preliminary manuscript of violin music in print. New York, R. R. Bowker, 1963. 471 p.

A preliminary edition reproduced by offset from typescript, listing currently available works for violin, and violin ensemble, from some 150 publishers. Unaccompanied works are listed separately. Users are invited to submit corrections or additions, or suggestions for improvement, which will be incorporated into a future comprehensive publication, String Music in Print. Arrangement is alphabetical by composer within a simple classification (violin unaccompanied; violin accompanied; 2 violins unaccompanied; 2 violins accompanied; etc.). Brief title entries, publisher indicated. There are also sections devoted to violin study material and violin literature.

Review by Joel H. Berman in Notes, 20 (1963) p. 229.

578. FEINLAND, ALEXANDER. The combination violin and violoncello without accompaniment. Paramaribo, Netherlands Guyana, Printed by J. H. Oliveira, 1944. 121 p.

Classified catalog, including manuscripts of music from the baroque to the present. Original publisher or location given. Biographical sketches of composers represented.

579. FOSTER, LEVIN W. A directory of clarinet music. Pittsfield, Mass., Printed by A. E. Johnson & Son, 1940. 128 p.

"Lists practically all the music known to be published for the clarinet." Classified arrangement, alphabetical by composer within each classification; publishers indicated. Some transcriptions and arrangements included, as well as more than 50 methods and studies.

580. FRISKIN, JAMES and IRWIN FREUNDLICH. Music for the piano. A handbook of concert and teaching material from 1580 to 1952. New York, Rinehart, 1954. 432 p. (The field of music, 5)

Selective listing of standard works in the piano repertory. Classified arrangement. Remarks concerned largely with the technical requirements of the material and with its interpretative treatment.

581. GIRARD, ADRIEN. Histoire et richesses de la flûte. Paris, Libraire Gründ, 1953. 143 p.

A handsome illustrated volume, printed in an edition of 1,500 copies. Chap. IV, "Les flûtistes," lists the principal performers from the 15th to the 20th centuries, with brief comments on each. Chap. V, "Littérature," is a chronological listing of important composers of flute music, with their works, from Louis Couperin to the present, followed by an alphabetical listing, by composer, of works for solo flute accompanied by keyboard, harp, or orchestra. Manuscript works included.

582. GRATIA, L. E. Répertoire pratique de pianiste ... Préface de I. Philipp. Paris, Delagrave, 1931. 117 p.

A list of 2,500 piano pieces by 271 composers, arranged alphabetically by composer with categories of varying degrees of difficulty. Four-hand pieces, p. 112-17.

583. GRODNER, MURRAY. Comprehensive catalogue of literature for the string bass ... a complete listing of solos, etudes, methods and chamber music for the string bass. ⌐Bloomington, Indiana, School of Music, Indiana University⌐ 1958. 58 p.

Lists works in print, 1955. Solos and ensembles, for 2 to 13 instruments, using string bass. A few works in manuscript given. Each entry gives composer, title, instrumentation, grade of difficulty, publisher, price, and comments on availability.

Review by Darius Thieme in Notes, 16 (1959) p. 258.

584. GRÜNBERG, MAX. Führer durch die Literatur der
Streichinstrumente ... Kritisches, progressiv geordnetes
Repertorium von instruktiven Solo- und Ensembelwerken ....
Leipzig, Breitkopf & Härtel, 1913. 218 p. (Handbücher der
Musiklehre ... hrsg. von X. Scharwenka, 10)

A listing of music for violin, viola, cello, and ensemble from
the baroque through the 19th century, classified according to
genre and degree of difficulty. Publishers, prices indicated.
Bibliography, p. 206-09. Index.

585. HELM, SANFORD M. Catalog of chamber music for
wind instruments. Ann Arbor ⊏ The Author, University of
Michigan, School of Music ⊐ 1952. 85 p. (National Association of
College Wind and Percussion Instrument Instructors. Publication
no. 1)

Chamber music for 3 to 12 instruments employing at least one
wind instrument; classified according to size and instrumentation,
giving publisher, date, and American agent for currently available
editions. Composer index.

586. HOUSER, ROY. Catalogue of chamber music for wood-
winds. 2nd ed. Bloomington, Indiana, Indiana University, 1960.
158 leaves (typescript)

Material for from 3 to 10 instruments, classified according
to ensemble. P. 147-48: A list of woodwind music found in the
Moravian archives at Winston-Salem, North Carolina, and at
Bethlehem, Pennsylvania. P. 152-55: Selected publications from
the catalog of the Donemus Foundation, Amsterdam.

Supplement: Woodwind ensembles bibliography.

587. INTERNATIONAL MUSIC COUNCIL. Répertoires internationaux de musique contemporaine à l'usage des amateurs et
des jeunes. I. Musique symphonique de 1880 à 1954. Frankfurt,
New York, C. F. Peters, 1957-   (v. 1, 63 p.)

A catalog of recently composed symphonic works suitable for
young people's and amateur orchestras. Material listed

alphabetically by country; publisher, date, and instrumentation given. Indexes of composers, types of ensemble. A list of music publishers.

588. KAGEN, SERGIUS. Music for the voice; a descriptive list of concert and teaching material. New York, Rinehart, 1949. 507 p. (The field of music, 3)

Selective list of works in the standard vocal repertory from the 17th century to the present. Classified arrangement. Each entry gives compass, type of voice required, and brief descriptive remarks.

589. KNAPP, J. MERRILL. Selected list of music for men's voices. Princeton, N. J., Princeton University Press, 1952. 165 p.

Original works and arrangements, published and unpublished. Alphabetical by composer within main classifications. Each entry gives dates of composer, scoring, language, publisher, and editor. Index of composers.

Review by Archibald Davison in Notes, 10 (1952) p. 104-05.

590. LEMACHER, HEINRICH. Handbuch der Hausmusik. Graz, A. Pustet, 1948. 454 p.

The second part of the volume (p. 221 to end) lists works for solo instruments and various chamber ensembles. Many lesser-known works included. Arranged alphabetically by composer within various categories. Publisher and brief description of works given. Bibliography, p. 435-39. Index.

591. LETZ, HANS. Music for the violin and viola. New York, Rinehart, 1948. 107 p. (The field of music, 2)

A selective graded list of music for unaccompanied violin or violin and piano, p. 1-94, followed by a similar list of music for viola, p. 96-106.

592. LOCKE, ARTHUR W. Selected list of choruses for

women's voices. 2nd ed., rev. & enl. Northampton, Mass., Smith College, 1946. 237 p. (Smith College monographs, 2)

Original works and arrangements, published and unpublished, octavo and in collections. Alphabetical by composer within chronological divisions. Each entry gives dates of composer, scoring, language, publisher, and edition. Index of composers, authors, and first lines and titles.

593. MOLDENHAUER, HANS. Duo-pianism; a dissertation. Chicago, Chicago Musical College Press, 1951. 400 p.

Contains a list of original 2-piano music, arranged alphabetically by composer. Publishers indicated. The main part of the dissertation concerns itself with practical rather than historical aspects of the subject.

"Original Two-Piano Music," p. 340-62; "Recorded Two-Piano Music," p. 363-73.

594. MÜLLER-REUTER, THEODOR. Lexikon der deutschen Konzertliteratur; ein Ratgeber für Dirigenten, Konzertveranstalter, Musikschriftsteller und Musikfreunde. Leipzig, G. F. Kahnt nachf., 1909. v. 1. 626 p.

Nachtrag zu Band I. Leipzig, Kahnt, 1921. 236 p.

The standard guide to the orchestral and chamber music of the major composers of the romantic period, with detailed information as to date of composition, first performance, duration, instrumentation, relation to composer's other works. Band I covers the following composers: Schubert, Mendelssohn, Schumann, Berlioz, Liszt, Raff, Wagner, Draeseke, Reinecke, Bruch, Gernsheim, and Richard Strauss. The Nachtrag is devoted to Beethoven, Brahms, and Haydn (symphonies only).

Buschkötter's Handbuch ... (no. 575) is intended to supplement Müller-Reuter and bring it up to date.

595. MÜNGER, FRITZ. Choralbearbeitungen für Orgel. Verzeichnis zu den Chorälen des Deutschen Evangelischen

Kirchengesangbuches und des Gesangbuches der evang.-reform.
Kirchen der deutschsprachigen Schweiz. Kassel, Bärenreiter
⌐1952⌐ 148 p.

Alphabetical listing by chorale text incipit, locating each in
the German or Swiss chorale books, and indicating the organ
settings available in some 56 collections of chorale preludes.

596. NATIONAL ASSOCIATION OF SCHOOLS OF MUSIC.
Solo literature for the wind instruments. 32 p. (The Bulletin of
the National Association of Schools of Music, no. 31,
January, 1951)

Lists of solos, including concertos, for flute, oboe, clarinet,
bassoon, French horn, cornet and trumpet, trombone. Graded
as to difficulty, brief critical or descriptive annotations.
Publisher indicated.

597. NOGUE, ÉDOUARD. La littérature du violoncelle ...
Préface de M. Paul Bazelaire .... Paris, Delagrave, 1925.
152 p.

Lists nearly 2,000 works for violoncello, solo or with other
instruments. Classified and graded, with short descriptions of
most of the works. Publisher indicated.

598. OPPERMAN, KALMEN. Repertory of the clarinet.
New York, Ricordi, 1960. 140 p.

Classified index of music for the clarinet, including methods,
etudes, and music for the instrument as solo as well as in combination with other instruments. Listing of publishers given, and
a short bibliography of books on the clarinet.

Review by Roger P. Phelps in Notes, 18 (1960) p. 63-64.

599. PARENT, CHARLOTTE F. H. Répertoire encyclo-
pedique du pianiste; analyse raisonnée d'oeuvres choisis pour le
piano, du XVIe siècle, avec renseignements pratiques; degré du
difficulté, nombre de pages, éditeur et prix .... Paris,
Hachette et Cie. (1900-07) 2 v.

600. PROTESTANT EPISCOPAL CHURCH IN THE U.S.A.
JOINT COMMISSION ON CHURCH MUSIC. Service music and
anthems for the nonprofessional choir. Greenwich, Conn.,
Seabury Press, 1955. 56 p.

Service music classified by liturgical use; anthems, by the
church year. Information includes degree of difficulty, number
of parts, presence of solos, type of accompaniment, publisher,
and series number.

601. RICHTER, JOHANNES F. Kammermusik-Katalog.
Verzeichnis der von 1944 bis 1958 veröffentlichten Werke für
Kammermusik und für Klavier vier- und sechshändig sowie für
zwei und mehr Klaviere. Leipzig, Hofmeister, 1960. 318 p.

Successor to Wilhelm Altmann's work of the same title (no.
567). Covers chamber music from 1945 through 1958. A
classified bibliography, including chamber works with voice,
piano 4-hands, etc. Alphabetical index of composers and titles
of collections. List of publishers.

602. ROWLEY, ALEC. Four hands — one piano. A list of
works for duet players. London/New York, Oxford Univ. Press,
1940. 38 p.

Classified list, with composer index, of original works for
the medium, 1750 to date. Alphabetical arrangement within each
class (the classics, the French school, etc.). Entries give
composer's name and dates; title, usually in the original
language; opus number; publisher.

603. RUTHARDT, ADOLF. Wegweiser durch die Klavier-
Literatur. 10. Aufl. Leipzig und Zürich, Hug & Co., 1925.
398 p.

First published in 1888.

Selective list of keyboard music, including works for 4 or
more hands, from the Renaissance to the early 20th century,
classified according to genre and degree of difficulty. Brief
descriptions of lesser-known works. Bibliography of writings

on keyboard music, p. 354-76. Index.

604. SATORIUS, RICHARD H. Bibliography of concertos for organ and orchestra. Evanston, Ill., Instrumentalist Co. ⊏1961⊐ 68 p.

Includes primary sources as well as modern publications. Extensive annotations, biographical and descriptive of the music. Locations of original materials given. The list includes much material not exclusively for organ, i.e. concertos for "harpsichord or organ."

605. SALTONSTALL, CECILIA D. and H. C. SMITH. Catalogue of music for small orchestra. Washington, D.C., Music Library Association, 1947. 267 p.

Selective list of works for orchestras with basic strings plus from 2 to 8 winds. Arranged by composer. Entries give movements, scoring, timing, and publisher. Many American compositions included. Indexed by title, and by number of wind instruments employed.

606. SCHÜNEMANN, GEORG. Führer durch die deutsche Chorliteratur. Wolfenbüttel, Verlag für Musikalische Kultur & Wissenschaft, 1935-36. 2 v.

Vol. 1: Männerchor. Vol. 2: Gemischter Chor.

Classified according to type of composition. Entries give composer, title, publisher, grade of difficulty, number of parts, duration. Indexed by first line of text, title, composer and arranger, author of text. Includes both secular and sacred works.

607. STELLHORN, MARTIN H. Index to hymn preludes ... and other organ compositions, based on hymns, chorales, and carols. A listing of 2,200 selections of various publishers according to key, difficulty, and length. St. Louis, Concordia Pub. House, 1948. 151 p.

608. SWAN, ALFRED J. The music director's guide to

musical literature (for voices and instruments). New York, Prentice-Hall, 1941. 164 p.

P. 117-64: A selected list of works from the early Middle Ages through the 20th century. Arranged chronologically, with subdivisions by genre and country. Occasional annotations. The earlier part of the book contains brief comments on the composers represented in the bibliography.

609. TEICHMÜLLER, ROBERT und KURT HERRMANN. Internationale moderne Klaviermusik, ein Wegweiser und Berater. Leipzig und Zürich, Hug & Co., 1927. 199 p.

Supplement, 1934.

Critical and selective bibliography of piano compositions from about 1890 to date of publication, arranged alphabetically by composer, with an index by country. Gives date of composition, opus number, title, publisher, price, grade, and critical comment.

610. TOTTMANN, ALBERT K. Führer durch die Violin-literatur ... 4. wesentlich vervollständigte, bus auf die Gegenwart seit 1901 forgeführte und neu bearbeitete Auflage von Wilhelm Altmann. Leipzig, J. Schuberth, 1935. 472 p.

Title varies, first published as Führer durch den Violin-Unterricht, 1873; 2nd ed., 1886; 3rd ed., 1902.

Classified bibliography, including etudes, solo or accompanied violin works, duos, trios, quartets, etc. for violins. Gives full bibliographical information and brief critical annotations. Supplements Altmann's Kammermusik-Katalog (no. 567) for solo works.

611. TUTHILL, BURNET C. "The concertos for clarinet," in Journal of Research in Music Education, 10 (1962) p. 47-58

Brief introduction to the history of clarinet concerto literature, followed by an annotated listing, alphabetical by composer, of clarinet concertos from the 18th century to the present.

612. VALENTIN, ERICH. Handbuch der Chormusik. Hrsg.

im Auftrag der Arbeitsgemeinschaft Deutscher Chorverbände.
Regensburg, Bosse ⌐1953-58⌐ 2 v.

These volumes serve as general source books of information
useful to choral directors. Special sections include a discography
of choral music, listings of the contents of Denkmäler, writings
on choral conducting. Major sections devoted to classified bibliographies of choral music, with full performance details. Each
volume has a composer index.

613. WEIGL, BRUNO. Handbuch der Orgelliteratur....
Leipzig, F. E. C. Leuckart, 1931. 318 p.

Classified listing of compositions for organ solo, or organ
with orchestra, other instruments, or voices. Original works
and transcriptions listed separately. International coverage.

614. WEIGL, BRUNO. Handbuch der Violoncell-Literatur;
systematisch geordnetes Verzeichnis der solo- und instruktiven
Werke ... 3. ... Auflage. Wien, Universal, 1929. 357 p.

Classified listing of compositions for cello and orchestra,
cello and piano, cello solo or accompanied by other instruments.
Comparable in arrangement and content to his Handbuch der
Orgelliteratur (above).

615. WINTERFELD, LINDE H. VON & HARALD KUNZ.
Handbuch der Blockflöten-Literatur. Berlin/Wiesbaden, Bote &
Bock, 1959. 139 p.

Listings of music for recorder, solo, ensemble, and in
combination with other instruments. Publisher and price given.
Composer and title index, and a short list of books on the
recorder.

EARLY MUSIC IN MODERN EDITIONS (Including Collected
Editions and Monuments)

The purpose of the bibliographies listed in this category is to
direct the user to new editions of old music, one of the most
pressing needs of the performer, the teacher, and the music

historian. Some of the items listed below are focused on the contents of the major critical editions (Denkmäler, Gesamtausgaben); others emphasize the more practical, performing editions of early music. In either case such listings are soon out of date. To keep abreast of new publications in this area, one should consult the music review sections of current periodicals (Notes, Music and Letters, Die Musikforschung, JAMS, etc.) as well as such regular listings as may be found in Fontes artis musicae (see no. 621).

See also the entries in this volume under "Guides to Systematic and Historical Musicology." Many of the works listed there have bibliographical supplements which cite and evaluate historical editions and monuments.

616. APEL, WILLI. "Editions, historical." In his Harvard Dictionary of Music. Cambridge, Mass., Harvard Univ. Press, 1944. p. 226-34, 826

A list of 31 important serial publications of early music, from plainsong through the 18th century. Contents of such large collections as the German and Austrian Denkmäler arranged alphabetically by composer.

617. BUKOFZER, MANFRED F. "A checklist of instrumental ensemble music before Haydn." In Music Teachers' National Association Proceedings, 1946. p. 470-79

Includes only practical editions available through American publishers at the time of compilation.

618. BUKOFZER, MANFRED F. "List of editions ⌐of Baroque music ⌐." In his Music in the Baroque Era. New York, Norton, 1947. p. 461-69

A selective list grouped under 4 main categories: 1. general anthologies; 2. historical collections; 3. smaller collections and performing editions; and 4. complete or collected editions of individual composers. Minimum bibliographical information.

619. "DENKMÄLER DER TONKUNST" ⌐by Wolfgang

Schmieder₃. In <u>MGG</u>, v. 4, col. 164-92

Lists 213 major editions, practical and scholarly, with contents given in considerable detail. Classified in terms of national or international coverage.

620. "DENKMÄLER UND GESAMTAUSGABEN." In <u>Repertorium der Musikwissenschaft</u> ... bearb. von Willi Kahl und Wilhelm-Martin Luther. Kassel & Basel, Bärenreiter, 1953. p. 232-43

140 entries for major historical sets. Full bibliographical information, but no listing of contents.

621. "ÉDITIONS ET RÉÉDITIONS DE MUSIQUE ANCIENNE (avant 1800)." In <u>Fontes artis musicae</u>, no. 1-   Paris, Assoc. Internationale des Bibliothèques Musicales, 1954-

One of the few current listings of new editions of early music. International coverage. Full bibliographical information, including price.

622. "EDITIONS, HISTORICAL." In <u>Reference Works in Music and Music Literature in Five Libraries of Los Angeles County</u>. Ed. by Helen W. Azhderian. Los Angeles, University of Southern California, 1953. p. 116-37

360 editions listed, both critical and practical. No detailed content analysis, but good coverage of important sets.

623. EITNER, ROBERT. Verzeichnis neuer Ausgaben alter Musikwerke aus der frühesten Zeit bis zum Jahre 1800. Berlin, Trautwein, 1871. 208 p. (Beilage zu den <u>Monatshefte für Musikgeschichte</u>)

<u>Nachträge,</u> published in <u>Monatshefte</u>, 9 (1877); "Register zu den Nachträgen" as its Beilage, 1877; and 10 (1878).

Still useful as a guide to the contents of early historical collections, including music in histories. Abtheilung I: annotated list of collections and literary works containing music;

Abtheilung II: index of composers and their works, with separate listings of anonymous works and of German secular song through the 16th century.

624. "GESAMTAUSGABEN" ⌐By Wolfgang Schmieder⌐ In MGG, v. 4, col. 1850-76

A valuable discussion of definitions and of the historical development of critical editions of individual composers, followed by entries for 84 such editions, with detailed listings of contents.

625. HEYER, ANNA H. Historical sets, collected editions and monuments of music, a guide to their contents. Chicago, American Library Association, 1957. 485 p.

An indispensable guide to editorial work in the field of early music. Detailed listings of contents of sets, including important publishers' series (e.g. Bärenreiter's Hortus musicus, Nagel's Musik Archiv, Kistner & Siegel's Organum. Numerous cross-references. Comprehensive index of composers, editors, titles.

Review by Irene Millen in Notes, 15 (1958) p. 390-91; by Harriet Nicewonger in Library Journal, Sept. 1958, p. 2380.

626. HIRSCH, PAUL and KATHI MEYER. "Sammelwerke und Gesamtausgaben." In their Katalog der Musikbibliothek Paul Hirsch, Bd. IV. Cambridge, Eng., Cambridge Univ. Press, 1947. p. 331-409

Lists 90 complete editions and collections, with a detailed survey of their contents.

627. "NOVAE EDITIONES MUSICAE CLASSICAE." In Acta, v. 3- Leipzig and Copenhagen, International Gesellschaft für Musikwissenschaft, Jan. 1931-

A regular listing of new editions of early music, arranged alphabetically by composer, giving title, scoring, editor, place, publisher, date, and price. Discontinued after 1952.

628. SCHERING, ARNOLD. "Übersicht über die

musikgeschichtlichen Sammelwerke und kritische Gesamtausgaben der Werke der grossen Meister der Musik aus dem Verlage von Breitkopf & Härtel." In his Tabellen zur Musikgeschichte. Leipzig, Breitkopf & Härtel, 1934. Anhang, 30 p.

A useful breakdown of the contents of the critical editions published by Breitkopf & Härtel.

629. SCHIEDERMAIR, LUDWIG. "Gesamtausgaben und Publikationsreihen in Ubersichten." In his Einführung in das Studium der Musikgeschichte. Bonn, F. Bümmlers Verlag, 1947. Anhang, p. 104-61

Surveys the contents of the major sets and publishers' series.

630. VERZEICHNIS DER NEUDRUCKE ALTER MUSIK. Herausgegeben im Auftrage des Staatlichen Instituts für deutsche Musikforschung von Walter Lott. Leipzig, F. Hofmeister, 1937-43. 7 v.

An annual bibliography of new editions of music composed before 1800, covering the years 1936-42. Includes separate works and contents of collections. German publications emphasized. Works listed by composer, with medium and title index.

PRIMARY SOURCES OF EARLY MUSIC: PRINTS

Items in this section will direct users to bibliographies of original printed source materials, chiefly those prior to 1800. Lists devoted exclusively to manuscript sources will be found in the section immediately following, i.e., "Bibliographies of Music. Primary Sources of Early Music: Manuscripts."

This list is highly selective. Nearly every dissertation or research study devoted to early music contains its bibliography of primary sources. Some of these bibliographies are of considerable value, but an attempt to cite tham all would be far beyond the scope of the present guide.

It should be obvious that one of the most important approaches

to the sources of early music will be found in the section devoted
to "Catalogs of Music Libraries and Collections." Another useful
approach, not employed here, apart from one or two exceptions,
is through the catalogs of the leading antiquarian music and book
dealers, such as Leo Liepmannssohn, Otto Haas, and Maggs Bros.

See also the section "Histories and Bibliographies of Music
Printing and Publishing" for bibliographies of the output of some
of the major music publishing houses of the 16th through 18th
centuries.

631. BÄUMKER, WILHELM. Das katholische deutsche
Kirchenlied in seinen Singweisen, von den frühesten Zeiten bis
gegen Ende des 17. Jahrhunderts. Freiburg, Herder'sche
Verlagshandlung, 1883-1911. 4 v.

Reissue projected, 1963, by Georg Olms, Hildesheim.

Bäumker is the basic study of German Catholic church song.
The main body of the work consists of quotations and discussion
of the individual melodies, classified according to the church
year, or liturgical use. Each volume contains an extensive
bibliography of early printed song collections, arranged chronologically. Entries cover the period from 1470 to 1800. Transcriptions from the prefaces of early song collections.

632. BECKER, CARL FERDINAND. Die Tonwerke des XVI.
und XVII. Jahrhunderts, oder systematisch-chronologische
Zusammenstellung der in diesen zwei Jahrhunderten gedruckten
Musikalien. Zweite ... Ausgabe. Leipzig, E. Fleischer, 1855.
356 cols.

First published in 1847.

An early classified bibliography, chronologically arranged
under categories, with an index by composers and a chronological
index to the whole, attempting to list all musical compositions
published in the 16th and 17th centuries to which actual or
approximate dates could be assigned. An abridgement of
Rimbault's Bibliotheca madrigaliana (no. 656) is included as a
supplement.

632A. BOHN, EMIL. "Bibliothek des gedruckten mehr-stimmigen weltlichen deutschen Liedes vom Anfange des 16. Jahrhunderts bis ca. 1640." In the author's Fünfzig historische Concerte in Breslau, 1881-1892. Breslau, Hainauer, 1893. p. 77-188.

A bibliography of German printed secular polyphonic song. The collections are listed chronologically to 1625; the volumes containing works by a single composer are listed alphabetically by composer. Detailed bibliographical information, but contents not given. A useful guide to the primary sources of early German song prints.

633. BRESLAUER, MARTIN (Firm, Booksellers, Berlin). Das deutsche Lied, geistlich und weltlich bis zum 18. Jahrhundert. Berlin, M. Breslauer, 1908. ⸤304 p.⸥ (Documente frühen deutschen Lebens. Reihe 1)

An important dealer's catalog listing 556 items in the field of early German song. Full bibliographical entries with descriptive annotations. Numerous facsimiles of title pages. Prices given. Index of first lines of song texts, melodies, persons.

634. BRITISH MUSEUM. DEPARTMENT OF PRINTED BOOKS. Hand-list of music published in some British and foreign periodicals between 1787 and 1848, now in the British Museum. London, The Trustees of the British Museum, 1962. 80 p.

Indexes the music, chiefly songs, in 12 periodicals. 1,855 entries arranged by composer.

This item also appears as no. 832.

635. THE BRITISH UNION-CATALOGUE OF EARLY MUSIC PRINTED BEFORE THE YEAR 1801. A record of the holdings of over 100 libraries throughout the British Isles. Editor: Edith B. Schnapper. London, Butterworths Scientific Publications, 1957. 2 v.

One of the major tools for work with early printed sources, the B.U.C. provides the key to the material in British libraries.

Brief bibliographical entries, locations established in more than 100 libraries in England, Scotland, Ireland.

Review by A. Hyatt King in Music & Letters, 39 (1958) p. 77-79; by Richard S. Hill in Notes, 15 (1958) p. 565-68; by Richard Schaal in Die Musikforschung, 12 (1959) p. 367-69.

636. BRIDGMAN, NANIE. "Musique profane italienne des 16e et 17e siècles dans les bibliothèques françaises," in Fontes artis musicae, 2 (1955) p. 40-59

Full bibliographical descriptions of 32 16th- and 17-century prints of Italian secular music in French libraries.

637. BROOK, BARRY S. La symphonie française dans la seconde moitié du XVIIIe siècle. Paris, Publications de l'Institut de Musicologie de l'Université de Paris, 1962. 3 v.

Vol. 1 is a study of the French symphony of the latter half of the 18th century, with important bibliographical supplements: Annexe IV: "Index thematique arrangé par tonalites et temps" (p. 511-73); Annexe V: "Index alphabetique des incipits trans-posés en do majeur ou do mineur et indiqués par les lettres" (p. 574-84); Annexe VI: "Inventaire sommaire de la symphonie et de la symphonie concertante françaises" (p. 585-633); Annexe VII: "Reeditions et enregistrements" (p. 634-39). Bibliography (p. 643-65); General index.

Vol. 2: "Catalogue thématique et bibliographique." Full descriptions of the works, location of sources. Short biographies of each composer.

Vol. 3: Scores of 6 unedited symphonies.

The work treats some 1,200 symphonies by 150 composers.

638. CHAILLON, PAULE. "Les fonds musicaux de quelques bibliothèques de Province," in Fontes artis musicae, 2 (1955) p. 151-63

A listing of libraries in 24 French provincial centers with a description of their catalogs, if any; followed by a list of unica or rare and unusual works in their collections.

639. DAVIDSSON, ÅKE. Catalogue critique et descriptif des imprimés de musique des XVIe et XVIIe siècles conservés dans les bibliothèques suédoises (Excepté la Bibliothèque de l'Université Royale d'Upsala). Upsala [Almquist & Wiksells] 1952. 471 p.

Early music in 18 Swedish libraries, excluding the University of Uppsala, which is treated elsewhere (see no. 927). Full descriptions, with listings of contents and bibliographical references. P. 455-71: bibliography of works cited.

640. DEAKIN, ANDREW. Outlines of musical bibliography. A catalog of early music and musical works printed or otherwise produced in the British Isles; the whole chronologically arranged with descriptive and critical notes on the principal works. Birmingham, 1899. 112 p.

This work was projected on a large scale, but not completed. P. 5-18 list manuscript sources only; p. 19-96, chiefly music prints of the 16th and 17th centuries, a few manuscripts included. Entries are not precise and the locations given are indefinite. Indexed by composer and title.

641. DICHTER, HARRY and ELLIOTT SHAPIRO. Early American sheet music, its lure and its lore, 1768-1889 ... including a directory of early American music publishers .... New York, R. R. Bowker Co., 1941. 287 p.

A cross-section of important or interesting publications, classified according to subject matter. Composer, main title, publisher, and date included. The directory of publishers is an alphabetical listing of firms active from 1768 to 1889, and carries their histories to 1940. Additional list of lithographers and artists concerned with music publications before 1870. Plates of illustrated title pages. Index.

642. DICHTER, HARRY. Handbook of American sheet music ... first annual issue, 1947. Philadelphia, Harry Dichter [1947] 100 p.

<u>Second Series</u>, with Bernice Larrabee. Philadelphia, 1953.

Catalogs of early American sheet music for sale by Harry Dichter; full of useful bibliographical information. Classified under selected headings: topic, author, title. Prices given. No index. The 1947 volume lists over 2,000 items.

643. DRAUDIUS, GEORG. Verzeichnisse deutscher musikalischer Bücher, 1611 und 1625. In originalgetreuem Nachdruck herausgegeben von Konrad Ameln. Bonn, Deutschen Musikverleger-Verband ⌐1957⌐

Facsimile reprint of the music sections from the 1611 and 1625 editions of Draudius' <u>Bibliotheca librorum germanicorum classica</u>. One of the early examples of the bibliography of music. ("Musikalischer Bücher" here means "scores"). Classified according to types of composition. Primarily of historical interest.

644. EITNER, ROBERT and F. X. HABERL ⌐et al.⌐ Bibliographie der Musik-Sammelwerke des XVI. und XVII. Jahrhunderts. Berlin, L. Liepmannssohn, 1877. 964 p.

Supplemented by additions and corrections published in the <u>Monatshefte für Musikgeschichte,</u> 14 (1882) p. 152-55; 161-64.

Chronological bibliography of some 795 collections of music published between 1501 and 1700, with full bibliographical description, summary of contents, lists of composers represented, and library locations of individual copies. The second part of the bibliography, p. 297-938, is a first-line index of vocal settings arranged alphabetically under composers. One of the major bibliographical tools for historical research in music, Eitner has been superseded, in part, by the first volume of the <u>International Inventory</u> (see no. 651).

645. EITNER, ROBERT. Biographisch-bibliographisches Quellen-Lexikon der Musiker und Musikgelehrten der christlichen Zeitrechnung bis zur Mitte des 19. Jahrhunderts .... Leipzig, Breitkopf & Härtel, 1900-04. 10 v.

Reprinted in photo-offset by Musurgia, New York, 1947.

Neuauflage.... Wiesbaden, Breitkopf & Härtel, 1959-60.

Supplemented by Miscellanea musicae bio-bibliographica (no. 63) and by G. Radiciotti's "Aggiunte e correzioni ai dizionari biografici dei musicisti" (no. 68).

The Quellen-Lexikon remains the primary reference tool for locating primary sources of music before 1800. Early prints and manuscripts included, with their locations in European libraries. The work is badly out of date, much of the information, particularly regarding locations, being no longer correct. It will be superseded upon completion of the new International Inventory of Musical Sources, now in progress.

Eitner is also cited, for its biographical treatment, as no. 50.

646. FRIEDLAENDER, MAX. Das deutsche Lied im 18. Jahrhundert, Quellen und Studien .... Stuttgart und Berlin, Cotta, 1902. 2 v. in 3

Vol. 1:1, p. 1-62: A chronological listing of 798 German songbooks of the 18th century (1689-1799), followed by detailed commentary on the most important examples. Vol. 1:2: A collection of musical examples. Vol. 2: Devoted to the poets, with indexes of names, text incipits.

647. FROST, MAURICE. English and Scottish psalm and hymn tunes, c. 1543-1677. London, Oxford Univ. Press, 1953. 531 p.

P. 3-50: a bibliography of English-Scottish "Old Version" psalters from 1556 to 1677, with full descriptions and lists of contents. The main body of the work is an edition of 457 psalm tunes or harmonized versions thereof.

648. GÖHLER, ALBERT. Verzeichnis der in den Frankfurter und Leipziger Messkatalogen der Jahre 1564 bis 1759 angezeigten Musikalien.... Leipzig, C. F. Kahnt Nachf., 1902 ⌐ 4 parts in 1 v., 20, 64, 96, 34 p.⌐

A bibliography of the music listed in the Frankfurt and Leipzig trade catalogs from 1564 to 1759. 16th, 17th, and 18th century works listed separately, arranged alphabetically by composer. Works identified by type.

649. GROPPO, ANTONIO. "Catalogo di tutti i drammi per musica recitati ne' Teatri di Venezia dell'anno 1637, in cui ebbero principio le pubbliche rappresentazioni de' medesimi fin all'anno presente 1745." In Bollettino bibliografico musicale. Nuova Serie. Milano, 1952.

Published serially in 4 instalments.

Lists 811 operas performed in Venice between 1637 and 1745, in chronological order, with title, librettist, composer, theater, and date of performance. Title index given in the last instalment.

650. INTERNATIONAL ASSOCIATION OF MUSIC LIBRARIES. RADIO COMMISSION. Catalogue of rare materials, and first supplement. Editor: Folke Lindberg. Stockholm, 1959. 185 leaves

Supplement I: leaves 175-85.

651. INTERNATIONAL INVENTORY OF MUSICAL SOURCES. Recueils imprimés XVIe - XVIIe siècles. Ouvrage publié sous la direction de François Lesure. I. Liste chronologique. München-Duisburg, G. Henle Verlag, 1960-   640 p.

This volume is Part I of the systematic-chronological section of a comprehensive bibliography of musical sources to be compiled under the joint auspices of the International Musicological Society and the International Association of Music Libraries. The present volume supersedes Eitner's Bibliographie der Musik-Sammelwerke (no. 644), and, when completed, the project will replace the Quellen-Lexikon (no. 645) as the major tool for locating primary source materials in the music field. The present volume lists collections of music published between 1501 and 1700, with a summary of their contents and with locations of copies in major European and American libraries. Index of editors and printers, and of titles and authors.

Review by Vincent Duckles in Notes, 18 (1961) p. 225-27; by Jack A. Westrup in Music & Letters, 42 (1961) p. 76.

LOEWENBERG, ALFRED. Annals of opera, 1597-1940.... See no. 224.

652. MEYER, ERNST H. "Quellennachweise." In his Die mehrstimmige Spielmusik des 17. Jahrhunderts in Nord- und Mittel-Europa .... Kassel, Bärenreiter, 1934. p. 128-258 (Heidelberger Studien zur Musikwissenschaft, 2)

A bibliography of primary source materials, printed and in manuscript, of 17th-century North European chamber music. Partially thematic for the English school. Locations given.

653. NISSER, CARL M. Svensk instrumentalkomposition, 1770-1830. Nominalkatalog. Stockholm, Bokförlaget Gothia ⌐ 1943 ⌐ 467 p.

Swedish instrumental music, native composers or composers living in Sweden. Alphabetical listing by composer, with detailed bibliographical and analytical descriptions, including key, movements, time signature, measure count. Bibliographical references. Index of names and places.

654. RIAÑO, JUAN F. Critical and bibliographical notes on early Spanish music .... London, B. Quaritch, 1887. 154 p.

Manuscripts and printed music to 1600, classified, giving descriptions and library locations of manuscripts. Numerous facsimile plates.

655. RIEDEL, FRIEDRICH W. Quellenkundliche Beiträge zur Geschichte der Musik für Tasteninstrumente in der zweiten Hälfte des 17. Jahrhunderts (vornehmlich in Deutschland). Kassel und Basel, Bärenreiter, 1960. 224 p. (Schriften des Landesinstituts für Musikforschung Kiel, 10)

A "source study" concerned with late 17th-century prints and manuscripts of keyboard music, with emphasis on the German school. Numerous useful lists and inventories incorporated into

the work, e.g. "Verzeichnis der von 1648-1700 im Druck
veröffentlichen Musik für Tasteninstrumente" (p. 57-72);
"Quellenregister" ⌐Handschriften⌐ (p. 219-24).

656. RIMBAULT, EDWARD F. Bibliotheca madrigaliana.
A bibliographical account of the musical and poetical works
published in England during the 16th and 17th centuries under the
titles of madrigals, ballads, ayres, canzonets, etc. London,
1847. 88 p.

A chronological list of vocal music published in England, 1588
to 1638, giving full bibliographical descriptions and contents,
source references. First line index of madrigals and songs.
Composer index.

657. SARTORI, CLAUDIO. Bibliografia della musica
strumentale italiana stampata in Italia fino al 1700. Firenze,
Olschki, 1953. 652 p. (Biblioteca di bibliografia italiana, 23)

Chronological list of instrumental music, collections of vocal
music containing one or more instrumental pieces, or vocal music
with one or more instrumental parts, published in Italy to 1700.
Includes a few works by Italian composers published outside Italy.
Excludes lute music and dramatic music. Complete bibliographical data, including dedications, prefaces, tables of contents.
Composer index.

Review by Dragan Plamenac in Notes, 10 (1953) p. 616-19;
by Harvey Olnick in MQ, 40 (1954) p. 98-102; by Willi Apel in
JAMS, 7 (1954) p. 84-86; by Richard Schaal in Die
Musikforschung, 7 (1954) p. 342.

658. SARTORI, CLAUDIO. "Finalmente svelati i misteri
delle biblioteche italiane," in Fontes artis musicae, 2 (1955)
p. 15-37; 3 (1956) p. 192-202

A product of the International Inventory in Italy, this article
contains a summary report of the holdings of 40 Italian libraries,
and an alphabetical listing of early printed music newly discovered
in these collections.

659. SCHEURLEER, DANIEL F. Nederlandsche liedboeken; lijst der in Nederland tot het jaar 1800 uitgegeven liedboeken .... 's-Gravenhage, M. Nijhoff, 1912. 321 p.

Erste supplement. 1923.

A bibliography of song books published in the Netherlands from 1487 to 1800, with or without music, arranged chronologically under main headings of sacred and secular music, with index by author, editor, publisher, main word of title. 3,887 titles in main work, 660 in supplement.

660. SCHANZLIN, HANS PETER. "Musik-Sammeldrucke des 16. und 17. Jahrhunderts in schweizerischen Bibliotheken." In Fontes artis musicae, 4 (1957) p. 38-42

661. SCHANZLIN, HANS PETER. "Musik-Sammeldrucke des 18. Jahrhunderts in schweizerischen Bibliotheken (I)." In Fontes artis musicae, 5 (1959) p. 20-26; II. ibid., 7 (1960) p. 26-29

Preliminary reports prepared by the Swiss office of the International Inventory of Musical Sources.

662. SCHREIBER, MAX. Kirchenmusik von 1500-1600, Originaldrucke und Manuskripte chronologisch zusammengestellt .... ⌐Regensburg⌐ Druckerei St. Georgsheim Birkeneck, 1932. 88 p.

Chronological list of 16th-century sacred music, printed and manuscript sources. Entered alphabetically by composer under year of issue. Brief titles, and locations in British and continental libraries. Index of composers, and classified index of forms.

663. SCHREIBER, MAX. Kirchenmusik von 1600-1700, Originaldrucke und Manuskripte chronologisch zusammengestellt .... ⌐Regensburg⌐ Druckerei St. Georgsheim Birkeneck, 1934.

Treats 17th-century sacred music as in the entry above.

664. SONNECK, OSCAR G. T. A bibliography of early secular American music (18th century) ... rev. and enl. by W. T. Upton. Washington, D. C., Library of Congress, Music Division, 1945. 617 p.

Title list, with full bibliographical descriptions, including first lines of texts, completely indexed, with lists of composers, first lines, publishers, etc. First published in 1905.

665. THIBAULT, GENEVIÈVE et LOUIS PERCEAU. Bibliographie des poésies de P. de Ronsard mises en musique au XVIe siècle. Paris, Droz, 1941. 121 p. (Publications de la Société Française de Musicologie, 2 sér., t. 8)

Chronological bibliography, 1552-1629, of some 148 collections containing settings of lyrics by Ronsard. Full bibliographical citations of the collections, with Ronsard settings listed for each. Index of text incipits, of collections and names.

666. VOGEL, EMIL. Bibliothek der gedruckten weltlichen Vocalmusik Italiens. Aus den Jahren 1500-1700 .... Berlin, A. Haack, 1892. 2 v.

Partially revised and enlarged by Alfred Einstein, under running title "Italian Secular Vocal Music," in Notes 2 (1945) - 5 (1948). 232 p. in all. Einstein's revision treats only the second part of Vogel's original work, namely, the collections containing works by two or more composers.

Unaltered reissue. Hildesheim, Olms, 1962. 2 v. This issue incorporates Einstein's revision as published in Notes.

Vogel's Bibliothek is the basic source of information concerning early printed secular vocal music in Italy. In two parts, the first of which gives publications of the work of individual composers, arranged alphabetically by composer; the second gives collections, listed chronologically from 1501 to 1697. Full bibliographical citations, lists of contents, locations in European libraries. Index of collections, or places and publishers, of authors of texts and persons to whom the works are dedicated.

A complete revision of Vogel is badly needed. Einstein's revision concerned only the collections. Such a revision is being undertaken by Claudio Sartori and François Lesure, and is scheduled for publication in the series <u>Bibliotheca musicae</u>, Milan ⌐1964?⌐

667. WACKERNAGEL, PHILIPP. Bibliographie zur Geschichte des deutschen Kirchenliedes im XVI. Jahrhundert. Hildesheim, Olms, 1961. 718 p.

Unaltered reprint of the edition, Frankfurt am Main, 1855.

A chronological listing of 1,050 editions of German sacred song published during the 16th century. Detailed bibliographical descriptions, with annotations. Transcriptions given of the introductions to 110 of the collections.

668. WIEL, TADDEO. I teatri musicali veneziani del settecento. Catalogo delle opere in musica rappresentate nel secolo XVIII in Venezia (1701-1800). Venezia, Fratelli Visentini, 1897. 600 p.

Chronological listing of operas performed in the Venetian theater during the 18th century. 1,274 items. Entries give librettist, composer, place of performance, cast if known, ballet if included. Indexes of titles, librettists, composers, singers, dancers, etc. Introductory essay of 80 p. on the Venetian musical theater.

669. WOTQUENNE, ALFRED. Table alphabétique des morceaux mesurés contenus dans les oeuvres dramatiques de Zeno, Metastasio et Goldoni. Leipzig, Breitkopf & Härtel, 1905. 77 p.

An alphabetical first-line index of aria and ensemble texts by Zeno, Metastasio, and Goldoni, citing volume and page numbers in the standard editions of the works of these librettists, and title of the work from which the incipit is derived. Table of librettos by the three authors.

670. ZAHN, JOHANNES. Die Melodien der deutschen

evangelischen Kirchenlieder, aus den Quellen geschöpft und mitgeteilt.... Gütersloh, Bertelsmann, 1889-93. 6 v.

Reprint of the original edition by Olms, Hildesheim, 1963. Zahn is primarily an edition, giving 8,806 melodies, derived from the earliest sources, for the German Protestant liturgy. Classified according to metrical form.

Vol. 5, p. 399-494: biographical notices of 463 chorale composers or editors of chorale collections. Index of composers; first-line index of texts.

Vol. 6: a bibliography of 1,408 items, listing the sources of the melodies, arranged chronologically from 1507 to 1892, with locations in the principal European libraries. Further supplements give non-German sources, and manuscript sources.

PRIMARY SOURCES OF EARLY MUSIC: MANUSCRIPTS

Included here are reference works of three types: (1) lists or inventories of early source materials for the study of medieval or Renaissance music; (2) compilations of musicians' autographs; (3) union lists or bibliographies of manuscripts compiled on a national or regional scale.

Coverage in the first of these areas will be greatly improved with the publication of the volumes of the International Inventory designed to list early sources in manuscript. Until these volumes appear, the best approaches remain through Eitner's Quellen-Lexikon, through the catalogs of libraries with important manuscript holdings, through the source lists appended to monographs and editions in the fields of medieval and Renaissance music. The reader should be reminded of the valuable listings of manuscript sources in MGG under such articles as "Ars antiqua," "Ars nova," "Chanson."

In the preceding section are a few works which list both manuscripts and points.

671. ALBRECHT, OTTO E. A census of autograph music

manuscripts of European composers in American libraries. Philadelphia, Univ. of Pennsylvania Press, 1953. 331 p.

Lists 2,017 manuscripts now in America by 571 European composers, giving title, pagination, dimensions, and descriptive notes. Current and former owners indicated. Arrangement is alphabetical by composer. Index of owners.

Review by Jack A. Westrup in Music Review, 16 (1955) p. 84-85.

672. APEL, WILLI. "Sources, musical, prior to 1450." In his Harvard Dictionary of Music. Cambridge, Mass., Harvard Univ. Press, 1944. p. 702-03

A listing of some of the major sources of Gregorian chant, secular monophonic and polyphonic music to 1450. Locations of the sources given; references to modern editions, if any.

673. BESSELER, HEINRICH. "Studien zur Musik des Mittelalters: 1. Neue Quellen des 14. und beginnenden 15. Jahrhunderts. 2. Die Motette von Franko von Köln bis Philipp von Vitry." In Archiv für Musikwissenschaft, 7 (1925) p. 167-252, and 9 (1927) p. 137-258

Two articles which are basic source studies for the music of the late medieval period, containing numerous inventories and descriptions of ars nova manuscripts. They supplement the work of Ludwig covering the ars antiqua sources (see no. 683).

674. BIBLIOTHECA MUSICO-LITURGICA. A descriptive handlist of the musical and Latin-liturgical mss. of the Middle Ages preserved in the libraries of Great Britain and Ireland. Drawn up by W. H. Frere ... and printed for the members of the Plainsong and Mediaeval Music Society.... London, B. Quaritch, 1901-32. 2 v.

Vol. 1 (nos. 1-545): manuscripts at Lambeth and Oxford; Vol. 2 (nos. 546-1031): manuscripts in cathedral chapter libraries and at Manchester, Dublin, Cambridge, etc. Full descriptions of the manuscripts. 17 plates. Indexes of service

books, places, persons, and of Bodleian and Cambridge
University Library manuscripts.

675. BORREN, CHARLES VAN DEN. "Inventaire des manuscrits de musique polyphonique qui se trouvent en Belgique." In
Acta 5 (1933) p. 66-71, 120-27, 177-84; 6 (1934) p. 23-29,
65-73, 116-21

Detailed description, with listings of contents, of the manuscripts of polyphonic music in the libraries in Brussels, Ghent,
Liège, Louvain, Malines, and Tournai.

676. CHEVALIER, ULYSSE. Repertorium hymnologicum.
Catalogue des chants, hymnes, proses, séquences, tropes en
usage dans l'église latine depuis les origines jusqu'à nos jours.
Louvain, 1892-1921. 6 v.

The standard bibliography of Latin rhymed poetic texts for
liturgical use. A volume of additions and emendations was prepared by Clemens Blume under the title Repertorium repertorii,
Leipzig, 1901.

677. FISCHER, KURT VON. Studien zur italienischen Musik
des Trecento und frühen Quattrocento. Bern, P. Haupt ⌐ c. 1956⌐
132 p. (Publikationen der Schweizerischen Musikforschenden
Gesellschaft, ser. 2, v. 5)

A catalog of Italian secular music of the 14th and early 15th
centuries. Text incipits, arranged alphabetically, for 177
madrigals, 25 cacce, and 423 ballate, with information as to
sources and modern editions.

Review by Hans Tischler in Notes, 15 (1958) p. 405-06.

678. GEERING, ARNOLD. Die Organa und mehrstimmigen
Conductus in den Handschriften des deutschen Sprachgebietes vom
13. bis 16. Jahrhundert. Bern, P. Haupt ⌐1952⌐ 99 p.
(Publikationen der Schweizerischen Musikforschenden Gesellschaft,
ser. 2:1)

A study concerned with the sources of early polyphony in

German-speaking countries, with a listing of the relevant manuscripts and an inventory of the organum and conductus settings
they contain.

679. GENNRICH, FRIEDRICH. Bibliographie der ältesten
französischen und lateinischen Motetten. Darmstadt, Selbstverlag, 1957. 124 p. (Summa musicae medii aevi, 2)

A bibliography of the 13th-century motet, serving also as a
guide to manuscript sources and a record of scholarly work done
in this field. Gennrich expands the work begun by Friedrich
Ludwig in his Repertorium (see no. 684). Motets are grouped
under their respective tenors, with references to all known concordances and modern editions. Supplementary bibliographies of
literature, manuscript sources, indexes of Latin and French
tenors, and of incipits to motettus and triplum parts.

Review by Hans Tischler in Notes, 16 (1959) p. 561-62.

680. GENNRICH, FRIEDRICH. Der musikalische Nachlass
der Troubadours. Kommentar. Darmstadt, 1960. 176 p.
(Summa musicae medii aevi, 4)

A complete bibliography of the surviving musical settings of
troubadour songs, 302 in all, with detailed information as to
source, editions of text and music, verse form, use of the melody
as a contrafactum. Songs numbered consecutively but grouped
under composer, with full bibliographical references to work
done on the individual troubadours. 25 manuscript sources
described and discussed.

Vol. 3 of the series Summa musicae medii aevi (1958) is the
musical edition of the surviving troubadour melodies.

681. GRÖNINGER, EDUARD. Repertoire-Untersuchungen
zum mehrstimmigen Notre Dame-Conductus. Regensburg, Bosse,
1939. 163 p. (Kölner Beiträge zur Musikforschung, 2)

An introductory essay of 59 p., followed by tabulations of the
polyphonic conductus compositions found in the four major Notre

Dame sources: Wolfenbüttel 1 & 2, Florence and Madrid manuscripts. Concordances given.

682. LINKER, W. Music of the Minnesinger and early Meistersinger, a bibliography. Chapel Hill, University of North Carolina Press [1961] 79 p.

A bibliography of German medieval song arranged alphabetically under composers' names. A preliminary list gives 40 manuscript sources, and 41 modern publications of literary history, music, and text editions.

683. LUDWIG, FRIEDRICH. "Die Quellen der Motetten ältesten Stils." In Archiv für Musikwissenschaft, 5 (1923) p. 185-222, 273-315

A basic source study of medieval polyphony, in which the author describes and gives complete or partial contents for some 50 manuscripts containing motets of the ars antiqua period.

This study is reprinted as a supplement to Gennrich's reissue of Ludwig's Repertorium, Abteilung 2 (see next item).

684. LUDWIG, FRIEDRICH. Repertorium organorum recentioris et motetorum vetustissimi stili. Band 1: Catalogue raisonné der Quellen. Abteilung 1: Handschriften in Quadrat-Notation. Halle, Niemeyer, 1910. 344 p.

Ludwig's Repertorium, although incomplete, is the starting point for all studies in the music of the ars antiqua period. It is essentially an inventory, with concordances, of the contents of the major manuscripts of the Notre Dame repertory.

Band 1, Abteilung 2: Handschriften in Mensuralnotation. Besorgt von Friedrich Gennrich. Langen bei Frankfurt, 1961. (Summa musicae medii aevi, 7)

This portion of Ludwig's Repertorium appeared in proof copy but was never published. It consists chiefly of inventories of two major sources of the 13th-century motet, the Montpellier Codex and the Clayette MS. Included as a supplement to this volume is a reprint of Ludwig's study of "Die Quellen der Motetten ältesten Stils, " which appeared first in the Archiv für Musikwissenschaft, 5 (1925). See no. 683 above.

Band 2: Musikalisches Anfangs-Verzeichnis des nach Tenores geordneten Repertorium. Besorgt von Friedrich Gennrich. Langen bei Frankfurt, 1962. 71 p. (Summa musicae medii aevi, 8)

A thematic catalog of 515 motets based on 50 tenors taken from the liturgy of the Mass. Reprinted, incomplete, from the author's unpublished proof copy.

A further reissue of the Repertorium, edited and with an introduction by Luther A. Dittmer, has been announced for publication (1963 ?) by the Institute of Mediaeval Music, New York. To be published jointly with Olms, Hildesheim.

685. MUSIKER HANDSCHRIFTEN ... ⌐Band I⌐ von Palestrina bis Beethoven; ⌐Band II⌐ von Schubert bis Strawinsky. Zürich, Atlantis Verlag ⌐1960-61⌐ 2 v.

Two handsome volumes made up chiefly of facsimile plates of autograph manuscripts by famous musicians, with brief descriptive commentary and identification of the sources. 159 plates in Vol. 1, 140 plates in Vol. 2. Editor, Walter Gerstenberg.

686. PILLET, ALFRED. Bibliographie der Troubadours. Erg. , weitergeführt und herausgegeben von Dr. Henry Carstens. Halle, Niemeyer ⌐1933⌐ 518 p. (Schriften der Königsberger Gelehrten Gesellschaft. Sonderreihe, 3)

Based on a bibliography of troubadour songs compiled by Karl Bartsch in 1872. Songs arranged alphabetically by first word of text, with inclusive numeration and subseries of numbers for works by individual authors. Emphasis directed toward literary scholarship.

687. RADO, POLYCARPE. Répertoire hymnologique des manuscrits liturgiques dans les bibliothèques publiques de Hongrie. Budapest, Stephaneum Nyomda, 1945. 59 p. (Az

orsza´gos sze´chenyi könyvta´r kiadva´nyai, 20)

Alphabetical listing of 727 hymns found in 146 liturgical manuscripts in libraries in Hungary.

688. RAU, ALBERT G. and HANS DAVID. A catalogue of music by American Moravians, 1724-1842, from the Archives of the Moravian Church at Bethlehem, Pa. Bethlehem, Pennsylvania, The Moravian Seminary and College for Women, 1938. 118 p.

Short biographies and lists of compositions by 17 American-Moravian composers. Appendix of 24 plates of selected compositions and interesting pages from the original manuscripts.

689. RAYNAUD, GASTON. Bibliographie des altfranzö-sischen Liedes. Neu bearbeitet und ergänzt von Hans Spanke. Erster Teil. Leiden, E. J. Brill, 1955. 286 p.

The first part of a projected revision of Raynaud's Biblio-graphie des chansonniers français des XIIIe et XIVe siècles. Paris, 1884. 2 v. This work serves as a guide to trouvère songs, similar to that offered by nos. 680 and 686 for the troubadour. Lists more than 2,130 songs, arranged according to the rhyme word of the first stanza, with references to the manuscript source and to literary and musical studies concerned with the item. P. 1-32 give a bibliography of the manuscript sources, and of modern editions and studies related to the work of the individual authors.

690. SCHÜNEMANN, GEORG. Musiker-Handschriften von Bach bis Schumann. Berlin, Atlantis Verlag ⌐1936⌐ 106 p. 80 plates

Facsimiles of 96 autographs in the Berlin State Library, with extensive commentaries by the author.

691. STEVENSON, ROBERT. "Sixteenth and seventeenth century resources in Mexico." In Fontes artis musicae, 1 (1954) p. 69-78; 2 (1955) p. 10-15

The first instalment is concerned with the manuscript resources of the Puebla Cathedral music archive comprising some 365 sacred works by 36 composers. Arranged alphabetically by composer. The second part is a description of a 16th-century manuscript of sacred music in the library of Canon Octaviano Valdés of Mexico City.

692. WALTHER, HANS. Initia carminum ac versuum medii aevi posterioris latinorum. Alphabetisches Verzeichnis der Versanfänge mittellateinischer Dichtungen .... Göttingen, Vanderhoeck & Ruprecht, 1959. 1,186 p. (Carmina medii aevi posterioris latina, 1)

Not a music bibliography, but a most valuable reference tool for musicologists working in the field of medieval studies. Alphabetical index of text incipits for more than 20,000 medieval Latin lyrics, with references to manuscript sources and modern editions. Bibliography of literature; index of names and subjects.

693. WINTERNITZ, EMANUEL. Musical autographs from Monteverdi to Hindemith. Princeton, N. J., Princeton University Press, 1955. 2 v.

Vol. 1 is devoted to commentary on the plates, with two introductory chapters: "The Written Sign" and "The Writing Act." Vol. 2 contains 195 full-page plates of autographs.

694. WOLF, JOHANNES. Handbuch der Notationskunde. I. Teil: Tonschriften des Altertums und des Mittelalters ... II. Teil: Tonschriften der Neuzeit, Tabulaturen, Partitur, Generalbass und Reformversuche. Leipzig, Breitkopf & Härtel, 1913-19. 2 v. (Kleine Handbucher der Musikgeschichte)

The Wolf Handbuch is cited here because of its useful listings of early manuscript sources in connection with the author's discussion of notational practices. For example: "Quellen der ars antiqua" (Vol. 1, p. 258-63); "Die ars nova" (Vol. 1, p. 351-54); "Handschriftliche Quellen des 15. und 16. Jahrhunderts" (Vol. 1, p. 444-65); "Verzeichnis einiger wichtiger deutscher Lautentabulaturen" (Vol. 2, p. 47-50); "Italienische

Lautentabulaturen" (Vol. 2, p. 66-71); "Quellen französischer Lautentablatur" (Vol. 2, p. 95-106); "Guitarretabulaturen" (Vol. 2, p. 209-18).

FOLK SONG AND BALLADS

This section should be used in conjunction with the section "Bibliographies of Music Literature. Special and Subject: Ethnomusicology." There will be found listings of studies and monographs pertaining to folk song and ballad, while here the emphasis is on the music itself. The user should bear in mind, however, that a work such as Haywood's Bibliography of North American Folklore and Folksong (no. 442) contains numerous entries for music, both printed and on sound recordings. Also relevant in certain respects are such bibliographies as Fuld's American Popular Music (no. 432), Sears' Song Index (no. 545), and the Sonneck and Upton Bibliography of Early Secular American Music (no. 664), which serve to bridge that uncertain area between folk and popular song.

695. BRONSON, BERTRAND H. The traditional tunes of the Child ballads, with their texts, according to the extant records of Great Britain and America. v. 1- Princeton, N. J., Princeton University Press, 1959-

Vol. 1: Ballads 1-53; Vol. 2 (1962): Ballads 54-113.

A monumental work of scholarship in the field of the English-Scottish ballad, based on the work of Francis J. Child, but far exceeding it in scope and authority. The literary and musical tradition of each ballad is discussed, with a complete printing of all known variants.

696. CALIFORNIA UNIV. DEPT. OF MUSIC. Check list of California songs. Archives of California folk music ... pt. 1. Berkeley, Calif., University of California, 1940.

A list, alphabetical by title, of more than 2,500 songs from texts, either published or known to have circulated in California, with an index of first lines. P. 157-60: bibliography of songsters and broadsides.

697. DEAN-SMITH, MARGARET. Guide to English folk-song collections. Liverpool, University Press of Liverpool, in association with The English Folk Dance & Song Society, 1954. 119 p.

Foreword by Gerald Abraham.

Indexes approximately 62 collections of English folk songs, 1822-1952. Main entry by song title with cross-references from text incipit. Chronological list of collections. Detailed annotations.

Review by Bertrand H. Bronson in JAMS, 8 (1955) p. 57-58.

698. MERWE, F. Z. VAN DER. Suid-Afrikaanse musiek-bibliografie 1787-1952. Pretoria, J. L. Van Schaik, 1958. 410 p.

A comprehensive bibliography of music related to South Africa (by South African composers wherever published, writings on South African themes or subject matter). The largest part of the material consists of songs, marches, dance music of a popular nature, although a few studies and monographs are interfiled. Entries are unclassified, arranged alphabetically by composer or author. Index of South African composers and musicians. The language is Afrikaans.

699. SIDEL'NIKOV, V. M. Russkaĩa narodnaĩa pesnĩa: bibliograficheskiĭ ukazatel' 1735-1945. Moskva, Izd. Akademii Nauk SSSR, 1962.

At head of title: Akademĩa Mauk SSSR, Institut mirovoi literatury im. A. M. Gor'kogo.

Part I: texts of folk poetry and folk songs, published in journals, newspapers, etc., with or without music. Part II: books, articles, etc. about Russian folk songs. Index of names.

CATALOGS OF MUSIC LIBRARIES AND COLLECTIONS

A knowledge of the published catalogs of the major music libraries
and collections is essential for locating source materials for study
or research. There are at least two comprehensive listings of
such catalogs in recent encyclopedia articles: (1) "Musik-
bibliotheken und Sammlungen, " by Alfons Ott, in MGG, 9, col.
1034-78, and (2) "Libraries and Collections, " by Charles
Cudworth, in Grove's, 5th edition, Vol. 5, pp. 160-223. Comprehensive as these articles are, they do not supply full bibliographical information. The following list covers the catalogs of
the principal music libraries, and also includes a number of
important exhibition catalogs and union lists. A few articles
descriptive of the holdings of certain libraries have also been
cited. Excluded are the auction or sale catalogs of music collections which have been dispersed, with the exception of the
famous Wolffheim catalog (no. 952), a bibliographical tool of first
importance.

It goes without saying that a great many musical source
materials have never been listed in special music catalogs, and
must be sought in general library catalogs of early prints or
manuscripts. The music manuscripts in the Bodleian Library at
Oxford, for example, must be extracted from the seven volumes
of F. Madan's Summary Catalogue of Western Manuscripts in the
Bodleian Library ... (1895-1953). Similarly, Cambridge University music manuscripts are to be found in the series of college
library manuscript catalogs by Montague Rhodes James. No
attempt has been made to cite general catalogs of this kind, but, in
this connection, the reader's attention may be called to the invaluable guide to Latin Manuscript Books Before 1600, a List of
the Printed Catalogues and Unpublished Inventories of Extant
Collections by Paul Kristeller (rev. ed. , Fordham Univ. Press,
1960).

In the following list the catalogs have been grouped, as far as
is possible, by place. Place is ordinarily designated as a city

followed by the appropriate country. Places within the United
States are entered under the name of the city, followed by the
state. Certain national union catalogs appear under the country
alone (cf. Germany, Great Britain, Sweden, etc.) There remain
a few catalogs of important private collections which have been
dispersed, or which have changed their locations in recent years
(cf. Hirsch, Koch, Wolffheim, etc.). These will be found in
their alphabetical positions under the collectors' names.

Aarhus, Denmark

700. STATSBIBLIOTEKET. Fagkataloger ⌐redigeret af
Erling Winkel og Ingeborg Heilmann⌐ 2. for∅gede udg. Aarhus,
Aarhuus Stiftsbogtrykkerie, 1946-57. 4 v.

⌐Afdeling⌐ 3. Musikalier: 1. Udenlandsk musik. Del 1.
Samlingsvaerker og musik for eet instrument, 1951. Del 2.
Kammermusik og orkestermusik, 1955. Del 3. Vokalmusik,
dramatisk musik, folkemusik, 1957.

⌐Afdeling⌐ 4. Musik: Musikfilisofi, musikteori, musikhistorie, biografi, 1946.

Three volumes cover scores, one, music literature. Entries
for scores include collections and separate publications, with
contents given for collections.

ALDRICH, RICHARD. A catalogue of books relating to
music .... See no. 740.

Amsterdam, Holland

701. VERENIGING VOOR NEDERLANDSE MUZIEK-
GESCHIEDENIS. BIBLIOTHEEK. Catalogus van de bibliotheek
der Vereniging voor Nederlandse Muziekgeschiedenis. Amsterdam,
G. Alsbach, 1919. 274 p.

Classified catalog, including both early and recent works.
Contains a special section on manuscripts. Index of names and
titles.

Assisi, Italy

702. LA CAPPELLA DELLA BASILICA DI S. FRANCESCO.
BIBLIOTECA. I. Catalogo del fondo musicale nella Biblioteca
Comunale di Assisi, a cura di Claudio Sartori. Milano, Istituto
Editoriale Italiano, 1962. 449 p. (Bibliotheca musicae, 1)

Expands and enlarges the work of Francesco Pennacchi
published in the series Associazione dei musicologi italiani (see
no. 802 below). Lists early printed music, books, and manuscripts separately. Most of the material is pre-1800, but some
19th-century manuscripts are included. Entries give contents of
early items; locations for rarities. Descriptive annotations.

Augsburg, Germany

703. SCHLETTERER, HANS M. Katalog der in der Kreis-
und Stadtbibliothek dem Städtischen Archive und der Bibliothek des
Historischen Vereins zu Augsburg befindlichen Musikwerke.
Augsburg, Fidelis Butsch Sohn, 1879. 138 p. (Monatshefte für
Musikgeschichte. Beilage, Jahrgang 10 und 11, 1878-79)

Barcelona, Spain

704. DIPUTACIÓN PROVINCIAL. BIBLIOTECA CENTRAL.
Catàlech de la Biblioteca Musical ... per en Filipe Pedrell.
Barcelona, Palau de la Diputació, 1908-09. 2 v.

Classified catalog of 1,271 entries, including theory, history,
practical music. Full bibliographical entries, collations, extensive notes, facsimiles, and musical quotations. Items listed by
signature number, with alphabetical index in Vol. 2.

705. DIPUTACIÓN PROVINCIAL. BIBLIOTECA CENTRAL.
La música española desde la edad media hasta nuestros días;
catálogo de la exposición histórica ... por Higinio Anglés.
ⵉBarcelonaⵉ Diputación provincial de Barcelona, Biblioteca
Central, 1941. 82 p.

Exposition catalog commemorating the centennial of the birth
of Filipe Pedrell. 171 items, manuscripts and prints, associated
with the history of Spanish music, assembled from a variety of

collections. Chronological arrangement, full entries, 52 facsimiles.

Basel, Switzerland

706. UNIVERSITÄT. BIBLIOTHEK. Catalog der Schweizerischen Musikbibliothek. Herausgegeben von der Öffentlichen Bibliothek der Universität Basel. I. Musikgeschichtliche und theoretische Werke. Basel, Buchdr. E. Birkhäuser, 1906. 39 p.

A collection of writings on music. The catalog of musical compositions, which was to form Vol. 2, was issued as Vol. 1 of the Library's Katalog der Musikabteilung der Öffentlichen Bibliothek ... (see next item).

707. UNIVERSITÄT. BIBLIOTHEK. Katalog der Musikabteilung der Öffentlichen Bibliothek der Universität Basel und in ihr enthaltenen Schweizerischen Musikbibliothek. Band 1: Musikalische Kompositionen ⌐ hrsg. Edgar Refardt⌐ Basel, Universitätsbibliothek, 1925, 141 p.

Works listed in alphabetical order by composer, important collections analyzed. Separate listing of collections, followed by a summary of the contents of a number of manuscript collections of music by Swiss composers bequeathed to the library. Index of editors, arrangers, librettists.

708. UNIVERSITÄT. BIBLIOTHEK. Katalog der Musik-Sammlung auf der Universitäts-Bibliothek in Basel (Schweiz) ... von Julius Richter. Leipzig, Breitkopf & Härtel, 1892. 104 p. (Monatshefte für Musikgeschichte. Beilage, Jahrgang 23 und 24)

Full descriptions, contents, musical quotations, for manuscripts and early printed music.

709. UNIVERSITÄT. BIBLIOTHEK. Thematischer Katalog der Instrumentalmusik des 18. Jahrhunderts in den Handschriften der Universitätsbibliothek Basel. Von Edgar Refardt. Bern, P. Haupt, 1957. 56 p. (Publikationen der Schweizerischen Musikforschenden Gesellschaft, ser. 2, v. 6)

The major part of the collection was assembled by the Basel silk manufacturer Lucas Sarasin (1730-1802). Some 473 of the works were once part of his library. With these are incorporated the collection of the Basel Collegium musicum and that of the de Pury family. References made to 18th-century and modern printings of the works here found in manuscript.

Berea, Ohio

710. BALDWIN-WALLACE COLLEGE. RIEMENSCHNEIDER MEMORIAL BACH LIBRARY. Catalog of the Emilie and Karl Riemenschneider Memorial Bach Library. Edited by Sylvia W. Kenney. New York, Published for Baldwin-Wallace College by Columbia University Press, 1960. 295 p.

Numbered catalog of 2,537 items, of which the first 520 are writings on Bach and his time. Nos. 521-31: music of contemporaries and sons of J. S. Bach; no. 532 to end: music of J. S. Bach. The principal grouping is by musical forms; manuscripts listed separately; index of cantatas, general index.

Review by Walter Emery in Music & Letters, 42 (1961) p. 376-77.

Berkeley, California

711. UNIVERSITY OF CALIFORNIA. MUSIC LIBRARY. Thematic catalog of a manuscript collection of eighteenth-century Italian instrumental music in the University of California, Berkeley, Music Library. By Vincent Duckles and Minnie Elmer. Berkeley & Los Angeles, University of Calif. Press, 1963. 403 p.

A collection comprising some 990 manuscripts containing works by 82 composers. The central figures are Giuseppe Tartini and Michele Stratico, and the collection itself has close connections with Tartini's school of violin playing at Padua. Preliminary chapters discuss the historical background of the collection and tabulate the handwritings and the watermarks represented.

Berlin, Germany

712. INTERNATIONALE MUSIKLEIHBIBLIOTHEK. Katalog. Berlin, 1952. 276 p.

Classified catalog of an international lending library of instrumental, vocal, and choral works. Includes parts for orchestral music. Strong in works by Soviet composers, but other countries well represented. Composer index.

713. JOACHIMSTHALSCHES GYMNASIUM. BIBLIOTHEK. Katalog der Musikaliensammlung des Joachimsthalschen Gymnasium zu Berlin. Verfasst von Robert Eitner. Berlin, T. Trautwein, 1884. 106 p. (Monatshefte für Musikgeschichte. Beilage, Jahrgang 16)

This collection incorporates the library of Princess Anna Amalie, sister of Frederick the Great. Strong in 18th-century music of the North-German school. 627 numbered items, manuscripts and early prints. Author-composer index.

714. JOACHIMSTHALSCHES GYMNASIUM. BIBLIOTHEK. Thematischer Katalog der von Thulemeir'schen Musikalien-Sammlung in der Bibliothek des Joachimsthal'schen Gymnasiums zu Berlin. ⌐ By Rudolf Jacobs, edited by Robert Eitner ⌐ Leipzig, Breitkopf & Härtel, 1899. 110 p. (Monatshefte für Musikgeschichte. Beilage, Jahrgang 30-31)

The collection covers the period 1700-1800.

715. KÖNIGLICHE HAUSBIBLIOTHEK. Katalog der Musiksammlung aus der Königlichen Hausbibliothek im Schlosse zu Berlin. Verfasst und erläutert von Georg Thouret .... Leipzig, Breitkopf & Härtel, 1895. 356 p.

Brief entries, alphabetical by composer. 6,836 items, printed and in manuscript, with a special section of works dedicated to members of the royal family, and a supplementary alphabet for military music.

Neue Erwerbungen der Königliche Hausbibliothek zu Berlin. (Monatshefte für Musikgeschichte. Beilage, Jahrgang 35, 1903) 4 p.

716. STAATSBIBLIOTHEK, MUSIKABTEILUNG. ... Manuscrits de musique. Berlin, 1927. 45 p.

At head of title: Exposition internationale de musique, Genève, 1927. Preussische Staatsbibliothek.

P. 39-46: "La Section de musique de la Preussische Staats-bibliothek" ⌐ signed: Wilhelm Altmann ⌐ .

717. STAATSBIBLIOTHEK. Die Bach-Handschriften der Berliner Staatsbibliothek, von Paul Kast. Trossinger, Hohner-Verlag, 1958. 150 p. (Tübinger Bach-Studien, 2/3)

A catalog of manuscripts of music by members of the Bach family, once a part of the collection of the Prussian State Library and now distributed between the Westdeutsche Bibliothek in Marburg and the Universitätsbibliothek in Tübingen. Essentially a finding list for one of the world's greatest collections of Bach materials, now dispersed. Brief entries. Indexes of composers, scribes, and former owners of the manuscripts.

Bern, Switzerland

718. SCHWEIZERISCHE LANDESBIBLIOTHEK. Katalog der Schweizerischen Landesbibliothek. Musik Werke der Mitgleider des Schweizerischen Tonkünstlervereins veröffentlicht von 1848-1925, von Tonkünstlerverein und von der Landesbibliothek gemeinsam herausgegeben. ⌐ Ed. by K. Joss ⌐ Bern-Bümpliz, Buchdruckerei Benteli, 1927. 152 p.

About 5,000 titles, abridged to indispensable information, in a classified arrangement.

Bologna, Italy

ARCHIVIO DELLA ACCADEMIA FILARMONICA. See no. 790.

ARCHIVIO DI S. PETRONIO. See no. 790.

BIBLIOTECA AMBROSINI. See no. 790.

719. CONSERVATORIO DI MUSICA "G. B. MARTINI." BIBLIOTECA. Catalogo della biblioteca del Liceo musicale di Bologna, compilato da Gaetano Gaspari, compiuto e pubblicato da

Federico Parisini per cura del municipio .... Bologna, Libreria Romagnoli dall'Acqua, 1890-1943. 5 v.

Vol. 1: music theory; Vol. 2: sacred vocal music (ed. Luigi Torchi); Vol. 3: secular vocal music and opera (ed. Luigi Torchi); Vol. 4: instrumental music and pedagogy (ed. Raffaele Caldolini); Vol. 5: librettos (ed. Ugo Sesini).

Vols. 1-4 were reissued in photo-offset with corrections by Napoleone Fanti, Oscar Mischiati, and Luigi Ferdinando Tagliavini. Bologna, Arnaldo Forni, 1961. A supplementary volume of recently added material is projected.

This catalog provides access to one of the richest collections of early music, incorporating the library of the 18th-century scholar Padre Martini. Complete bibliographical description, contents given for collections, numerous prefaces and dedications transcribed. Entries are alphabetical within each category. General index of names.

Bonn, Germany

720. BEETHOVEN-HAUS. Katalog der Handschriften des Beethoven-Hauses und Beethoven-Archivs Bonn. Bearbeitet von Dr. Joseph Schmidt-Görg. Bonn, Beethoven-Haus, 1935. 75 p.

275 numbered items, including letters, sketches, manuscripts and early editions of music by Beethoven and by his contemporaries.

721. BEETHOVEN-HAUS. Katalog der mit der Beethoven-Feier zu Bonn am 11.-15. Mai 1890 verbundenen Ausstellung von Handschriften, Briefen, Bildnissen, Reliquien Ludwig van Beethoven's, sowie sonstigen auf ihn und seine Familie bezüglichen Erinnerungen. Bonn, Verlag des Vereins Beethoven-Haus, 1890. 75 p.

360 numbered items, including portraits, music, letters and other documents by Beethoven and his contemporaries. Full transcriptions of numerous letters and excerpts from the "Conversationsheften."

722. UNIVERSITÄTSBIBLIOTHEK. "Die musikalischen Autographen der Universitäts-Bibliothek Bonn" ⌐ By Theo Clasen⌐ In Festschrift Joseph Schmidt-Görg zum 60. Geburtstag. Bonn, Beethoven-Haus, 1957. p. 26-65

The collection comprises 12 albums containing autograph letters, cards, sketches, etc. by 245 musicians. Material listed by author.

Bordeaux, France

723. BIBLIOTHÈQUE MUNICIPALE. Catalogue des livres composant la bibliothèque de la ville de Bordeaux. Musique. ⌐ By I. Delas⌐ Bordeaux, 1856. 127 p.

Boston, Massachusetts

724. PUBLIC LIBRARY. Catalogue of the Allen A. Brown collection of music. Boston, Mass., 1910-16. 4 v.

A dictionary catalog of composers, titles, subjects, with explicit contents and analytics for all collections. Rich in operas and orchestral scores, primarily 19th-century editions.

Brandenburg, Germany

725. ST. KATHARINENKIRCHE. BIBLIOTHEK. Die musikalischen Schätze der St. Katharinenkirche zu Brandenburg a.d. Havel. Ein Beitrag zur musikalischen Literatur des 16. und 17. Jahrhunderts ⌐ von Johann F. Täglichsbeck⌐ Brandenburg, A. Müller, 1857. 50 p.

Manuscripts and printed works, 1564-1671, chronologically arranged, with full bibliographical information and descriptive notes. 51 entries.

Brasov, Rumania

726. HONTERUSGYMNASIUM. BIBLIOTHEK. Die Musik-sammlung der Bibliothek zu Kronstadt, von Erich H. Müller. Kronstadt, J. Gött's Sohn, 1930. 176 p.

Manuscripts, printed music, and books. Brief biographical

sketches of authors or composers. Publication dates, plate numbers.

Breslau, Germany

727. BOHN, EMIL. Bibliographie der Musik-Druckwerke bis 1700 welche in der Stadtbibliothek, der Bibliothek des Acad. Inst. für Kirchenmusik, und der K. und Universitäts-Bibliothek zu Breslau aufbewahrt werden .... Berlin, A. Cohn, 1883. 450 p.

The three collections cataloged here are outstanding for their 16th- and 17th-century manuscripts and prints, particularly of liturgical and vocal music. P. 1-31: theoretical works; p. 32-351: practical works (music); p. 371-74: collections in chronological order; p. 374-440: continuation of practical works. Full bibliographical descriptions.

728. STADTBIBLIOTHEK. Die musikalischen Handschriften des XVI. und XVII. Jahrhunderts der Stadtbibliothek zu Breslau ... von Emil Bohn. Breslau, Commissions-Verlag von J. Hainauer, 1890. 423 p.

356 items, with full inventories of contents. Numerous indexes and supplementary lists: first line incipits of vocal texts, anonymous compositions, composer index, etc.

729. STAATS- UND UNIVERSITÄTS-BIBLIOTHEK. Beschreibendes Verzeichnis der alten Musikalien-Handschriften und Druckwerke, des Königlichen Gymnasiums zu Brieg. Bearbeitet von Friedrich Kuhn. Leipzig, Breitkopf & Härtel, 1897. 98 p. (Monatshefte für Musikgeschichte. Beilage, Jahrgang 29)

Collection placed in the library of Breslau University in 1890. 54 manuscripts and some 110 prints, chiefly 16th-century. Contents given for manuscript collections, full bibliographical description for prints. Index.

Brieg, Germany

KÖNIGLICHEN GYMNASIUM. See no. 729 above.

Bristol, England

730. PUBLIC LIBRARIES. Catalogue of music scores.
Bristol, 1959. 305 p.

Brussels, Belgium

731. BIBLIOTHÈQUE ROYALE DE BELGIQUE. Catalogue de
la bibliothèque de F. J. Fétis, acquise par l'État belge.
Bruxelles, C. Muquardt, 1877. 946 p.

The Fétis library was acquired by the Bibliothèque Royale in
1872. 7,325 items classified under two main headings:
(1) "Bibliothèque générale," and (2) "Bibliothèque musicale."

732. BIBLIOTHÈQUE ROYALE. Exposition de documents
musicaux (Manuscrits — Imprimés — Estampes) 11-30
Septembre, 1955. Brussels, Bibliothèque Royale de Belgique
[1955] 23 p.

An exposition catalog of 113 items, assembled from the
music collections of the Bibliothèque Royale. Prepared for the
International Congress of Libraries and Documentation Centers by
the Ministry of Public Instruction, Brussels, 1955.

733. CONSERVATOIRE ROYAL DE MUSIQUE.
BIBLIOTHÈQUE. Catalogue de la bibliothèque ... par A.
Wotquenne. Bruxelles, Coosemans, 1898-1912. 4 v.

Annexe I. Libretti d'opéras et d'oratorios italiens du XVIIe
siècle. Bruxelles, O. Schlepens, 1901. 189 p.

A classified catalog of one of the richest European collections.
Prints and manuscripts interfiled.

Budapest, Hungary

734. ORSZÁGOS SZÉCHÉNYI KÖNYVTÁR. "Catalogue
raisonné der Esterházy-Opernsammlung, in chronologischer
Ordnung der Premìeren." In Haydn als Opernkapellmeister; die
Haydn-Dokumente der Esterházy-Opernsammlung. Bearbeitet
von Dénes Bartha und László Somfai. Budapest, Verlag der
Ungarischen Akademie der Wissenschaften, 1960. p. 179-403.

A chronological listing of the operatic works preserved in the
Esterházy archive now in the National Széchényi Library at
Budapest. Each work is fully described, with special attention
given to Haydn's annotations on works performed under his direction. An important study opening new dimensions in Haydn research

735. ORSZÁGOS SZÉCHÉNYI KÖNYVTÁR. Haydn

compositions in the music collection of the National Széchényi
Library, Budapest. Published on the occasion of the 150th anniversary of Haydn's death (1809-1959) ⊏ Edited by Henö Vécsey .... ⊐
Budapest, Publishing House of the Hungarian Academy of Sciences,
1960. 167. (Pubn. of the National Széchényi Library, 48)

Also published in Hungarian and German.

A classified listing of 372 items, 73 of which are Haydn
autographs. 42 facsimiles of Haydn manuscripts, prints, and
other documents.

736. ORSZÁGOS SZÉCHÉNYI KÖNYVTÁR. Zenei kéziratok
jegyzéke. Budapest, Kiadja a Magyar Nemzeti Múzeum Orzágos
Széchényi Kónyvtár, 1921-40. 2 v. (Catalogus bibliothecae
musaei nat. hungarici. Musica, I & II)

Vol. 1: Editor, Isoz Kálmán. Catalog of 1449 autograph
letters of musicians in the National Széchényi Library, including
some by Haydn and Liszt. Vol. 2: Editor, Lavotta Rezsö.
Catalog of music manuscripts.

Cambrai, France

737. COUSSEMAKER, EDMOND DE. Notice sur les
collections musicales de la Bibliothèque de Cambrai et des
autres villes du Départment du Nord .... Paris, Techener,
1843. 180, 40 p.

Concerned chiefly with 16 manuscripts and 4 printed collections in the Cambrai library. The descriptions are brief, faulty,
and outdated.

Cambridge, England

738. UNIVERSITY. FITZWILLIAM MUSEUM. LIBRARY.
Catalogue of the music in the Fitzwilliam Museum, Cambridge,
by J. A. Fuller-Maitland and A. H. Mann. London, C. J. Clay
& Sons, 1893. 298 p.

209 manuscripts, 196 prints, and an important collection of
Handel materials.

739. UNIVERSITY. PETERHOUSE COLLEGE. LIBRARY.
Catalogue of the musical manuscripts at Peterhouse, Cambridge;

compiled by Anselm Hughes. Cambridge, University Press, 1953. 75 p.

Important materials for the study of English church music of the 16th and 17th centuries, comprising 4 Latin partbooks of c. 1540 and 2 sets of English partbooks c. 1630–40.

Cambridge, Massachusetts

740. HARVARD UNIVERSITY. MUSIC LIBRARY. A catalogue of books relating to music in the library of Richard Aldrich. New York, 1931 ⌐Printed at the Plimpton Press, Norwood, Mass.⌐ 1931. 435 p.

A classified catalog of music literature, primarily of the 19th and 20th centuries, with a small collection of books printed before 1800 (p. 35–55). This library has been incorporated into the Harvard University music collection.

741. CATALOGUS MUSICUS. A series of catalogues and bibliographies. ⌐ General editor, Harald Heckmann⌐ v. 1–Kassel, Bärenreiter ⌐ for the International Association of Music Libraries⌐ 1963–

Vol. 1: Das Musikarchiv im Minoritenkonvent zu Wien, 1963. See no. 940.

Cesena, Italy

742. BIBLIOTECA COMUNALE. "Catalogo delle opere musicali a stampa dal'500 al'700 conservate presso la Biblioteca Comunale di Cesena." ⌐ By Sergio Paganelli⌐ In Collectanea musicae, 2 (1957) p. 311–38

95 early prints of vocal and instrumental music; 6 theory works.

Coimbra, Portugal

743. UNIVERSIDADE. BIBLIOTECA. Inventário dos inéditos e impressos musicais (subsídios para um catálogo). Fasc. I. Prefaciado por Santiago Kastner. Coimbra, Impresso nas oficinas da "Atlántida, " 1937. 47 p. (Publicacões da Biblioteca da Universidade)

Separate alphabets for manuscripts and early printed works. Full descriptions.

Cologne, Germany

744. UNIVERSITÄTS- UND STADTBIBLIOTHEK. Katalog der in der Universitäts- und Stadtbibliothek Köln vorhandenen Musikdrucke des 16., 17., und 18. Jahrhunderts. ⸢ By Willi Kahl ⸣ Köln, 1958. 20 p.

Prepared for distribution at the 7th Congress of the International Musicological Society, Cologne, June 23-26, 1958. 118 items. Bibliographical references.

Copenhagen, Denmark

745. KOMMUNEBIBLIOTEKER. Katalog over dansk og udenlandsk musik og musiklitteratur. 2. udgave. København, B. Lunos Bogtrykkeri, 1932. 157 p.

First published in 1921. 72 p.

Tilvaext ⸢supplement⸣ 1932-39. København, B. Lunos, 1939. 53 p.

746. KOMMUNEBIBLIOTEKER. Katalog over musik og musiklitteratur. København, Nordlunde, 1954-56(?) 5 v.

Del 1: Orkestermusik, Kammermusik, Enkelte Instrumenter, 1956. 72 p. Del 2: Klaver, Orgel, Harmonium, 1954. 65 p. Del 3: ⸢Vokalmusik, 195-(?)⸣ Del 4: Operaer, Operetter, Balletter, 1955. 46 p. Del 5: ⸢Musikteori, Musikhistorie, Biografier, 195-(?)⸣

747. CORTOT, ALFRED. Bibliothèque Alfred Cortot .... v. 1. Catalogue établi par Alfred Cortot et rédigé par Frederik Goldbeck, avec la collaboration de A. Fehr. Préface de Henry Prunières. ⸢Argenteuil, Sur les presses de R. Coulouma, 1936⸣ 212 p.

Première partie (all published): Traités et autres ouvrages théoriques des XVe, XVIe, XVIIe & XVIIIe siècles.

The holdings of the private library of Alfred Cortot in the field of music theory. Full bibliographical citations, with descriptive annotations.

Cremona, Italy

748. MOSTRA BIBLIOGRAFICA DEI MUSICISTI CREMONESI DAL RINASCIMENTO ALL'OTTOCENTO, 1949. Mostra bibliografica dei musicisti cremonesi: catalogo storico-critico degli autori e catalogo bibliografico. Cremona, Biblioteca Governativa e Libreria Civica, 1951. 149 p. (Annali della Biblioteca Governativa e Libreria Civica di Cremona, 2)

P. 1-106: biographical notices of Cremonese musicians; p. 107-45: exhibition catalog, chronologically arranged, about 140 items related to the history of music in Cremona.

CZECHOSLOVAKIA

749. TERRAYOVÁ, MÁRIA J. "Súpis archívnych hudobných fondov na Slovensku." In Hudobnovedné štúdie, IV. Bratislava, Vydavateľstvo Slovenskej Akadémie Vied, 1960. p. 197-328

Thematic catalog of the music manuscripts in two hitherto undescribed Czech archives: the archive of the Catholic Pfarrkirche of Púchov (on deposit in the Musicological Institute of the Slovakian Academy of Sciences), and the archive of the Prílesský-Ostrolúcky family (on deposit in the Slovakian National Museum in Martin). The manuscripts are chiefly of late 18th-century instrumental and vocal music by Italianate Czech composers of the period.

The catalog is described as the beginning of a projected complete thematic catalog of early music in Czech archives.

See also no. 552, a listing of the music accessions in ten major Czech libraries.

Dagenham, England

750. PUBLIC LIBRARIES. Catalogue of music; a complete catalogue of the scores, miniature scores, recorded music and

books ... in the Dagenham Public Libraries. Compiled by W. C. Pugsley & G. Atkinson. Dagenham ⌐Essex⌐ 1958. 299 p.

Danzig (Gdansk), Poland

751. STADTBIBLIOTHEK. Die musikalischen Handschriften der Stadtbibliothek und in ihrer Verwaltung befindlichen Kirchenbibliotheken von St. Katharinen und St. Johann in Danzig. ⌐Von Otto Günther⌐ Danzig, 1911. (Katalog der Handschriften der Danziger Stadtbibliothek, 4)

Darmstädt, Germany

752. HOFBIBLIOTHEK. "Musik-Handschriften der Darmstädter Hofbibliothek." ⌐Beschreiben von F. W. E. Roth⌐ In Monatshefte für Musikgeschichte, 20 (1888) p. 64-73, 82-92

117 items, 10th to 19th centuries. Brief descriptions.

753. HOFBIBLIOTHEK. "Zur Bibliographie der Musikdrucke des XV. bis XVII. Jahrhunderts in der Darmstädter Hofbibliothek." ⌐Von F. W. E. Roth⌐ In Monatshefte für Musikgeschichte, 20 (1888) p. 118-25, 134-41, 151-61

75 items, fully described.

754. KRANICHSTEINER MUSIKINSTITUT. Katalog. ⌐Vorwort: Dr. Wolfgang Steinecke⌐ Darmstädt, Kranichsteiner Musikinstitut ⌐1956-⌐ (Expandable looseleaf format)

An international lending library, established in 1948, to further the study and performance of 20th-century music. Classified catalog, chiefly scores and performance materials, but with a small section of books on music.

Denton, Texas

755. NORTH TEXAS STATE COLLEGE. MUSIC LIBRARY. A bibliography of contemporary music in the Music Library of North Texas State College, March 1955. Compiled by Anna Harriet Heyer .... Denton, Texas, 1955. 128 leaves (typescript)

Alphabetical listing by composer, and by title under composer. Chiefly scores and chamber music with parts. No indexes.

Review by Dorothy A. Linder in Notes, 13 (1956) p. 656-57.

Dresden, Germany

756. SÄCHISCHE LANDESBIBLIOTHEK. MUSIKABTEILUNG. Katalog der Musik-Sammlung der Kgl. öffentlichen Bibliothek zu Dresden (im Japanischen Palais). Bearb. von Robert Eitner und Otto Kade .... Leipzig, Breitkopf & Härtel, 1890. 150 p. (Monatshefte für Musikgeschichte. Beilage, Jahrgang 21 & 22)

Contents: music manuscripts to the present day; prints and books on music to 1700.

Edinburgh, Scotland

757. UNIVERSITY. REID LIBRARY. Catalogue of manuscripts, printed music and books on music up to 1850, in the library of the Music Department at the University of Edinburgh (Reid Library) edited by Hans Gál. Edinburgh, Oliver and Boyd, 1941. 78 p.

Important for its holdings in 18th-century music, printed and manuscript, from the private collection of John Reid, 1721-1807. Brief entries.

Ferrara, Italy

BIBLIOTECA COMUNALE. See no. 799.

Florence, Italy

BIBLIOTECA DEL R. ISTITUTO MUSICALE. See no. 792.

758. BIBLIOTECA NAZIONALE. Catalogo dei manoscritti musicali della Biblioteca Nazionale di Firenze. ⊏By⊐ Bianca Becherini. Kassel, Bärenreiter, 1959. 178 p.

144 numbered items; detailed descriptions, contents of collections. Indexes of text incipits, musicians, poets, and names mentioned in the descriptive notes.

Review by Frank Ll. Harrison in Music & Letters, 42 (1961)
p. 281; by Nanie Bridgman in Fontes artis musicae, 8 (1961)
p. 31-33; by Walther Dürr in Die Musik-Forschung, 14 (1961)
p. 234-35.

759. BIBLIOTECA NAZIONALE. Mostra bibliografica di
musica italiana dalle origini alla fine del secolo XVIII. Firenze,
L. S. Olschki, 1937. 102 p.

An exhibition catalog. Preface signed: Anita Mondolfo.

760. CONSERVATORIO DI MUSICA "LUIGI CHERUBINI. "
Esposizione nazionale dei Conservatori Musicali e delle
Biblioteche. Palazzo Davanzati, 27 Ottobre 1949-8 Gennaio 1950.
Firenze, G. Barbera, 1950. 121 p.

Exposition catalog for the 100th anniversary of the founding of
the Conservatorio "Luigi Cherubini. " Includes manuscripts,
prints, and some musical instruments.

761. GALLERIA DEGLI UFFIZI. I desegni musicali del
Gabinetto degli "Uffizi" e delle minori collezioni pubbliche a
Firenze. ⌐ By⌐ Luigi Parigi. Firenze, L. S. Olschki, 1951.
233 p.

A catalog of prints and drawings with musical content or
subject matter: musicians, musical instruments, performance
practice, etc. Indexed by instruments and by subjects.

762. GALLERIA DEGLI UFFIZI. Mostra di strumenti
musicali in disegni degli "Uffizi. " Catalogo a cura di Luisa
Marcucci con prefazione di Luigi Parigi. Firenze, L. S. Olschki
⌐ 1952 ⌐ 47 p.

An exhibition of 65 items from the Uffizi print collection;
25 plates.

763. GALLERIA DEGLI UFFIZI. Gli strumenti musicali
nei dipinti della Galleria degli Uffizi. ⌐ By ⌐ Marziano Bernardi e
Andrea Della Corte. ⌐ Torino, Edizioni Radio Italiana, 1952.⌐
177 p. 51 plates

A handsome volume devoted to representations of musical activity in paintings in the Uffizi gallery. Index of artists and of instruments depicted.

764. ILLUSTRAZIONI DI ALCUNI CIMELI CONCERNENTI L'ARTE MUSICALE IN FIRENZE ... ⌐ Di Riccardo Gandolfi ⌐ In Firenze, a cura della Commissione per la Esposizione di Vienna, 1892.

A lavish, illustrated catalog prepared for the exposition in Vienna in 1892. Limited edition, elephant folio. 39 facsimile plates of Italian musical documents from the 11th to the 19th centuries. Historical introduction and brief notes on the plates.

Frankfurt am Main, Germany

765. INTERNATIONAL EXHIBITION "MUSIC IN THE LIFE OF THE PEOPLE," 1927. Katalog der Internationalen Ausstellung "Musik im Leben der Völker," von Kathi Meyer. ⌐ Frankfurt am Main, Hauserpresse Werner U. Winter, 1927⌐ 340 p.

Catalog of the large international music exhibition held June 11 - August 28, 1927. The catalog follows the systematic arrangement of the exhibition halls. Includes prints, manuscripts, instruments, pictures, and artifacts. 49 plates.

766. INTERNATIONAL EXHIBITION "MUSIC IN THE LIFE OF THE PEOPLE," 1927. Catalogo della sezione Italiana. Roma, 1927. 161 p.

A separate listing of the Italian part of the above exhibition. 35 plates.

767. LESSING-GYMNASIUM. BIBLIOTHEK. Die musikalischen Schätze der Gymnasialbibliothek und der Peterskirche zu Frankfurt a. M., von Carl Israël. Frankfurt a. M., Mahlau & Waldschmidt, 1872. 118 p.

Covers the period to about 1800; full bibliographical data.

768. STADTBIBLIOTHEK. Kirchliche Musikhandschriften

des XVII. und XVIII. Jahrhunderts; Katalog von Carl Süss, im
Auftrage der Gesellschaft der Freunde der Stadtbibliothek, bearb.
und hrsg. von Peter Epstein. Berlin, Frankfurter Verlags-
Anstalt ⌈1926⌉ 224 p.

Chiefly cantatas arranged alphabetically under composer,
with a separate section of 834 works by G. P. Telemann. Entries
give title, date if known, and instrumentation.

Freiberg, Germany

769. KADE, OTTO. Die alteren Musikalien der Stadt
Freiberg in Sachsen. Leipzig, Breitkopf & Härtel, 1888. 32 p.
(Monatshefte für Musikgeschichte. Beilage, Jahrgang 20)

Genoa, Italy

BIBLIOTECA UNIVERSITARIA. See no. 797.

GERMANY

770. KAHL, WILLI und WILHELM-MARTIN LUTHER.
Repertorium der Musikwissenschaft. Musikschrifttum, Denkmäler
und Gesamtausgaben in Auswahl (1800-1950) mit Besitzvermerken
deutscher Bibliotheken und musikwissenschaftlicher Institute.
Kassel, Bärenreiter, 1953. 271 p.

This item is cited here because of its character as a union
list of musicological holdings in postwar German libraries. It is
also entered as no. 362.

Glasgow, Scotland

771. ANDERSON'S COLLEGE. LIBRARY. EUING
COLLECTION. The Euing musical library. Catalogue of the
musical library of the late Wm. Euing, Esq., bequeathed to
Anderson's University, Glasgow .... Glasgow, Printed by W. M.
Ferguson, 1878. 256 p.

Classified catalog. The collection contains primarily theoretical works from 1487, and liturgical music of the Church of
England, 16th to 19th centuries.

Göttingen, Germany

772. NIEDERSÄCHSISCHE STAATS- UND UNIVERSITÄTS-
BIBLIOTHEK. Johann Sebastian Bach Documenta. Hrsg ... von
Wilhelm Martin Luther zum Bachfest 1950 in Göttingen. Kassel,
Bärenreiter ⌐1950⌐ 148 p.

545 numbered items from an exhibition illustrating J. S.
Bach's influence from his own time to the present day; covers a
wide area of Bach documentation. 54 plates.

773. NIEDERSÄCHSISCHE STAATS- UND UNIVERSITÄTS-
BIBLIOTHEK. Die Musikwerke der Kgl. Universitäts-Bibliothek
in Göttingen. Verzeichnet von Albert Quantz. Berlin, T.
Trautwein, 1883. 45 p. (Monatshefte für Musikgeschichte.
Beilage, Jahrgang 15)

45 theoretical works and some 100 music prints of the 16th
and 17th centuries; good representation of German composers.

Granada, Spain

774. CAPILLA REAL. ARCHIVO. "El Archivo de musica
de la Capilla Real de Granada." ⌐ By José López Calo ⌐ In
Anuario musical, 13 (1958) p. 103-28

Small collection of manuscripts, early prints, and documents.
Contents fully listed for the polyphonic sources.

GREAT BRITAIN

775. BIBLIOTHECA MUSICO-LITURGICA. A descriptive
handlist of the musical and Latin-liturgical mss. of the Middle
Ages preserved in the libraries of Great Britain and Ireland.
Drawn up by W. H. Frere ... and printed for the members of the
Plainsong and Mediaeval Music Society .... London, B. Quaritch,
1901-32. 2 v.

Also entered as no. 674.

776. THE BRITISH UNION-CATALOGUE OF EARLY MUSIC
PRINTED BEFORE THE YEAR 1801. A record of the holdings of
over 100 libraries throughout the British Isles. Editor: Edith B.

Schnapper. London, Butterworths Scientific Publications, 1957. 2 v.

Also entered as no. 635.

Grimma, Germany

777. KÖNIGL. LANDESSCHULE. BIBLIOTHEK.
Verzeichniss der in der Bibliothek der Königl. Landesschule zu
Grimma vorhandenen Musikalien aus dem 16. und 17. Jahrhundert,
von N. M. Petersen .... Grimma ⌐ G. Gensel, 1861 ⌐ 24 p.

Guadalupe, Spain

778. SANTA MARÍA (Franciscan Monastery). Catalogo del
archivo musical del Monasterio de Guadalupe, por Arcángel
Barrado. Badajoz, Diputación Provincial, Institución de Servi-
cios Culturales, 1945. 181 p.

18th-century sacred music. 947 works by 98 composers.

The Hague, Holland

779. GEMEENTEMUSEUM. Nederlandsche muziekleven
1600-1800. 's-Gravenhage, Gemeentemuseum, 6 Juni-6
September, 1936. 124 p.

Catalog of an exhibition on Dutch musical life of the 17th and
18th centuries. Includes prints, manuscripts, musical instruments, and paintings with musical subjects. Illustrated.
Introductions by D. J. Balfoort.

780. MUZIEKHISTORISCH MUSEUM VAN DR. D. F.
SCHEURLEER. Catalogus van de Muziek-werken en de Boeken
over Muziek. 's-Gravenhage, M. Nijhoff, 1923-25. 3 v.

This catalog was preceded by two earlier compilations,
1885-87 (in 2 volumes) and 1893-1910 (in 3 volumes).

Classified catalog; Vol. 3 is a general index. Numerous
facsimiles of early title pages. An outstanding working library,
as well as containing many rarities. It is now the property of the
city of The Hague, housed in the Gemeentemuseum and the Royal
Library.

Halle, Germany

781. HÄNDEL-HAUS. Katalog zu den Sammlungen des Händel-Hauses in Halle. v. 1-   Halle an der Saale ⌐Händel-Haus⌐ 1961-

1. Teil: Handschriftensammlung. 1961. 330 p.

2. Teil: Bildsammlung, Porträts. 1962. 288 p.

The first two volumes of a series projected to cover all of the collections of the Händel-Haus. Teil 1 includes both musical and literary manuscripts. Rich in materials related to early 19th-century German song. The letters and documents are transcribed in full. Teil 2 is concerned with iconography, classified as to paintings, engravings, busts, and medals, with reproductions given for all items. Bibliography of Händel iconography: p. 283-88.

Heilbronn, Germany

782. GYMNASIUM. BIBLIOTHEK. Alter Musikschatz, geordnet und beschreiben von Edwin Mayser. Heilbronn, C. F. Schmidt, 1893. 82 p. (Mitteilungen aus der Bibliothek des Heilbronner Gymnasiums, 2)

783. HEYER, WILLIAM. Musikhistorisches Museum von Wilhelm Heyer in Cöln. Katalog von Georg Kinsky. Band 4: Musik-Autographen. Leipzig, Breitkopf & Härtel, 1916. 870 p.

1,673 items, one of the finest collections of musical autographs ever assembled. Dispersed and sold at auction in 1926 by the firm of Henrici and Liepmannssohn. Kinsky's catalogs of the Heyer collection are monuments of music bibliography, full of biographical and descriptive detail. 64 facsimile plates.

For other volumes of the Heyer Katalog, see no. 970.

784. HIRSCH, PAUL. Katalog der Musikbibliothek Paul Hirsch ... Frankfurt am Main, herausg. von K. Meyer und P. Hirsch .... Berlin, M. Breslauer, 1928-47. 4 v. (v. 4 has imprint: Cambridge Univ. Press)

Vol. 1: Theoretische Drucke bis 1800; Vol. 2: Opern-Partituren; Vol. 3: Instrumental- und Vokalmusik bis etwa 1830; Vol. 4: Erstausgaben, Chorwerke in Partitur, Gesamtausgaben, Nachschlagewerke, etc. Ergänzungen zu Bd. I-III.

The Paul Hirsch Library, one of the finest private music collections ever assembled, was removed from Frankfurt to Cambridge, England, just prior to World War II, and was acquired by the British Museum in 1946.

See also nos. 833-34.

HUNGARY

See no. 687.

Iowa City, Iowa

785. UNIVERSITY LIBRARY. An exhibit of music and materials on music, early and rare. Preface by Albert T. Luper. Iowa City, The Graduate College and The University Libraries, State University of Iowa, April 1953. 39 p.

An annotated exhibition catalog of materials borrowed from the Library of Congress, The Newberry Library, The University of Illinois Libraries, The Sibley Musical Library, and private sources. Part I: autograph scores (13 items); Part II: early music editions and manuscripts (43 items); Part III: books on music, mainly 17th and 18th century (45 items).

786. UNIVERSITY LIBRARY. Rare musical items in the libraries of the University of Iowa, by Frederick K. Gable. Foreword by Albert T. Luper. Iowa City, The University Libraries, University of Iowa, 1963. 130 p.

A carefully annotated catalog of 275 items. Part I: books on music; Part II: music scores. Index of names and of selected subjects. Selected bibliography.

ITALY

787. ASSOCIAZIONE DEI MUSICOLOGI ITALIANI. Catalogo generale delle opere musicali, teoriche o pratiche, manoscritto o

stampate, di autori vissuti sino ai primi decenni del XIX secolo, esistenti nelle biblioteche e negli archivi d'Italia .... Parma, Fresching, 1911-38. 18 v.

The Associazione catalogs are of mixed quality and completeness, but in many cases they represent the best available listings of the holdings of important Italian libraries. Their coverage is confined to music and theoretical works written or published before 1810.

788. 1. ⊏1⊐. Cittа di Parma. ⊏Compilatori ... Guido Gasperini ... Nestore Pellicelli (sic)⊐ ⊏1909⊐ -11. 295 p.

789. ⊏ i(2)⊐. Cittа di Reggio-Emilia. ⊏Compilatori ... Guido Gasperini ... Nestore Pellicelli (sic)⊐ 1911. 24 p.

790. vii ⊏sic, ii⊐ Cittа di Bologna. Archivio della R. accademia filarmonica. ⊏Biblioteca dell'Avv. Raimondo Ambrosini; Archivio di S. Petronio⊐ ⊏Compilatore ... Alfredo Bonora, Emilio Giani⊐ 1910-11-⊏38⊐ 124 p. incomplete.

791. iii. Cittа di Milano. Biblioteca ambrosiana. Compilatore ... Gaetano Cesari. 1910-11. 20 p. incomplete.

792. iv ⊏1⊐. Cittа di Firenze. Biblioteca del R. istituto musicale. Compilatori ... Riccardo Gandolfi e ... Carlo Cordara. 1910-11. 321 p.

793. iv ⊏2⊐. Cittа di Pistoia. Archivio capitolare della cattedrale. Compilatore ... Umberto de Laugier. 1936-37. 106 p.

794. v. Cìttа di Roma. ⊏Biblioteca della R. accademia di S. Cecilia. Compilatore ... Otello Andolfi ⊐ 1912-13. incomplete.

795. vi ⊏1⊐. Cittа di Venezia. Biblioteca Querini Stampalia. ⊏Museo Correr⊐ Compilatore ... Giovanni Concina. ⊏1913?⊐ -14. 113 p.

796. viɾ2ᴣ. Città di Vicenza. ɾBiblioteca bertoliana ...
de Sebastiano Rumor; Archivio della cattedrale ... da
Primo Zanini ᴣ 1923. 48 p.

797. vii. Città di Genova. R. biblioteca universitaria.
ɾSchedatore: Raffaele Bresciano ᴣ ɾn.d.ᴣ 21 p.

798. vii ɾsicᴣ -viii. Città di Modena. R. biblioteca
estense. ɾCompilatore ... Pio Lodi ᴣ ɾ1916-24ᴣ 561 p.

799. ix. Città di Ferrara. Biblioteca comunale. ɾda
Emanuele Davia ... Allessandro Lombardi ᴣ 1917. 40 p.

800. xɾ1ᴣ. Città di Napoli. Archivio dell'Oratorio dei
Filippini. ɾ Compilatore ... Salvatore di Giacomo ᴣ 1918.
108 p.

801. xɾ2ᴣ. Città di Napoli. Biblioteca del R. conservatorio
di S. Pietro a Majella. Compilatori ... Guido Gasperini
... Franco Gallo. ɾ 1918ᴣ -34. 696 p.

802. xi. Città di Assisi. Biblioteca comunale. Compilatore
... Francesco Pennacchi. 1921. 45 p.

803. xii. Città di Torino. R. biblioteca nazionale.
ɾCompilatore ... Attilio Cimbro (Alberto Gentili)ᴣ 1928.
38 p.

804. xiii. Biblioteche e archivi della città di Pisa.
Compilatore ... Pietro Pecchiai. 1932-33- ɾ35ᴣ 90 p.

805. xiv. Città di Verona. Biblioteca della Soc. accademica
filarmonica di Verona. Fondo musicale antico. Compilatore ... Giuseppe Turini. 1935-36. 54 p.

806. BIBLIOTHECA MUSICAE. Collana di cataloghi e
bibliografie diretta da Claudio Sartori. 1962-   Milano, Istituto
Editoriale Italiano.

A projected series of catalogs of Italian libraries and collections under the general editorship of Claudio Sartori. The first volume to appear (1962) covered the musical collection of the Biblioteca Comunale of Assisi; this volume is cited as no. 702.

Jena, Germany

807. UNIVERSITÄTSBIBLIOTHEK. Die geistlichen Musikhandschriften der Universitätsbibliothek Jena, von Karl Erich Roediger. Jena, Frommannsche Buchhandlung Walter Biedermann, 1935. 2 v.

Vol. 1: Textband; Vol. 2: Notenverzeichnis. Primarily a study, with inventory, of 18 choirbooks, Burgundian-Netherland repertory, in the Jena University Library.

Vol. 1 is a detailed study of the sources and their contents, with indexes of liturgical settings, cantus firmi, composers represented and their works. Vol. 2 is a thematic catalog of the choirbooks.

Vol. 1, p. 111-14: a listing of 63 16th-century music prints in the library at Jena.

Kassel, Germany

808. DEUTSCHES MUSIKGESCHICHTLICHES ARCHIV. Katalog der Filmsammlung. Zusammengestellt und bearbeitet von Harald Heckmann. Band I, Nr. 1- Kassel, Bärenreiter, 1955- (5 v. issued to Summer, 1962).

Title varies: Nr. 1, Mitteilungen und Katalog ... A series of catalogs, in progress, of the holdings of a unique microfilm archive of primary source materials for the study of German music history. Includes manuscripts and early prints. Prints listed alphabetically under composer or author; printed collections chronologically; manuscript collections under place. For a description of the Archiv and its catalogs, see: Harald Heckmann, "Archive of German Music History," in Notes, 16 (1958) p. 35-39.

809. LANDESBIBLIOTHEK. Übersichtlicher Katalog der Musikalien der ständischen Landesbibliothek zu Cassel, bearb.

von Carl Israël. Cassel, A. Freyschmidt, 1881. 78 p.

Works from the 16th and early 17th centuries, manuscripts and prints. Church and chamber music, German and Italian.

810. KOCH, LOUIS. COLLECTION. Katalog der Musik-autographen Sammlung ... Manuskripte, Briefe, Dokumente, von Scarlatti bis Stravinsky. Beschreiben und erläutert von Georg Kinsky. Stuttgart, Hoffmannsche Buchdruckerei F. Krais, 1953. 360 p.

The catalog of a rich private collection of musical autographs. Strong in German music of the classic and romantic periods. 21 facsimile plates.

Review by Richard S. Hill in Notes, 11 (1953) p. 119-20.

Königsberg, Germany

811. STAATS- UND UNIVERSITÄTS-BIBLIOTHEK. BIBLIOTHECA GOTTHOLDIANA. Die musikalischen Schätze der Königsberg in Pr., aus dem Nachlasse Friedrich August Gotthold's. Nebst Mittheilungen aus dessen musikalischen Tagebüchern. Ein Beitrag zur Geschichte und Theorie der Tonkunst von Joseph Müller. Bonn, A. Marcus, 1870. 431 p.

Important collection, 55,000 volumes, with primary emphasis on 17th-century church music, manuscript and printed, and vocal music from the 16th to 19th centuries. Classified list of collec-tions, with author index. Works by various Königsberger Kapell-meister, such as Eccard, Stobaeus, Sebastiani, and first editions of Beethoven, Haydn, Mozart. Full bibliographical citations.

Kraków, Poland

812. UNIWERSYTET JAGIELLÓNSKI. BIBLJOTEKA. Ksiazki o muzyce w Bibljotece Jagiellónskiej. Kraków, 1924-38. 3 v.

At head of title: Josef Reiss.

Leipzig, Germany

813. BREITKOPF & HÄRTEL (Publisher). Catalogo delle sinfonie, partite, overture, soli, trii, quattri e concerti per il violino, flauto traverso, cembalo ad altri stromenti, che si trovano in manuscritto nella Officina musica di Giovanni Gottlob Breitkopf in Lipsia ⌐6 parts⌐ Leipzig, 1762-65.

Supplemento I-XVI ⌐1766-87⌐

Reprint projected, with an introduction by Barry S. Brook, New York, Dover Publications, 1964(?) An important 18th-century thematic catalog of instrumental music in manuscript in the Breitkopf archives. Useful in tracing or identifying works of the period.

814. BREITKOPF & HÄRTEL. Katalog des Archivs von Breitkopf & Härtel, Leipzig, im Auftrage der Firma hrsg. von Wilhelm Hitzig. Leipzig, Breitkopf & Härtel, 1925-26. 2 v. in 1

1. Musik-Autographe; 2. Briefe.

348 autograph scores from Händel to Hindemith, fully described with a composer index. Autograph letters are limited to persons born before 1780. Separate index to letters.

815. MUSIKBIBLIOTHEK PETERS. Katalog der Musik-bibliothek Peters, neu bearb. von Rudolf Schwartz. Band I: Bücher und Schriften. Leipzig, C. F. Peters, 1910. 227 p.

An earlier edition by Emil Vogel (1894) included both books and music. A music reference library maintained by the publishing house. Classified, with an author index.

816. MUSIKBIBLIOTHEK DER STADT LEIPZIG. Quellen-werke zur Händelforschung: Katalog. Hrsg. anlässlich der wissenschaftlichen Konferenz zur Händel-Ehrung der D. D. R., 11-19 April, 1959, in Halle. ⌐Leipzig, 1959⌐ 29 p.

817. MUSIKBIBLIOTHEK DER STADT LEIPZIG. Erst- und Frühdrucke von Robert Schumann in der Musikbibliothek

Leipzig. Leipzig, 1960. 64 p. (Bibliographische Veröffentlichungen der Musikbibliothek der Stadt Leipzig)

Also includes pictures, autographs, and Schumann literature.

Leningrad, Russia

818. GOLUBOVSKIĬ, I. V. Muzykal'nyĭ Leningrad.
Leningrad, Gosundarstvennoe Muzykalnoe Izdatel'stvo, 1958.

"Biblioteki i muzei", p. 351-411.

Describes in general terms the musical content of 14 libraries,
2 record libraries, and 12 museums. Lists manuscripts of
Russian composers, and mentions a few examples of Western
manuscripts and early books in various collections. Details as to
organization, cataloging, circulation, etc.

Liège, Belgium

819. CONSERVATOIRE ROYAL DE MUSIQUE. FONDS
TERRY. Catalogue de la Bibliothèque du Conservatoire Royal de
Musique de Liège. ⌐Par⌐ Eugene Monseur. Fonds Terry:
Musique dramatique. ⌐Liège, Conservatoire Royal de Musique,
1960⌐ 75 p.

Opera scores in the collection of Léonard Terry, acquired
by the Liège conservatory in 1882. Consists chiefly of works
from 1780 to 1880. Broadly classified as to full or vocal scores,
and by language of the libretto (French or foreign).

820. CONSERVATOIRE ROYAL DE MUSIQUE. FONDS
TERRY. ... Musique instrumentale. ⌐Liège, Conservatoire
Royale de Musique, 1960⌐ 51 p.

Instrumental music in the Terry collection; chiefly late 18th-
and early 19th-century material, both prints and manuscripts.

Lille, France

821. BIBLIOTHÈQUE. Catalogue des ouvrages sur la
musique et des compositions musicales de la Bibliothèque de Lille.

Lille, Imprimerie de Lefebvre-Ducrocq, 1879. 752 p.

2, 721 items. The collection is particularly rich in late 18th-
and early 19th-century French operas, which exist here in complete sets of performance materials. Also a large collection of
symphonies, overtures, chamber music.

Liegnitz, Germany

822. RITTER-AKADEMIE. "Katalog der in der Kgl. Ritter-
Akademie zu Liegnitz gedruckten und handschriftlichen Musikalien
nebst den hymnologischen und musikalisch-theoretischen Werken."
⌐ By Robert Eitner ⌐ In Monatshefte für Musikgeschichte, 1 (1869)
p. 25-39, 50-56, 70-76 (incomplete).

823. RITTER-AKADEMIE. Die Musik-handschriften der
Königl. Ritter-Akademie zu Liegnitz. Verzeichnet von Ernst
Pfudel. ⌐ Leipzig, Breitkopf & Härtel, 1886-89 ⌐ 74 p. (Monats-
hefte für Musikgeschichte. Beilage. Jahrgang 18 & 21)

Lisbon, Portugal

824. LIBRARY OF JOÃO IV, KING OF PORTUGAL.
Primeira parte do index de livraria de musica do muyto alto, e
poderoso Rey Dom João o IV ... Por ordem de sua Mag. por
Paulo Crasbeck. Anno 1649. ⌐ Edited by J. de Vasconcellos.
Porto, 1874-76 ⌐ 525 p.

Reprinting of a catalog, compiled in 1649 by Paul Crasbeck,
for the royal library in Lisbon, which was destroyed in the
earthquake of 1755. The catalog, although of a nonexistent collection, remains an important bibliographical tool for the study
of early Spanish and Portuguese music.

Liverpool, England

825. PUBLIC LIBRARY. MUSIC LIBRARY. Catalogue of
the music library. Liverpool, Central Public Libraries, 1954.
572 p.

Supersedes an earlier catalog, 1933. 374 p.

About 45,000 entries for books and music published for the most part after 1800. Brief entries.

London, England

826. BRITISH MUSEUM. Henry Purcell, 1659(?)-1695, George Frederic Handel, 1685-1759; catalogue of a commemorative exhibition, May-August 1959. London, Published by the Trustees, 1959. 47 p.

66 items related to Purcell, 180 to Handel. Introduction, annotations, 8 full-page plates.

827. BRITISH MUSEUM. Mozart in the British Museum. London, Published for the Trustees, 1956. 27 p. 12 plates

An exhibition catalog of 196 prints, autographs, early editions, etc., drawn from various collections, including the Department of Prints and Drawings, Burney collection, Maps, Hirsch, and Zweig collections.

828. BRITISH MUSEUM. DEPARTMENT OF MANU-SCRIPTS. Catalogue of manuscript music in the British Museum, by A. Hughes-Hughes. London, 1906-09. 3 v.

Vol. 1: sacred vocal music; Vol. 2: secular vocal music; Vol. 3: instrumental music, treatises, etc.

Each volume indexed by author, title, first lines of songs. Entries classified by genre or form, which means that the contents of the manuscript collections are often separated and distributed through the three volumes of the catalog.

829. BRITISH MUSEUM. DEPARTMENT OF MANU-SCRIPTS. Catalogue of the musical manuscripts deposited on loan in the British museum by the Royal Philharmonic Society of London. ⌐ London ⌐ Printed by order of the Trustees, 1914. 16 p.

830. BRITISH MUSEUM. DEPARTMENT OF PRINTED BOOKS. Catalogue of music. Accessions. v. 1- ⌐ London ⌐ 1884-

An annual publication compiled from the printed catalog slips.
It is ordinarily reserved for departmental use in the British
Museum, but there are copies in the New York Public Library and
the Library of Congress. Occasional volumes of special bibliographical interest have been given wider distribution. See nos.
833, 834.

831. BRITISH MUSEUM. DEPARTMENT OF PRINTED
BOOKS. Catalogue of printed music published between 1487 and
1800 now in the British Museum, by W. Barclay Squire. London,
Printed by order of the Trustees, 1912, 2 v.

First Supplement, 34 p. , bound in. Second Supplement, by
W. C. Smith. Cambridge Univ. Press, 1940. 85 p.

Includes early music of all countries, but is particularly
rich in British sources. Early theory and literary works included.
Brief entries with dates, or estimated dates, of publication.

832. BRITISH MUSEUM. DEPARTMENT OF PRINTED
BOOKS. Hand-list of music published in some British and foreign
periodicals between 1787 and 1848, now in the British Museum.
London, The Trustees of the British Museum, 1962. 80 p.

Indexes the music, chiefly songs, in 12 periodicals. 1, 855
entries arranged by composer. Printed from slips prepared for
entry in the British Museum catalog.

This item also appears as no. 634.

833. BRITISH MUSEUM. DEPARTMENT OF PRINTED
BOOKS. HIRSCH MUSIC LIBRARY. Books in the Hirsch Library,
with supplementary list of music. London, The Trustees of the
British Museum, 1959. 542 p. (Catalogue of printed books in the
British Museum. Accessions, 3rd ser. , Pt. 291B)

A catalog of over 11, 500 books on music, acquired by the
British Museum in 1946 as part of the Paul Hirsch library. Brief
entries printed from slips prepared for the Museum catalog.

Review by Richard S. Hill in Notes, 17 (1960) p. 225-27.

See also HIRSCH, PAUL. Katalog der Musikbibliothek ...
no. 784.

834. BRITISH MUSEUM. DEPARTMENT OF PRINTED
BOOKS. HIRSCH MUSIC LIBRARY. Music in the Hirsch Library.
London, The Trustees of the British Museum, 1951. 438 p.
(Catalogue of printed music in the British Museum. Accessions,
Pt. 53)

About 9,000 entries listed in two sections: "Music Printed
Before 1800," p. 1–112; "Music Printed Since 1800," p. 113 to
end. Brief listings from the Museum's catalog slips.

See also the "Supplementary List of Music" printed in the
catalog of Books in the Hirsch Library, above.

Review by Vincent Duckles in Notes, 10 (1952) p. 281–82.

See also HIRSCH, PAUL. Katalog der Musikbibliothek ...
no. 784.

835. BRITISH MUSEUM. KING'S MUSIC LIBRARY. Catalogue of an exhibition of music held in the King's Library,
October 1953. ⸢ London, 1953⸥ 52 p.

836. BRITISH MUSEUM. KING'S MUSIC LIBRARY. Catalogue of the King's Music Library, by William Barclay Squire and
Hilda Andrews. London, Printed by order of the Trustees, 1927–
29. 3 v.

Part I: The Handel manuscripts, by William Barclay Squire.
143 p. 5 facsimile plates. Part II: The miscellaneous manuscripts, by Hilda Andrews. 277 p. Part III: Printed music and
musical literature, by William Barclay Squire. 383 p.

837. HISTORICAL MUSIC LOAN EXHIBITION, 1885. ...
A descriptive catalogue of rare manuscripts and printed books,
chiefly liturgical ... by W. H. James Weale. London, B.
Quaritch, 1886. 191 p.

An exhibition held at Albert Hall, London, June–Oct., 1885.

Full bibliographical citations, with descriptive annotations,
for 23 liturgical manuscripts, 73 liturgical books, 46 theory
works, and some 56 items of early music, manuscripts and prints.
14 plates; bibliographical references.

838. MUSICIANS' COMPANY. An illustrated catalogue of the music loan exhibition held ... by the Worshipful Company of Musicians at Fishmongers' Hall, June and July, 1904. London, Novello, 1909. 353 p.

Includes early printed music, manuscripts, instruments, portraits, concert and theater bills, etc. Descriptive annotations; numerous plates and facsimiles.

839. PLAINSONG & MEDIAEVAL MUSIC SOCIETY. LIBRARY. Catalogue of the Society's library. Nashdom Abbey, Burnham, Bucks., 1928. 39 p.

A short title catalog; 4 facsimile plates. This collection, formerly at Nashdom Abbey, is now on deposit in the Music Library of London University.

840. ROYAL COLLEGE OF MUSIC. LIBRARY. Catalogue of the manuscripts in the Royal College of Music, by William Barclay Squire, with additions by Rupert Erlebach ... ⊏London, 1931⊐ 568, 216 leaves (typescript)

This catalog was never printed. Typewritten copies are on deposit in the major British libraries, and microfilm of the catalog can be obtained. The Royal College manuscripts are currently on deposit in the British Museum.

841. ROYAL COLLEGE OF MUSIC. LIBRARY. Catalogue of printed music in the library of the Royal College of Music, by William Barclay Squire ... London, Printed by order of the Council ..., 1909. 368 p.

This collection, rich in English music, incorporates the holdings of the Sacred Harmonic Society, below, and the library of Sir George Grove.

842. SACRED HARMONIC SOCIETY. LIBRARY. Catalogue of the library ... new edition, revised and augmented. London, Published by the Society, 1872. 399 p.

First printed in 1862. Supplement to the Catalogue, 1882.

Classified catalog in three main divisions: printed music, manuscript music, musical literature. 2,923 numbered items. General index.

843. WESTMINSTER ABBEY. LIBRARY. Musik-katalog der Bibliothek der Westminster-Abtei in London. Angefertigt von William Barclay Squire. Leipzig, Breitkopf & Härtel, 1903. 45 p. (Monatshefte für Musikgeschichte. Beilage. Jahrgang 35)

Broadly classified catalog, including both prints and manuscripts of sacred and secular music.

Loreto, Italy

844. SANTA CASA DI LORETO. L'ARCHIVIO MUSICALE. L'Archivio musicale della Cappella Laurentana. Catalogo storico-critico. ⌐By⌐ Giovanni Tebaldini. Loreto, A cura dell'Amministrazione di S. Casa, 1921. 198 p.

Printed music, 16th-18th centuries; manuscripts of the same period; an archive of manuscript scores by Maestri della Cappella, anonymous works, etc. Full descriptions. Detailed history of the chapel, index of composers.

Lucca, Italy

845. LUCCA ALL'ESPOSIZIONE DELLA MUSICA E DEL TEATRO IN VIENNA NEL 1892. Lucca, Dalla Tipografia Giusti, 1882. 50 p.

A rare exposition catalog of music from Lucca displayed at the exposition in Vienna in 1892. 37 facsimile plates. Detailed discussion of plates, and a brief introduction on the history of music in Lucca.

846. BIBLIOTECA DEL SEMINARIO. "Il fondo di musiche a stampa della Biblioteca del Seminario di Lucca." ⌐By⌐ Claudio Sartori. In Fontes artis musicae, 2 (1935) p. 134-47.

Listing, alphabetical by composer, of the early music prints in the Seminary library, including, at end of list, 5 anthologies and 3 manuscripts.

847. BONACCORSI, ALFREDO. "Catalogo con notizie biografiche delle musiche dei maestri lucchesi esistenti nelle biblioteche di Lucca. " In Collectanea historiae musicae, 2 (1957) p. 73-95.

Sources listed from 3 libraries in Lucca: Seminario Arcivescovile; Istituto Musicale "L. Boccherini"; and Biblioteca Governativa.

Lübeck, Germany

848. STADTBIBLIOTHEK. Katalog der Musik-Sammlung auf der Stadtbibliothek zu Lübeck. Verzeichnet von Carl Stiehl. Lübeck, Druck von Gebrüder Borchers ⌐1893⌐ 59 p.

849. STADTBIBLIOTHEK. Die Musikabteilung der Lübecker Stadtbibliothek in ihren älteren Beständen: Noten und Bücher aus der Zeit von 12. bis zum Anfang des 19. Jahrhunderts, verzeichnet von Wilhelm Stahl. Lübeck, 1931. 61 p.

850. STADTBIBLIOTHEK. Musik-Bücher der Lübecker Stadtbibliothek, verzeichnet von Prof. Wilhelm Stahl. Lübeck, Verlag der Lübecker Stadtbibliothek, 1927. 42 p.

Classified catalog of 19th- and 20th-century music literature.

Lüneburg, Germany

851. RATSBÜCHEREI. Katalog der Musikalien der Rats-bücherei Lüneburg, von Friedrich Welter. Lippstadt, Kistner & Siegel, 1950. 332 p.

A catalog of music prints and manuscripts, theory and practical music, to 1850. Rich holdings in 17th- and 18th-century instrumental music, particularly in the manuscript collections which are listed separately. Numerous thematic incipits given.

Luzern, Switzerland

852. THEATER- und MUSIK-LIEBHABERGESELLSCHAFT. Die Haydndrucke aus dem Archiv der "Theater- und Musik-Liebhabergesellschaft zu Luzern, " nebst Materialien zum

Musikleben in Luzern um 1800. Von Wilhelm Jerger. Freiburg
in der Schweiz, Universitätsverlag, 1959. 45 p. (Freiburger
Studien zur Musikwissenschaft, 7)

Entries for 64 early Haydn prints, with a table of concordances with the Hoboken Thematisch-bibliographisches
Werkverzeichnis.

Madrid, Spain

853. AYUNTAMIENTO. BIBLIOTECA MUSICAL
CIRCULANTE. Catálogo. Ed. ilus. Madrid, Ayuntamiento, Sec-
ción de Culture e Información, 1946. 610 p. Apendice 1. 1954.
213 p.

Music arranged in 16 classes, by instrument and form.
Class T, "Bibliografia, " contains books on music, almost ex-
clusively in Spanish. No publishers or dates given for entries.
Many light or popular works. No index.

854. BIBLIOTECA MEDINACELI. "Catalogue of the music
in the Biblioteca Medinaceli, Madrid. " By J. B. Trend. In
Revue hispanique, 71 (1927) p. 485-554.

"The Medinaceli library is notable for possessing almost the
entire corpus of Spanish (Castilian) madrigals. " 34 items fully
described, with inventories of contents and biographical sketches
of the composers. Appendix: musical settings of famous poets.

855. BIBLIOTECA NACIONAL. Catálogo músical de la
Biblioteca Nacional de Madrid, por Higinio Anglés y José Subirá.
Barcelona, Consejo Superior de Investigaciones Científicas,
Instituto Español de Musicología, 1946-51. 3 v.

Contents: t. I: Manuscritos (490 p. , 27 facsimile plates);
t. II: Impresos: Libros litúrgicos y teóricos musicales (292 p. ,
12 facsimile plates); t. III: Impresos: Música práctica (410 p. ,
13 facsimile plates).

Entries for 234 manuscripts, 285 liturgical and theoretical
prints, 337 music prints; full descriptions, with bibliographical
references, lists of contents.

856. BIBLIOTECA NACIONAL. Esposicion de música
sagrada española. Catalogo de los codices, manuscritos y libros
musicales expuestos por Jaime Moll Roqueta. Madrid, 1954.
41 p.

120 items. 12 facsimile plates.

857. LA CASA DE ALBA. La música en la Casa de Alba;
estudios históricos y biográficos, por José Subirá. Madrid
⌐ Establecimiento tipográfico "Sucesores de Rivadeneyra"⌐ 1927.
374 p.

Not a catalog, but full of bibliographical information concerning the holdings in early music and books on music in the
library of the Casa de Alba. Numerous early prints and manuscripts cited and described, with 60 plates, chiefly facsimiles of
manuscripts and early editions.

Mainz, Germany

858. GUTENBERG–MUSEUM. Tausend Jahre Mainzer
Musik; Katalog der Ausstellung, 1957. ⌐ Text: Adam Gottron⌐
Mainz, 1957. 32 p. (Kleiner Druck der Gutenberg-Gesellschaft,
63)

An illustrated catalog of 138 items of materials related to
the history of music in Mainz.

859. STADTBIBLIOTHEK. "Zur Bibliographie der Musikdrucke des XV. – XVIII. Jahrhunderts der Mainzer Stadtbibliothek, von F. W. E. Roth. " In Monatshefte für
Musikgeschichte, 21 (1889) p. 25-33.

A catalog of 45 early music prints, including both theoretical
works and practical music. Full bibliographical citations for
some items, otherwise references to citations in available
catalogs of other collections.

860. MEYER, ANDRÉ. MUSIC COLLECTION. Collection
musicale André Meyer: manuscrits, autographes, musique
imprimée et manuscrite, ouvrages théoriques, historiques et
pédagogiques, livrets, iconographie, instruments de musique.

Abbeville, F. Paillart ⌐1960⌐ 118 p. Catalog compiled by François Lesure and Nanie Bridgman. An important private collection of manuscripts and prints of early music, particularly noteworthy for its holdings in iconography. Beautifully illustrated by 292 plates.

Milan, Italy

BIBLIOTECA AMBROSIANA. See no. 791.

861. CAPPELLA DEL DUOMO. ARCHIVIO. La Cappella del Duomo di Milano. Catalogo delle musiche dell'archivio. ⌐By Claudio Sartori⌐ Milano, A cura dell Ven. Fabbrica del Duomo ⌐1957⌐ 366 p.

The archive, established in 1394, contains important 15th-century manuscript holdings, and sacred vocal works to the 19th century. Catalog organized in two main sections: manuscripts and printed music. Brief entries; contents for collections.

862. CIVICA RACCOLTA DELLE STAMPE E DEI DISEGNI. CASTELLO SFORZESCO. Ritratti di musicisti ed artisti di teatro conservati nella raccolta delle stampe e dei disegni. Catalogo descrittivo. ⌐By⌐ Paolo Arrigoni e Achille Bertarelli. ⌐Milano⌐ Tipografia del "Popolo d'Italia," 1934. 454 p.

Index, alphabetical by subject, of a portrait collection. Main alphabet includes musicians, singers, comedians, dancers; separate sections for acrobats, extemporaneous poets, child prodigies, etc. Entries give full names of subjects, descriptions of pictures, biographical information. Numerous indexes: names, places, theatrical performances, etc. 30 plates.

863. CONSERVATORIO DI MUSICA GIUSEPPE VERDI. BIBLIOTECA. Indice generale dell'Archivio Musicale Noseda; compilato dal prof. Eugenio de' Guarinoni ... con una breve biografia del fondatore e con alcuni cenni intorno all'archivio stesso ed all Biblioteca del R. Conservatorio di musica di Milano. Milano, E. Reggiani, 1897. 419 p.

First published in the Annuario of the R. Conservatorio di musica di Milano, 1889-96. 10,253 titles.

864. MUSEO TEATRALE ALLA SCALA. Catalogo del
Museo treatrale alla Scala. Edito a cura del Consiglio direttivo;
compilato da Stefano Vittadini; pref. di Renato Simoni. Milano,
E. Bestetti, 1940. 401 p.

An illustrated catalog of the musical-theatrical collection at
La Scala. Bibliography: p. 375-93.

865. PARIGI, LUIGI. La musica nelle gallerie di Milano.
Con 21 illustrazioni in tavole fuori testo. Milano, F. Perrella,
1935. 71 p.

Paintings with musical subjects in the art galleries of Milan.
Description of each work and its subject matter. 21 plates.

Modena, Italy

BIBLIOTECA ESTENSE. See no. 798.

866. BIBLIOTECA ESTENSE. "Bibliografia delle stampe
musicali della R. Biblioteca Estense. " ⊏ By⊐ Vittorio Finzi.
In Rivista delle biblioteche (1892-95): v. 3, p. 77-89, 107-14,
162-76; v. 4, 16-28, 174-85; v. 5, p. 48-64, 89-142.

Full descriptions of 321 works. Index.

867. BIBLIOTECA ESTENSE. "Repertorio dei libri musicali
di S. A. S. Francesco II d'Este nell'archivio di Stato di Modena. "
⊏ By E. J. Luin⊐ In Bibliofilia, 38 (1936) p. 419-45.

A catalog compiled in the late 17th century of the holdings of
the library of Francesco II d'Este. Much of the material has been
incorporated into the collection of the Biblioteca Estense of
Modena. Rich in late 17th-century operas, oratorios, cantatas,
etc. Includes both manuscripts and prints.

Montecassino, Italy

868. ARCHIVIO MUSICALE. "L'Archivio musicale di
Montecassino. " ⊏ By Eduardo Dagnino⊐ In Casinensia:
miscellanea di studi Cassinesi pubblicati in occasione del XIV
centenario della fondazione della Badia di Montecassino. v. 1
(1929) p. 273-96.

A summary account of the music holdings of the Montecassino archive, a collection of some 1,100 items including more than 100 full scores of 18th-century operas, oratorios, cantatas, etc. Four plates illustrating rarities from the collection.

Montserrat, Spain

869. LENAERTS, RENÉ B. "Niederländische polyphone Musik in der Bibliothek von Montserrat. " In Festschrift Joseph Schmidt Görg zum 60. Geburtstag. Bonn, Beethovenhaus, 1957. p. 196-201.

Describes 6 manuscripts containing Netherlands polyphony. (manuscript nos. 765, 766, 769, 771, 772, 778).

Moscow, Russia

870. PUBLICHNAÎA BIBLIOTEKA. OTDEL RUKOPISEĬ. Sobraniîa D. V. Razumovskogo i V. F. Odoevskogo. Arkhiv D. V. Razumovskogo. Opisaniîa pod radaktsiei I. M. Kudriâvtseva. Moskva, 1960. 261 p.

Catalog of manuscripts, 15th-19th centuries, primarily of church music in various notations. The Razumovskii collection contains 135 manuscripts, the Odoevskii, 35. Description of biographical material, papers, letters, etc., in the Razumovskii archive. Chronological index; index of names and titles.

Münster, Germany

871. KILLING, JOSEPH. Kirchenmusikalische Schätze der Bibliothek des Abbate Fortunato Santini, ein Beitrag zur Geschichte der katholischen Kirchenmusik in Italien. Düsseldorf, L. Schwann ⌐1910⌐ 516 p.

A study based on the material in the Santini collection, a library of early music scored from the original parts by Fortunato Santini (1778-1862), and acquired by the University Library at Münster about 1856.

P. 455-67: "Verzeichnis der in der Bibliothek Santini enthaltenen Druckwerke. " P. 469-516: "Verzeichnis von

Musikwerken, die in der Santinischen Bibliothek als Handschriften enthalten sind. "

872. UNIVERSITÄTSBIBLIOTHEK. Die musikalischen Schätze der Santinischen Sammlung. Führer durch die Ausstellung der Universitäts-Bibliothek ... Münster, Westfälische Vereinsdruckerei, 1929. 32 p.

Exhibition catalog prepared by K. G. Fellerer.

Munich, Germany

873. BAYERISCHE STAATSBIBLIOTHEK. Die musikalischen Handschriften der K. Hof- und Staatsbibliothek in München, beschreiben von Jul. Jos. Maier. Erster Theil: Die Handschriften bis zum Ende des XVII. Jahrhunderts. München, In Commission der Palm'schen Hofbuchhandlung, 1879. 176 p.

278 items, chiefly collections, containing about 6,380 pieces of music. One of the richest collections of 16th-century music, contained in a series of 74 choirbooks belonging to the original Bavarian court chapel. "Inhalts-Verzeichnis" of anonymous and attributed works.

874. STÄDTISCHE MUSIKBÜCHEREI. Kataloge der städtischen Musikbücherei München ... Erster Band: Klavier. Bearbeitet von Bibliotheksrat Dr. Willy Krienitz. München, 1931. 407 p.

Catalogs the keyboard music holdings of one of the major public music libraries in Germany. Some 40,000 items, classified. Includes works for piano solo, duet, and two pianos. Index of names.

875. THEATERMUSEUM. "Die vor 1801 gedruckten Libretti des Theatermuseums München. " ⌐By⌐ Richard Schaal. In Die Musikforschung, 10 (1957) p. 388-96, 487-94; 11 (1958) p. 54-69, 168-77, 321-36, 462-77; 12 (1959) p. 60-75, 161-77, 299-306, 454-61; 13 (1960) p. 38-46, 164-72, 299-306, 441-48; 14 (1961) p. 36-43, 166-83. Also published separately, Kassel, Bärenreiter, 1962.

983 librettos, listed alphabetically by title, with date and place of first performance, name of composer, etc.

Naples, Italy

876. BIBLIOTECA NAZIONALE. "Il fondo musicale cinquecentesco della Biblioteca Nazionale di Napoli. " ⌐ By ⌐ Anna Mondolfi. In <u>Collectanea historiae musicae</u>, 2 (1957) p. 277-90.

Describes 51 16th-century works.

CONSERVATORIO DI MUSICA S. PIETRO A MAJELLA. See no. 801.

877. CONSERVATORIO DI MUSICA S. PIETRO A MAJELLA. Mostra autografi musicali della scuola napoletana ... Settembre-Ottobre 1936. Napoli, Confederazione Fascista dei Professionisti e degli Artisti ⌐1936⌐ 58 p.

An exhibition catalog of musical autographs and portraits of musicians of the Neopolitan school.

878. CONSERVATORIO DI MUSICA S. PIETRO A MAJELLA. Il Museo storico musicale di S. Pietro a Majella. Napoli, R. Stabilimento Tipografico Francesco Giannini & Figli, 1930. 153 p.

A collection of musicians' portraits, busts, autographs, musical instruments, medals, and photographs. 734 items. Special archives of material related to Vincenzo Bellini and Giuseppe Martucci.

ORATORIO DEI FILIPPINI. ARCHIVIO. See no. 800.

Newcastle, England

879. PUBLIC LIBRARY. Handlist of miniature scores ⌐in the ⌐ music section. 2nd ed. ⌐ Newcastle upon Tyne ⌐ 1958. 52 p.

New Haven, Connecticut

880. YALE UNIVERSITY. SCHOOL OF MUSIC. LIBRARY.

A temporary mimeographed catalog of the music manuscripts and related materials of Charles Edward Ives ... Compiled by John Kirkpatrick in 1954-60. ⊏ New Haven, Conn. , Yale School of Music⊐ 1960. 279 p. (typescript)

New York City, New York

881. NEW YORK PUBLIC LIBRARY. MUSIC DIVISION. Catalogue of Jos. W. Drexel's musical library. Part I: Musical writings. Philadelphia, King & Baird, 1869. 48 p.

The Drexel collection became part of the Astor Library, which, with the Lennox and Tilden Libraries, became the Reference Department of the New York Public Library. The Drexel collection is housed in the Music Division. This catalog contains only 1,536 of the more than 6,000 items in the collection. Especially rich in English prints and manuscripts of the 16th, 17th, and 18th centuries.

882. NEW YORK PUBLIC LIBRARY. MUSIC DIVISION. "Musicalia in der New York Public Library, mitgeteilt von Hugo Botstiber. " In Sammelbände der Internationalen Musik-Gesellschaft, 4 (1902-03) p. 738-50.

A summary account of some of the most interesting and important items in the Drexel collection. Gives a full inventory of the "Sambrook MS, " with brief entries for other manuscripts and early printed books. Includes a listing of musicians' autographs.

Oxford, England

883. UNIVERSITY. BODLEIAN LIBRARY. ⊏ Catalog, in manuscript, of the music manuscripts in the Bodleian Library, with a list of books given to the University by Dr. Heather ⊐ 1 v. , unpaged.

An unpublished, handwritten catalog made in the early 19th century, available for examination at the Bodleian Library. Gives detailed contents for some 303 of the Music School manuscripts, dating from the early 17th century.

884. UNIVERSITY. BODLEIAN LIBRARY. Medieval polyphony in the Bodleian Library, by Dom Anselm Hughes. Oxford, Bodleian Library, 1951. 63 p.

Descriptions, inventories of contents, for 51 manuscripts and fragments in the Bodleian Library. Index of text incipits and of composers and places of origin.

Review by Manfred Bukofzer in JAMS, 5 (1952) p. 53-56.

885. UNIVERSITY. BODLEIAN LIBRARY. "Seventeenth-century Italian instrumental music in the Bodleian Library, " by Denis Stevens. In Acta M, 26 (1954) p. 67-74.

The author lists some 85 sets of parts of early Italian instrumental music in the Bodleian, by composer in alphabetical order, with the essential bibliographical information. In an article in Collectanea historiae musicae, 2 (1957) p. 401-12, he discusses 9 unica from the above collection.

886. UNIVERSITY. CHRIST CHURCH COLLEGE. LIBRARY. Catalog of music manuscripts in the library of Christ Church, Oxford, by G. E. P. Arkwright ... London, Oxford Univ. Press, 1915-23. Part I: Works of ascertained authorship. 1915. 128 p. Part II:1: Manuscript works of unknown authorship. Vocal. 1923. 182 p. A thematic catalog of anonymous vocal works. Part II:2: ⌐Manuscripts of instrumental music of unknown authorship⌐ An unpublished catalog, completed in 1935; available for examination in the Christ Church College Library.

887. UNIVERSITY. CHRIST CHURCH COLLEGE. LIBRARY. Catalog of printed music published prior to 1801, now in the Library of Christ Church, Oxford. Edited by Aloys Hiff. London, Oxford Univ. Press, 1919. 76 p.

A collection rich in Italian and English music of the 16th and 17th centuries. Alphabetical arrangement by composer, with analytics for collections.

Padua, Italy

888. BASILICA DI SANT'ANTONIO. ARCHIVIO MUSICALE.

... L'Archivio musicale della Cappella Antoniana in Padova;
illustrazione storico-critica, non cinque eliotipie. Padova,
Tipografia e Libreria Antoniana, 1895. 175 p.

At head of title: Giovanni Tebaldini.

P. 1-92: historical essay on the chapel of St. Anthony.
P. 93-149: partial catalog of manuscripts and prints. Complete
lists of works for Vallotti, Sabbatini; thematic incipits for Tartini
concertos.

Paris, France

889. BIBLIOTHÈQUE DE L'ARSENAL. Catalogue des livres
de musique (manuscrits et imprimes) de la Bibliothèque de
l'Arsenal à Paris, par L. de La Laurencie ... et A. Gastoué ...
Paris, E. Droz, 1936. 184 p. (Publications de la Société
française de musicologie, 2. sér., t. 7)

Manuscripts and printed music arranged alphabetically by
composer, or catch word of title if anonymous, under main
divisions of sacred and secular. Manuscripts from the 10th
century; printed works of the 16th-18th centuries. Exceptionally
rich in editions of little-known French composers of the 18th
century.

890. BIBLIOTHÈQUE NATIONALE. Claude Debussy. Paris,
Bibliothèque Nationale, 1962. 73 p.

An exposition catalog of 335 items celebrating the centennial
of Debussy's birth. Arranged chronologically. 8 plates.

891. BIBLIOTHÈQUE NATIONALE. Frédéric Chopin.
Exposition du centenaire. Paris ⌈ Bibliothèque Nationale ⌉ 1949.
82 p.

234 items, 8 plates; documents arranged to parallel the
chronology of the composer's life.

892. BIBLIOTHÈQUE NATIONALE. Introduction à la
paléographie musicale byzantine. Catalogue des manuscrits de
musique byzantine de la Bibliothèque Nationale de Paris et des

bibliothèques publiques de France. ⌐ Paris, Impressions artistiques L. M. Fortin, 1928⌐ 99 p. (Publications de la Sociéte' internationale de musique. Section de Paris) Compiled by Amédée Gastoué.

893. BIBLIOTHÈQUE NATIONALE. Mozart en France. Paris ⌐ Bibliothèque Nationale ⌐ 1956. 76 p.

An illustrated exhibition catalog of 234 items related to Mozart's life in France. P. 67-76: a bibliography of early French editions of Mozart.

894. BIBLIOTHÈQUE NATIONALE. La musique française du moyen âge à la révolution, catalogue rédigé par Amédée Gastoué ⌐ et al. ⌐ ⌐ Paris ⌐ Édition des Bibliothèques Nationales de France, 1934. 196 p.

Illustrated catalog of 660 manuscripts, books, and works of art from major French public and private collections displayed at the "Exposition de la musique française, " 1933, in the Galérie Mazarine of the Bibliothèque Nationale.

895. BIBLIOTHÈQUE NATIONALE. DÉPARTEMENT DES IMPRIMÉS. Catalogue du fonds de musique ancienne de la Bibliothèque Nationale. ⌐ By ⌐ Jules Ecorcheville. Paris, 1910-14. 8 v.

Manuscripts, printed music, and theoretical and literary works on music not included in the general catalog of the library, to 1750. Partially thematic. Arranged alphabetically by composer, with collections analyzed by composer. Brief bibliographical descriptions.

896. BIBLJTEKA POLSKA. Frédéric Chopin, George Sand et leurs amis. Exposition à la Bibliothèque Polonaise. Paris, 1937. 63 p.

An exhibition of 638 items related to Chopin, George Sand, and their circle. Includes manuscripts, letters, portraits. Illustrated.

897. CONSERVATOIRE NATIONAL DE MUSIQUE ET DE
DÉCLAMATION. BIBLIOTHÈQUE. ... Catalogue bibliographique
... par J. B. Weckerlin, bibliothécaire. Paris, Firmin-Didot et
Cie., 1885. 512 p.

Covers the period to about 1800. Includes only part of the
early materials in the collection. Following a prefatory history
of the library, three sections are given: early treatises, vocal
music, early instrumental music of the French school.

898. CONSERVATOIRE NATIONALE DE MUSIQUE ET DE
DÉCLAMATION. BIBLIOTHÈQUE. FONDS BLANCHETON.

... Inventaire critique du Fonds Blancheton ... Paris, E.
Droz, 1930-31. 2 v. (Publications de la Société française de
musicologie. 2. sér., 2:1-2) At head of title: Lionel de La
Laurencie.

The Blancheton collection consists of 27 volumes containing
some 300 instrumental compositions by 104 composers. It was
assembled before 1750. Important source material for the
history of the symphony. Full descriptions, critical and biographical notes on the composers.

899. OPÉRA. BIBLIOTHÈQUE, ARCHIVES ET MUSÉE.
Bibliothèque musicale du Théâtre de l'Opéra. Catalogue
historique, chronologique, anecdotique ... rédigé par Théodore
de Lajarte. Paris, Librairie des Bibliophiles, 1878. 2 v.

A descriptive list of 594 stage works arranged in order of
their first production at the Paris Opéra, 1671-1876. Classified
by periods. Each period is concluded with a biographical section
in which composers and librettists are listed alphabetically.
Composer and title index to works in the repertoire.

Parma, Italy

900. BIBLIOTECA DEL CONSERVATORIO. "Biblioteche
musicali in Italia: La Biblioteca del Conservatorio di Parma e un
fondo di edizioni dei sec. XVI e XVII non compiese nel catalogo a
stampa." ⊏ By ⊐ Riccardo Allorto. In Fontes artis musicae, 2
(1955) p. 147-51.

Describes a collection of 31 sets of 16th- and 17th-century partbooks acquired by the library in 1925.

CITTÀ DI PARMA. See no. 788.

Philadelphia, Pennsylvania

901. FREE LIBRARY. The Edwin A. Fleischer Music Collection ... Philadelphia, 1933–45. 2 v.

Supplementary List, 1945–55. (1956) 33 p.

Catalog of a loan collection of orchestral music, much of the material unpublished. Entries give full names and dates of composers, instrumentation, duration of performance, dates of composition and first performance, etc.

902. FREE LIBRARY. DRINKER LIBRARY OF CHORAL MUSIC. Catalog. ⊏ By Henry S. Drinker ⊐ Philadelphia, 1957. 116 p.

First published in 1947 by the Association of American Choruses, Princeton, New Jersey. Supplement, July 1948.

Catalog of a lending library of choral materials, made available to members of the Association of American Choruses.

Piacenza, Italy

903. L'ARCHIVIO DEL DUOMO. "L'Archivio del Duomo di Piacenza e il Liber XIII di Constanzo Antegnati. " ⊏ By ⊐ Claudio Sartori. In Fontes artis musicae, 4 (1957) p. 28–37.

Description of the collection and catalog of its early printed music. Special attention given to a unique copy of the Liber XIII, sacred and secular vocal music by C. Antegnati.

Pisa, Italy

BIBLIOTECHE E ARCHIVI ... See no. 804.

Pistoia, Italy

ARCHIVIO CAPITOLARE DELLA CATTEDRALE. See no. 793.

Plasencia, Spain

904. CATEDRAL. ARCHIVO. "El archivo de música en la Catedral de Plasencia. " ⸤By⸥ Samuel Rubio. In Anuario musical, 5 (1950) p. 147–68.

A small collection of early manuscripts and prints, fully described and contents listed.

Prague, Czechoslovakia

905. CATHEDRAL. Catalogus collectionis operum artis musicae quae in bibliotheca Capituli metropolitani pragensis asservantur. Composuit Dr. Antonius Podlaha. Prague, Sumptibus S. F. Metropolitani capituli pragensis. Typis Typographicae archiepiscopalis Pragae, 1926. 85 p.

906. KNIHOVNA. Seznam hudebnin. ⸤Část⸥ 2–4. Praha, Nákladem obce pražské, 1925–35. 3 nos. (Spisy Knihovny hlavního města Prahy, 4, 9, 19)

Část 2: Klavírní výtahy hudby scénické. Melodram. Harmonium. Libretta. Část 3: Partitury. Komorní hudba ve hlasech. Část 4: Housle.

907. NATIONAL MUSEUM. Hudební sbírka Emiliána Troldy. ⸤The music library of Emilián Trolda⸥ ⸤By⸥ Alexandr Buchner. Prague, Národní museum, 1954. 132 p.

Reggio–Emilia, Italy

CITTÀ DI REGGIO–EMILIA. See no. 789.

Rio de Janeiro, Brazil

908. BIBLIOTECA NACIONAL. "Estudio Brasilenos I. Manuscritos musicales en la Biblioteca Nacional de Rio de Janeiro. " ⸤By⸥ Francisco Curt Lange. In Rivista de estudios musicales, 1 (April 1950) p. 98–194

Chiefly 19th–century composers. A: works by European composers; B: works by Brazilian composers or Europeans active in Brazil.

909. BIBLIOTECA NACIONAL. Música no Rio de Janeiro imperial 1822-1870. ⌐Rio de Janeiro⌐ Biblioteca Nacional, 1962. 100 p.

At head of title: "Exposicão comemorativa do primeiro decênie da secão de música e arquivo sonore. "

391 numbered items, chiefly Brazilian imprints of the period.

Rome, Italy

BIBLIOTECA DELLA R. ACCADEMIA DI S. CECILIA. See no. 794.

910. COLLECTION OF THE COMTESSE DORIA-PAMPHILJ. "Die Musiksammlung der Fürsten Doria-Pamphilj in Rom. " ⌐By⌐ Andreas Holschneider. In Archiv für Musikwissenschaft, 18 (1961) p. 248-64.

Description of the collection and inventory of contents, classified under five headings: 1. collections, 16th and 17th centuries; 2. sacred music, 16th and 17th centuries; 3. oratorios (early manuscripts); 4. operas (early manuscripts); 5. German instrumental music, 18th-century.

911. VATICAN. BIBLIOTECA VATICANA. Catalogo sommario della esposizione gregoriana aperta nella Biblioteca apostolica vaticana ... 2. ed., riveduta e aumentata. Roma, Tipografia, Vaticana, 1904. 74 p.

An exposition catalog devoted to materials related to Gregorian chant.

912. VATICAN. CAPPELLA SISTINA. ARCHIVIO. Bibliographischer und thematischer Musik-katalog des Päpstlichen Kapellarchives im Vatikan zu Rom ... von Fr. X. Haberl. Leipzig, Breitkopf & Härtel, 1888. 183 p. (Monatshefte für Musikgeschichte. Beilage. Jahrgang 19 u. 20)

Descriptions of 269 items, manuscripts and prints, with a thematic catalog, by composer, of early polyphonic works. Considerable documentary information about the Cappella Sistina and the musicians employed there. The catalog itself represents only part of the collection. See no. 913, below.

913. VATICAN. CAPPELLA SISTINA. ARCHIVIO. Capellae Sixtinae Codices musicis notis instructi sivi manu scripti sive praelo excussi. Rec. J. M. Llorens. Roma, Eitta del Vaticano, Biblioteca Apostolica Vaticana, 1960. 555 p. 10 facsimile plates.

A catalog of the collection treated by F. X. Haberl, above, but more compete, since Haberl covered only 269 of the 660 manuscripts and printed volumes present. Volumes listed by number, with detailed inventory of contents. Descriptive annotations in Latin. Thematic catalog for anonymous works, p. 477-98. Index of names and terms.

Review by Dragan Plamenac in Notes, 19 (1961) p. 251-52; by Peter Peacock in Music & Letters, 42 (1961) p. 168-69.

Salt Lake City, Utah

914. UNIVERSITY OF UTAH. LIBRARY. A catalogue of books and music acquired from the library of Hugo Leichtentritt ... Edited by Carol E. Selby. Salt Lake City, Univ. of Utah, 1954. 106 p. (Bulletin of the University of Utah, 45:10)

Catalog divided in two sections: books (p. 9-46); music (p. 49-106). A scholar's working library of music books and scores; a few early editions, but chiefly 19th- and 20th-century materials.

San Marino, California

915. HENRY E. HUNTINGTON LIBRARY AND ART GALLERY. Catalogue of music printed before 1801, now in the Huntington Library. Compiled by E. M. Backus. ⌐ San Marino, Calif. ⌐ The Library, 1949. 773 p.

"Music publications and publications without music notation but of distinct interest to musicians and musicologists ... " Excluded are manuscripts, song texts, opera librettos. Includes music published in periodicals. Entry is under composer, with anonymous works under title. Index to composers and editors, chronological index, first-line index of songs. The collection is strong in 17th- and 18th-century English music.

Review by Cyrus L. Day in <u>Notes</u>, 6 (1949) p. 601-10; and by Harold Spivacke in <u>MQ</u> 35 (1949) p. 640-42.

Schwerin, Germany

916. GROSSHERZOGLICHE REGIERUNGSBIBLIOTHEK. Die musikalien Sammlung des grossherzoglich Mecklenburg-Schweriner Fürstenhauses aus den letzten zwei Jahrhunderten. Schwerin, Druck der Sandmeyerschen Hofbuchdruckerei, 1893. 2 v.

Compiled by Otto Kade.

Primarily 18th- and 19th-century manuscripts and printed music. Part I is a thematic catalog, alphabetical by composer, with a classified section under <u>Anonyma</u>. Part II: librettos. Part III: index of dedications, autographs, etc.

917. GROSSHERZOGLICHE REGIERUNGSBIBLIOTHEK. Der musikalische Nachlass der Frau Erbgrossherzogin Auguste von Mecklenburg-Schwerin ... alphabetisch-thematisch verzeichnet und ausgearbeitet von Otto Kade. Schwerin, Druck der Sandmeyerschen Hofbuchdruckerei, 1899. 142 p.

Seville, Spain

918. BIBLIOTECA COLOMBINA. "La música conservada en la Biblioteca Colombina y en la Catedral de Sevilla." ⌐ By ⌐ Higinio Anglés. In <u>Anuario musical</u>, 2 (1947) p. 3-39.

88 manuscripts and prints from the Colombina library; 9 manuscripts and 22 prints from the cathedral archive. Bibliographical references and notes on all the items.

Sorau, Germany

919. HAUPTKIRCHE. Musikalienkatalog der Hauptkirche zu Sorau N. L. Hergestellt von G. Tischer und K. Burchard. ⌐ Langensalza, H. Beyer & Söhne, 1902 ⌐ 24 p. (Monatshefte für Musikgeschichte. Beilage. Jahrgang 34)

The collection contains 33 prints, chiefly 17th-century, and a small group of manuscripts in which Telemann, Petri, and C. G. Tag are well represented.

Stanford, California

920. STANFORD UNIVERSITY LIBRARY. Catalogue of the Memorial Library of Music, Stanford University, by Nathan van Patten. Stanford, Calif., Stanford University Press, 1950. 310 p.

A collection of manuscripts, prints, inscribed copies of books and scores; the emphasis is on "association items." 1,226 numbered items.

Review by Otto Albrecht in Notes, 8 (1951) p. 706-09.

Stuttgart, Germany

921. LANDESBIBLIOTHEK. Katalog über die Musik-Codices des 16. und 17. Jahrhunderts auf der K. Landesbibliothek in Stuttgart. Angefertigt von A. Halm. Langensalza, Beyer [1902-03] 58 p. (Monatshefte für Musikgeschichte. Beilage. Jahrgang 34-35, 1902-03)

Catalogs 70 manuscripts, with listings of contents for each. Index of text incipits under individual composers.

SWEDEN

Åke Davidsson has prepared union catalogs of early printed music, and of music theory works in Swedish libraries. See nos. 510 and 511.

Tenbury Wells, England

922. ST. MICHAEL'S COLLEGE. LIBRARY. The catalog of manuscripts in the library of St. Michael's College, Tenbury, compiled by E. H. Fellowes. Paris, Éditions de l'Oiseau Lyre, 1934. 319 p.

Manuscripts in the library bequeathed to the College by Sir Frederick Ouseley. 1,386 numbered items; rich in early English music. This library also incorporates the greater part of the so-called "Toulouse-Philidor Collection, " consisting of 290 volumes of manuscripts and 67 printed books, devoted to the repertory of early 18th-century French opera. Composer index.

923. ST. MICHAEL'S COLLEGE. LIBRARY. A summary catalog of the printed books and music in the library of St. Michael's College, Tenbury. Compiled by Edmund H. Fellowes, 1934. 143 leaves (manuscript).

An unpublished catalog maintained at St. Michael's of the printed music materials in the college library. Intended as a companion volume to the manuscript catalog above, but never published.

Tokyo, Japan

924. NANKI MUSIC LIBRARY. Catalog of the Nanki Music Library. Part I: Musicology. Tokyo, 1929. 372 p.

A reference library for the historical study of music. Much of the material came from the collection of W. H. Cummings.

925. NANKI MUSIC LIBRARY. Catalogue of the W. H. Cummings collection in the Nanki Music Library. ⌐ Tokyo ⌐ 1925. 70 p.

A special collection made up of the rarities of the W. H. Cummings library, acquired in its sale in 1918. About 450 volumes, including much important early English music. 5 facsimile plates.

Toledo, Ohio

926. MUSEUM OF ART: The printed note, 500 years of music printing and engraving, January 1957. ⌐ Toledo, Museum of Art, 1957 ⌐ 144 p.

Foreword by A. Beverly Barksdale.

A splendidly illustrated catalog of 188 items, on loan from major public and private collections, related to the history of music printing and engraving. Informative annotations. Bibliography of 67 items.

Toledo, Spain

927. BIBLIOTECA CAPITOLAR. "Les manuscrits poly-
phoniques de la Biblioth̀eque Capitulaire de Tolede. " ⌐By⌐ Reneé
Lenaerts. In <u>International Society for Musical Research, Fifth
Congress Report</u>, Utrecht, 1952, p. 267-81.

Brief descriptions and discussion of the contents of approximately 30 sources of polyphonic music in the Toledo library.

Turin, Italy

BIBLIOTECA NAZIONALE. See no. 803.

928. BIBLIOTECA NAZIONALE. Manoscritti e libri a
stampa musicali espositi dalla Biblioteca Nazionale di Torino.
Firenze, Tip. L. Franceschini, 1898. 24 p.

At head of title: Esposizione nazionale, Torino, 1898. Exposition catalog of 20 manuscripts, 12 ballets in manuscript, and 36
early prints, 16th-18th centuries.

Uppsala, Sweden

929. UNIVERSITET. BIBLIOTEK. Catalogue critique et
descriptif des imprimeés de musique des XVIe et XVIIe sìecles,
conserveés à la Biblioth̀eque de l'Université Royale d'Upsala; par
Rafael Mitjana, avec une introduction bibliographique par Isak
Collijn ... Upsala, Impr. Almqvist & Wiksell, 1911-51. 3 v.

Vol. 1: Musique religieuse, I, par Rafael Mitjana (1911).
Vol. 2: Musique religieuse, II, musique profane; musique dramatique; musique instrumentale; additions au Tome I, par Åke
Davidsson (1951). Vol. 3: Recueils de musique religieuse et
profane, par Åke Davidsson (1951).

Entries in Vols. 1 and 2 are arranged alphabetically within
each category; Vol. 3 is arranged chronologically, with an index
of the contents of the collections under composer. Index of
printers and publishers, and a bibliography of works cited. Full
bibliographical entries, with locations of copies of the works in
other libraries.

See also no. 511.

Valladolid, Spain

930. CATEDRAL. ARCHIVO MUSICAL. "El Archivo Musical de la Catedral de Valladolid. " ⌐ By ⌐ Higinio Anglés. In Anuario musical, 3 (1948) p. 59-108.

20 manuscripts and 97 early prints. Inventories given for the contents of the manuscripts. Full bibliographical citations for prints, with references to Eitner and other bibliographies.

Venice, Italy

931. BIBLIOTECA NAZIONALE MARCIANA. I codici musicali Contariniani del secolo XVII nella R. biblioteca di San Marco in Venezia, illustrati dal Dr. Taddeo Wiel. Venezia, F. Ongania, 1888. 121 p.

The Contarini collection is a specialized library of manuscript scores of 17th-century Venetian opera, by such composers as Cavalli, Cesti, Pallavicino, Ziani. 120 numbered items. Entries give information as to date of first performance, librettist, cast, general description of the work. Composer index.

BIBLIOTECA QUERINI STAMPALIA. See no. 795.

932. VENTURI, ANTONIO. BIBLIOTECA. "La collection Antonio Venture, Montecatini-Terme (Pistoia) Italie. " ⌐ By ⌐ Ramond Meylan. In Fontes artis musicae, 5 (1958) p. 31-44.

A private collection of late 18th-century and instrumental music.

Vercelli, Italy

933. ARCHIVIO DELLA CATTEDRALE. "Il fondo musicale dell' archivio della Cattedrale di Vercelli. " ⌐ By ⌐ Claudio Sartori. In Fontes artis musicae, 5 (1958) p. 24-31.

Verona, Italy

934. BIBLIOTECA CAPITOLARE. Il patrimonio musicale della Biblioteca Capitolare di Verona dal sec. XV al XIX. ⌐ By ⌐ Giuseppe Turrini. Verona, "La Tipografica Veronese, " 1952.

83 p. (Estratto dagli Atti dell'Accademia di Agricoltura, Scienze
e Lettere di Verona, ser. IV, v. 2)

Cites 57 manuscripts, 108 early prints, 21 theoretical works,
and 13 instruments of the 16th and 17th centuries. Composite
indexes of the contents of the manuscripts. A chapter on the
origin of the collections, with reference to some early inventories.

BIBLIOTECA DELLA SOC. ACCADEMICA FILARMONICA.
See no. 805.

Vicenza, Italy

ARCHIVIO DELLA CATTEDRALE. See no. 796.

BIBLIOTECA BERTOLIANA. See no. 796.

Vienna, Austria

935. BEETHOVEN-ZENTENARAUSSTELLUNG. Führer
durch die Beethoven-Zentenarausstellung der Stadt Wien.
"Beethoven und die wiener Kultur seiner Zeit." Wien,
Selbstverlag der Gemeinde Wien, 1927. 248 p.

An exhibition catalog of 1,070 items, including letters, documents, pictures, musical instruments, scores, and prints related
to Beethoven and his circle.

936. GESELLSCHAFT DER MUSIKFREUNDE. Geschichte
der K. K. Gesellschaft der Musikfreunde in Wien ... In einem
Zusatzbande: Die Sammlungen und Statuten, von Dr. Eusebius
Mandyczewski. Wien ⌐Adolf Holzhausen⌐ 1912. 2 v.

Vol. 1 is a history of the Gesellschaft, in two sections: 1812-
70 and 1870-1912. Vol. 2, "Zusatz-Band," is not a true catalog
but a summary listing of the holdings of the archive, library, and
museum. Of particular value is the listing of "Bücher und
Schriften über Musik. Druckwerke und Handschriften aus der
Zeit bis zum Jahre 1800" (p. 55-84). Also, "Musik-Autographe"
(p. 85-123).

937. INTERNATIONALE AUSSTELLUNG FÜR MUSIK- UND

THEATERWESEN. Fach-Katalog der Musikhistorischen Abtheilung von Deutschland und Oesterreich-Ungarn ... Wien, 1892. 591 p.

Catalog for a large and varied music exhibition held in Vienna in 1892. Includes prints, manuscripts, instruments, portraits, letters, and other documents, arranged roughly in chronological order from ancient times to the end of the 19th century.

938. KÜNSTLERHAUS. Katalog der Ausstellung anlässlich der Centenarfier Domenico Cimarosa's. Wien, Verlag des Comite's, 1901. 163 p.

Exhibition catalog of 524 items related to Cimarosa and his contemporaries; includes scores, portraits, medals, etc.

939. KUNSTHISTORISCHE MUSEUM. ESTENSISCHE SAMMLUNG. Die Estensischen Musikalien; thematisches Verzeichnis mit Einleitung ⌈by Robert Haas⌉ Regensburg, G. Bosse, 1927. 232 p.

Reissued, 1957, as Bd. VII of Forschungsbeiträge zur Musikwissenschaft. Regensburg, G. Bosse.

Catalog, largely thematic, of an important collection of 18th-century instrumental music originating in northern Italy. Includes a small group of cantatas and other vocal works. Classified within major sections of prints and manuscripts. Index of names, text incipits.

940. MINORITENKONVENT. Das Musikarchiv im Minoritenkonvent zu Wien (Katalog des älteren Bestandes vor 1784). ⌈By⌉ Friedrich Wilhelm Riedel. Kassel ⌈Bärenreiter, for the International Association of Music Libraries and the International Musicological Society⌉ 1963. 139 p. (Catalogus musicus, 1).

Catalog, broadly classified, of manuscripts and prints, chiefly of the 17th and 18th centuries. Strong in early keyboard music. Indexes of composers, copyists, and former owners of the sources.

941. NATIONALBIBLIOTHEK. "Die Musikbibliothek von

Raimund Fugger d. J. ; ein Beitrag zur Musiküberlieferung des 16. Jahrhunderts. " ⌐ By Richard Schaal ⌐ In <u>Acta M</u>, 29 (1957) p. 126-37.

Includes the catalog of the library copied from the original 16th-century manuscript in the Staatsbibliothek, Munich. The bulk of the Fugger family music collection is now in the Vienna National Library.

942. NATIONALBIBLIOTHEK. Tabulae codicum manu scriptorum praeter Graecos et Orientales in Bibliotheca Palatina Vindobonensi Asservatorum ... v. IX-X: Codicum musicorum, Pars I-II. Vindobonae, venum dat. C. Geroldi filius, 1897-99. 2 v. in 1.

Catalog of the manuscripts numbered 15,501 to 19,500, comprising the music holdings of the Vienna National Library. Introduction and descriptive annotations in Latin. Each volume has an index of names, and of subjects and text incipits.

Washington, District of Columbia

943. U.S. LIBRARY OF CONGRESS. MUSIC DIVISION. Catalog of early books on music (before 1800) by Julia Gregory ... Washington, D.C., Govt. Printing Office, 1913. 312 p.

Supplement (Books acquired by the Library, 1913-42) by Hazel Bartlett ... with a list of books on music in Chinese and Japanese. (1944) 143 p.

This catalog, and supplement, provide access to the Library of Congress' rich holdings in the field of early music theory. The citations conform to the Library's printed catalog cards.

944. U.S. LIBRARY OF CONGRESS. MUSIC DIVISION. Catalog of first editions of Edward MacDowell (1861-1908) by O. G. Sonneck. Washington, D.C., Govt. Printing Office, 1917. 89 p.

Includes works with and without opus numbers, compositions written under pseudonyms, and works edited by the composer. Indexes of class, titles, first lines of text, authors and translators, publishers.

945. U.S. LIBRARY OF CONGRESS. MUSIC DIVISION.
Catalog of first editions of Stephen C. Foster (1826–1864) by Walter
R. Whittlesey and O. G. Sonneck. Washington, D.C., Govt.
Printing Office, 1915. 79 p.

Works arranged by title; indexed by authors of text, publishers,
first lines. Detailed annotations.

946. U.S. LIBRARY OF CONGRESS. MUSIC DIVISION.
Catalogue of opera librettos printed before 1800, prepared by O.
G. T. Sonneck. Washington, D.C., Govt. Printing Office, 1914.
2 v.

The Library's collection of librettos began in 1909 with the
purchase of the Schatz collection. By 1914 it contained some
17,000 items and was particularly strong in first editions of 17th-
and 18th-century works. Vol. 1 is a title listing, with notes
giving date of first performance, place, name of composer if
known. Vol. 2 is an index by composer and by librettist, and of
titles of specific arias mentioned.

947. U.S. LIBRARY OF CONGRESS. MUSIC DIVISION.
Dramatic music. Catalog of full scores, compiled by O. G. T.
Sonneck. Washington, D.C., Govt. Printing Office, 1908. 170 p.

Full scores of operas in original editions, manuscript copies,
and some photo copies. Arranged alphabetically by composer.

948. U.S. LIBRARY OF CONGRESS. MUSIC DIVISION.
Orchestral music ... catalog. Scores. Prepared under the
direction of O. G. T. Sonneck. Washington, D.C., Govt. Printing
Office, 1912. 663 p.

Orchestral scores from about 1830 to date of publication.
Main entries under composer, with a class index and title index.

949. U.S. LIBRARY OF CONGRESS. MUSIC DIVISION.
ELIZABETH SPRAGUE COOLIDGE FOUNDATION. Coolidge
Foundation program for contemporary chamber music; preliminary
checklist of works available for loan (November 1961). Compiled

by Frances C. Gewehr. Washington, D.C., Library of Congress
⌐ 1961 ⌐ 38 p. (typescript)

<u>Supplement</u>, April 1963. 19 p. (typescript)

A classified list of contemporary chamber music scores and
parts which may be borrowed by qualified ensembles for study
purposes. Entries give publisher and price; recordings, if
available, are also cited.

U.S. LIBRARY OF CONGRESS. MUSIC DIVISION. DAYTON
C. MILLER FLUTE COLLECTION. See nos. 459 and 997.

950. WASHINGTON CATHEDRAL. LIBRARY. "The Douglas
collection in the Washington Cathedral Library." In <u>The Life and
Work of Charles Winfred Douglas</u>, by Leonard Ellinwood and Anne
Woodward Douglas. New York, Hymn Society of America, 1958.
p. 36-72. (Hymn Society of America. Papers, no. 23)

A library of hymnology and liturgical music formed by one of
the leading authorities on Episcopal church music.

Wolfenbüttel, Germany

951. HERZOG-AUGUST-BIBLIOTHEK. Die Handschriften
nebst den älteren Druckwerken der Musikabteilung ... Beschreiben
von Emil Vogel ... Wolfenbüttel, J. Zwissler, 1890. 280 p. (Die
Handschriften der Herzoglichen Bibliothek zu Wolfenbüttel ...
8 Abth.)

989 entries, manuscripts and printed works, arranged alphabetically by composer, with anonymous works grouped under
general headings. Covers the period to about 1800.

952. WOLFFHEIM, WERNER JOACHIM. LIBRARY.
Versteigerung der Musikbibliothek des Herrn Dr. Werner
Wolffheim ... durch die Firmen: M. Breslauer & L.
Liepmanssohn ... Berlin, 1928-29. 4 v. in 2.

"One of the finest collections ever brought together by a
private person ... the 2 volume catalog compiled at the time of
its sale will always rank as an indispensable work of reference"

(Grove's). Classified catalog of a library that included not only numerous rarities, but the standard reference works and editions as well. Full descriptions, with copious notes. Each volume has a "Tafel-band" of facsimile plates.

Zurich, Switzerland

953. ALLGEMEINE MUSIKGESELLSCHAFT. Katalog der gedruckten und handschriftlichen Musikalien des 17. bis 19. Jahrhunderts im Besitze der Allgemeinen Musikgesellschaft Zürich. Red. von Georg Walter. Zürich, Hug, 1960. 145 p.

A collection rich in 17th- and 18th-century instrumental music. Thematic incipits for works in manuscript.

Review by Donald Krummel in Notes, 19 (1961) p. 77.

Zwickau, Germany

954. RATSSCHULBIBLIOTHEK. Bibliographie der Musikwerke in der Ratsschulbibliothek zu Zwickau, bearb. ... von Reinhard Vollhardt. Leipzig, Breitkopf & Härtel, 1893-96. 299 p. (Monatshefte für Musikgeschichte. Beilage. Jahrgang 25-28, 1893-96)

764 numbered items, manuscripts and prints, including liturgical works, theoretical works, instrumental and vocal music. Chiefly 16th- and 17th-century materials.

CATALOGS OF MUSICAL INSTRUMENT COLLECTIONS

Collections of musical instruments are frequently annexed to music libraries. The reader will note that a number of the catalogs in the preceding section are concerned, in part, with holdings of Western or Oriental instruments. In the section which follows are listed the catalogs of some of the major specialized collections of musical instruments, along with a number of exhibition catalogs emphasizing this area of collecting activity. For a comprehensive and historical view of the field, see Alfred Berner's article "Instrumentensammlungen," in MGG 6, col. 1295-1310. There is also an illuminating paper by Georg Kinsky, "Musikinstrumentensammlungen in Vergangenheit und Gegenwart," in Jahrbuch Peters, 27 (1920) pp. 47-60. The article in Grove's, 5th edition, by Langwell (Vol. 4, pp. 509-15), provides the locations of the collections but no bibliographical information.

Ann Arbor, Michigan

955. UNIVERSITY OF MICHIGAN. STEARNS COLLECTION OF MUSICAL INSTRUMENTS. Catalog of the Stearns collection of musical instruments, by Albert A. Stanley. 2nd ed. Ann Arbor, Mich., University of Michigan, 1921. 276 p.

First published in 1918.

A catalog of 1,464 items, Western and Oriental. 13 plates, descriptive annotations. Bibliography and indexes of makers, geographical distribution, names of instruments.

Basel, Switzerland

956. HISTORISCHEN MUSEUM. Katalog der Musikinstrumente im Historischen Museum zu Basel. Von Dr. Karl Nef. Basel, Universitäts-Buchdruckerei von Friedrich Reinhardt, 1906. 74 p.

Bound with Festschrift zum zweiten Kongress der

Internationalen Musikgesellschaft, Basel, 1906. 294 instruments listed and described. 12 plates.

Berlin, Germany

957. INSTITUT FÜR MUSIKFORSCHUNG. Die Berliner Musikinstrumenten-Sammlung; Einführung mit historischen und technischen Erläuterungen von Alfred Berner. Berlin, 1952. 58 p. 11 plates.

Not strictly a catalog, but a guide to the principal types of instruments with reference to specific examples in the Berlin collection.

958. STAATLICHE AKADEMISCHE HOCHSCHULE FÜR MUSIK. Führer durch die Sammlung alter Musik-Instrumente, von Dr. Oskar Fleischer. Berlin, A. Haack, 1892. 145 p.

Classified catalog, chiefly early Western instruments, with a few Oriental instruments.

959. STAATLICHE AKADEMISCHE HOCHSCHULE FÜR MUSIK. Sammlung alter Musikinstrumente bei der Staatlichen Hochschule für Musik zu Berlin; beschreibender Katalog von Curt Sachs. Berlin, J. Bard, 1922. 384 cols. 30 plates.

Collection contains some 3,200 items, of which about 250 are non-European. Classified catalog. Entries give description of instrument, maker, date and place of manufacture. Index of instruments, places, makers, etc.

Boston, Massachusetts

960. MUSEUM OF FINE ARTS. LESLIE LINDSEY MASON COLLECTION. Ancient European musical instruments ... By N. Bessaraboff ... Pub. for the Museum ... by the Harvard Univ. Press, 1941. 503 p.

An authoritative catalog, well illustrated, 314 items. Provides a wealth of background material for the historical study of instruments. Bibliography, p. 453-69. Indexes of names and subjects. 16 plates and 72 illustrations in text. The collection of Canon Francis W. Galpin forms the basis of the Mason collection.

Braunschweig, Germany

961. STÄDTISCHEN MUSEUM. Verzeichnis der Sammlung alter Musikinstrumente im Städtischen Museum Braunschweig ... Instrumente, Instrumentenmacher und Instrumentisten in Braunschweig ... Braunschweig, E. Appelhans, 1928. 124 p. (Werkstücke aus Museum, Archiv und Bibliothek der Stadt Braunschweig, 3)

At head of title: Hans Schröder.

The catalog occupies p. 5-34; lists 113 items, all European. The remainder of the volume is devoted to studies of local instrument makers and performers.

Brussels, Belgium

962. CONSERVATOIRE ROYAL DE MUSIQUE. MUSÉE INSTRUMENTAL. Catalogue déscriptif et analytique du Musée ... par Victor-Charles Mahillon, conservateur ... 2nd ed. Gand, A. Hoste, 1893-1922. 5 v.

One of the great instrument collections of the world. More than 3,000 instruments of all cultures. Classified catalog. The description includes a precise indication of each instrument's pitch, tuning, and range.

Cairo, Egypt

963. MUSEUM OF EGYPTIAN ANTIQUITIES. Catalogue général des antiquités égyptiennes du Musée du Caire. Nos. 69201-69852: Instruments de musique, par Hans Hickmann. Le Caire, Imprimerie de l'Institut français d'archéologie orientale, 1949. 216 p. 116 plates.

Classified catalog of 651 ancient Egyptian instruments, or fragments thereof, with detailed descriptions and photo reproductions.

Cincinnati, Ohio

964. ART MUSEUM. Musical instruments. [Collection of the Cincinnati Art Museum] Cincinnati, 1949.

An illustrated brochure listing 110 instruments, 60 European, 50 non-European.

Copenhagen, Denmark

965. CARL CLAUDIUS COLLECTION. Carl Claudius' Samling af gamle musikinstrumenter. København, Levin & Munksgaards Forlag, 1931. 423 p.

A rich private collection of musical instruments, now administered by the University of Copenhagen. The catalog describes 757 items.

966. MUSIKHISTORISK MUSEUM. Das Musikhistorische Museum zu Kopenhagen: beschreibender Katalog von Angul Hammerich; deutsch von Erna Bobé. Mit 179 illustrationen. Kopenhagen, G. E. C. Gad; Leipzig, Kommissionsverlag von Breitkopf & Härtel, 1911. 172 p.

Danish edition appeared in 1909.

Classified catalog of 631 items, 582 of which are instruments, Western and Oriental, followed by a short listing of liturgical manuscripts and prints, and miscellany.

Eisenach, Germany

967. BACHHAUS. Verzeichnis der Sammlung alter Musik-instrumente im Bachhaus zu Eisenach. Hrsg. von der Neuen Bachgesellschaft zu Leipzig. Dritte, vermehrte Ausgabe. Leipzig, Breitkopf & Härtel, 1939. 64 p.

First published in 1913.

Classified catalog of 233 items. Illustrated with line drawings.

Florence, Italy

968. R. ISTITUTO LUIGI CHERUBINI. Gli strumenti musicali raccolti nel Museo del R. Istituto L. Cherubini a Firenze. ⊏By⊐ Leto Bargagna. Firenze, G. Ceccherini ⊏1911⊐ 70 p.

A catalog of 146 items, with 12 plates.

The Hague, Holland

969. GEMEENTEMUSEUM. Exotische en oude Europese muziekinstrumenten, in de muziekafdeling van het Haagse Gemeentemuseum; 25 afbeeldingen toegelicht. ⌐ By⌐ A. W. Ligtvoet. 's-Gravenhage, Nijgh & Van Ditmar ⌐1955⌐ 51 p.

A general introduction to the collection. Text in Dutch and English. 25 plates.

970. HEYER, WILHELM. Musikhistorisches Museum von Wilhelm Heyer in Cöln. Katalog von Georg Kinsky. Leipzig, Breitkopf & Härtel, 1910-16. 3 v.

The first two volumes of this catalog are concerned with the instrument collection. Vol. 1: Besaitete Tasteninstrumente. Orgeln und orgelartige Instrumente. Friktionsinstrumente. Vol. 2: Zupf- und Streichinstrumente. Vol. 3 (not published) intended to cover the wind instruments. The Heyer instrument collection was transferred to Leipzig in 1926, where it was destroyed in World War II.

Kinsky's catalog is a mine of information for the student of early instruments, copiously illustrated, rich in detail.

See also no. 783.

971. HEYER, WILHELM. Kleiner Katalog der Sammlung alter Musikinstrumente, verfasst von Georg Kinsky. Cöln, 1913. 250 p.

An abridgement of the material in the preceding catalog; valuable because it contains entries for the wind instruments in the Heyer collection, planned but not published as Vol. 3 of the above.

Holyoke, Massachusetts

972. MOUNT HOLYOKE COLLEGE. The Belle Skinner collection of old musical instruments ... A descriptive catalogue compiled under the direction of William Skinner. ⌐ Philadelphia,

New York, etc. Printed by the Beck Engraving Co.] 1933. 210 p.

Illustrated catalog of 89 instruments, including particularly fine examples of keyboard instruments. Colored plates.

Since 1959 this collection has been on loan to Yale University.

973. LACHMANN, ERICH. Erich Lachmann collection of historical stringed musical instruments. Los Angeles, Allan Hancock Foundation, Univ. of Southern Calif., 1950. 53 p.

A handsome catalog of 42 items; noteworthy for its photographic illustrations by Irvin Kershner.

Leipzig, Germany

974. UNIVERSITÄT. MUSIKWISSENSCHAFTLICHES INSTRUMENTEN-MUSEUM. Führer durch das Musikwissenschaftliche Instrumenten-Museum der Universität Leipzig. Hrsg. von Helmut Schultz. Leipzig, Breitkopf & Härtel, 1929. 85 p. 19 plates.

A classified catalog arranged according to the ground plan of the display.

975. KARL-MARX-UNIVERSITÄT. Führer durch des Musikinstrumentenmuseum der Karl-Marx-Universität Leipzig. Von Paul Rubardt. Leipzig, Breitkopf & Härtel, 1955. 84 p. 16 plates.

London, England

976. FENTON HOUSE. BENTON FLETCHER COLLECTION. Catalog of the Benton Fletcher collection of early keyboard instruments at Fenton House, Hampstead. London, Country Life, Ltd., for The National Trust, 1957. 26 p.

A descriptive brochure by Raymond Russell for a collection of early keyboard instruments maintained in playing condition in a late 17th-century house in Hampstead, London.

977. GALPIN SOCIETY. British musical instruments. August 7 - 30, 1951. [London, The Galpin Society, 1951] 35 p.

A classified exhibition catalog of instruments, chiefly of British make or use. Includes 151 woodwind, 61 brass, 27 keyboard, 62 of the violin family, 16 of the viol family, and 16 miscellaneous. Brief descriptions, with short introductions for each class of instruments.

978. HORNIMAN MUSEUM. The Adam Carse collection of old musical wind instruments ⊏ now in the Horniman Museum, London ⊐ London, Staples Press for the London County Council ⊏1951 ⊐88 p.

A collection of 320 items, briefly described, with historical notes for each instrument family. Illustrated by drawings.

979. ROYAL COLLEGE OF MUSIC. Catalog of historical musical instruments, paintings, sculpture and drawings. ⊏London, Royal College, 1952 ⊐16 p.

Foreword by George Dyson.

Contains the Donaldson collection of musical instruments. Brief inventory with minimum description.

980. ROYAL MILITARY EXHIBITION, 1890. A descriptive catalog of the musical instruments recently exhibited at the Royal Military Exhibition, London, 1890. Compiled by Charles Russell Day. London, Eyre & Spottiswoode, 1891. 253 p.

An exhibition confined to wind and percussion instruments. 457 wind instruments (percussion not inventoried). Plates.

981. SOUTH KENSINGTON MUSEUM. A descriptive catalog of the musical instruments in the South Kensington Museum ... By Carl Engel ... London, Printed by G. E. Eyre and W. Spottiswoode for H. M. Stationery Off., 1874. 402 p.

Preceded by an essay on the history of musical instruments.

LONDON. See also no. 838.

Lucerne, Switzerland

982. RICHARD WAGNER MUSEUM. Katalog der städtischen Sammlung alter Musikinstrumente in Richard-Wagner-Museum,

Tribschen, Luzern. Erstellt im Auftrag der Museums-Kommission von René Vannes, Brüssel. Luzern, Otto Dreyer, 1956. 40 p.

A catalog of 95 stringed instruments, 46 wind instruments, 11 idiophones, 37 exotic instruments. 16 plates.

Luton, England

983. MUSEUM AND ART GALLERY. The Ridley collection of musical wind instruments in the Luton Museum. The Corp. of Luton, Museum and Art Gallery, 1957. 32 p. 65 wind instruments. Historical note, p. 1-21. 8 plates.

Milan, Italy

984. CIVICO MUSEO DI ANTICHI STRUMENTI MUSICALI. Catalogo, descrittivo, a cura di Natale Gallini. Milan, Comune di Milano ⊏ 1958 ⊐ 128 p.

Classified catalog of 358 items, chiefly Western but with a few Oriental instruments. 77 plates.

985. CIVICO MUSEO DI ANTICHI STRUMENTI MUSICALI. Mostra di antichi strumenti musicali della Collezione N. Gallini (Maggio, 1953). Milano, Villa Comunale (Ex Reale) ⊏ 1953 ⊐ 43 p. 32 plates.

Preface signed by Natale Gallini.

An exhibition catalog of 200 items dating from the time when the Gallini collection was in private hands. It has since become the property of the city of Milan, and its complete catalog appears as no. 984, above.

986. CONSERVATORIO DI MUSICA GIUSEPPE VERDI. Gli strumenti musicali nel Museo del Conservatorio di Milano. Ed. E. Guarinoni. Milan, Hoepli, 1908.

A collection of 278 instruments, 177 European and 91 non-European. Classified arrangement; index of donors and of instruments.

Munich, Germany

987. BAYERISCHE NATIONALMUSEUM. Ausstellung alte Musik, Instrumente, Noten und Dokumente aus drei Jahrhunderten. Veranstaltet dur die Stadt München im Bayerischen Nationalmuseum, November-Dezember, 1951. Katalog. München, Musikverlag Max Hieber, 1951. 71 p. 23 plates.

An exhibition devoted to music in general cultural history. 636 items, of which the majority are early instruments.

New Haven, Connecticut

988. YALE UNIVERSITY. ART GALLERY. Musical instruments at Yale, a selection of Western instruments from the 15th to 20th centuries. Catalog by Sibyl Marcuse ... ⌐New Haven, Conn.⌐ Yale University Art Gallery ⌐1960⌐ 32 p.

An exhibition, Feb. 19-March 27, 1960, of 26 instruments, as well as paintings, drawings, prints, and manuscripts. Illustrated.

989. YALE UNIVERSITY. MORRIS STEINERT COLLECTION. The Morris Steinert collection of keyed and stringed instruments. New York, Tretbar ⌐1893⌐

New York City, New York

990. METROPOLITAN MUSEUM OF ART. CROSBY BROWN COLLECTION. Catalog of the Crosby Brown collection of musical instruments of all nations ... New York, Metropolitan Museum of Art, 1903-07. 3 v. in 4 (Hand-book no. 13)

Contents: 1. Europe (1904); 2. Asia (1903); 3. Instruments of savage tribes and semi-civilized people. Pt. 1. Africa (1907) Pt. 2. Oceanica (1907); 4. Historical groups (1905).

991. METROPOLITAN MUSEUM OF ART. ... Catalog of keyboard instruments. New York, Metropolitan Museum of Art, 1903. 313 p.

Paris, France

992. CONSERVATOIRE NATIONAL ... Le Musée du

Conservatoire national de musique. Catalogue descriptif et raisonné, par Gustave Chouquet. Nouvelle ed. Paris, Firmin-Didot, 1884. 276 p.

First published in 1875. Supplements by León Pillaut, in 1894, 1899, 1903.

A catalog of 1,006 instruments, subdivided into European and non-European sections. Index of instruments and of names.

Salzburg, Austria

993. MUSEUM CAROLINO AUGUSTEUM. Alte Musik-Instrumente in Museum Carolino Augusteum Salzburg. Führer und beschreibendes Verzeichnis, von Karl Geiringer. Leipzig, Breitkopf & Härtel, 1932. 46 p.

A catalog of 288 instruments, with an index of makers and 4 photographic plates showing 48 different instruments.

Vienna, Austria

994. KUNSTHISTORISCHE MUSEUM. Alte Musikinstrumente; die Sammlung des Kunsthistorischen Museums in der neuen Burg zu Wien. ⊏ By⊐ Victor Luithlen. Wien, H. Bauer ⊏ 1954 ⊐ 28 p.

995. MUSEUM FÜR VÖLKERKUNDE. Aussereuropäische Musikinstrumente. Wien, Museum für Völkerkunde ⊏ 1961 ⊐ 89 p.

Foreword by Alfred Janata.

Illustrated, classified catalog of 654 non-European instruments.

Washington, District of Columbia

996. U.S. LIBRARY OF CONGRESS. GERTRUDE CLARKE WHITTALL FOUNDATION. The Stradivari memorial at Washington, the national capital, by William Dana Orcutt. Library of Congress, Gertrude Clarke Whittall Foundation ⊏ 1938 ⊐ 49 p.

Description of the matched set of Stradivarius instruments donated to the Library of Congress.

997. U.S. LIBRARY OF CONGRESS. MUSIC DIVISION. The Dayton C. Miller flute collection, a checklist of the instruments. Compiled by Laura E. Gilliam and William Lichtenwanger. Washington, D.C., Library of Congress, 1961. 113 p.

Lists 1,593 instruments of the flute type. Indexes by maker, type of instrument, trade name, system, etc. Eight plates.

See also no. 459, for the Dayton C. Miller Catalog of Books ... Relating to the Flute.

998. U.S. NATIONAL MUSEUM. Handbook of the collection of musical instruments in the United States National Museum. By Frances Densmore. Washington, D.C., Govt. Printing Off., 1927. 164 p. 49 plates (Smithsonian Institution. United States National Museum. Bull. 136)

HISTORIES AND BIBLIOGRAPHIES OF MUSIC
PRINTING AND PUBLISHING

Included here are bibliographies of the output of some of the major
early music printers and publishers, such as Petrucci, Playford,
Walsh, Ballard, etc.; studies of music publishing in particular
regions or countries (England, Italy, Paris, Vienna); and a few
works concerned with the technical processes of music printing or
engraving. The most comprehensive bibliography on the history
of music printing has been compiled by Åke Davidsson: see no.
1005 below.

999. BERGMANS, PAUL. "La typographie musicale en
Belgique au XVIe siècle." In Histoire du livre et de l'imprimerie
en Belgique des origines à nos jours, 5 (Bruxelles, 1929) p.
47-75.

Illustrated account of 16th-century Belgian music printing.

1000. BOBILLIER, MARIE. "La librairie musicale en
France de 1653 à 1790, d'après les Registres de privilèges."
⌐ Par Michel Brenet, pseud. ⌐ In Sammelbände der Inter-
nationalen Musikgesellschaft, v. 8 (1906-07) p. 401-66.

An examination and transcription of the archives in the
Bibliothèque Nationale pertaining to licenses granted for the
publication of music and books on music in Paris from 1653 to
1790. Supplemented by Cucuel (no. 1004 below).

1001. CASTELAIN, RAOUL. Histoire de l'édition musicale;
ou, du droit d'éditer au droit d'auteur, 1501-1793. Préf. de
André Siegfried. Paris, H. Lemoine, 1957. 92 p.

Brief history of music publishing, with emphasis on legal
aspects.

1002. COHEN, PAUL. Musikdruck und Drucker zu Nürnberg

im 16. Jahrhundert, mit einem Verzeichnis der in Nürnberg im 16. Jahrhundert erschienenen Noten und Musikbücher ... Nürnberg, H. Zierfuss, 1927. 63 p.

Also issued as a dissertation (Erlangen) under the title Die Nürnberger Musikdrucker im sechzehnten Jahrhundert, 1927. Historical study, with brief accounts of the individual printers, followed by a chronological listing of 443 works published in Nürnberg from 1501 to 1600.

1003. DAVIDSSON, ÅKE. Danskt Musiktryck intill 1700-Talets mitt. Dänischer Musikdruck bis zur Mitte des 18. Jahrhunderts. Uppsala, Almqvist & Wiksells, 1962. 100 p. (Studia musicologica upsaliensia, 7)

A historical study of early Danish music printing, with a chronological listing of Danish prints issued during the period under consideration. Bibliography and index of names.

1004. CUCUEL, GEORGES. "Quelques documents sur la librairie musicale au XVIIIe siècle." In Sammelbände der Internationalen Musikgesellschaft, v. 13 (1911-12) p. 385-92.

Supplements the article by Bobillier (no. 1000 above).

1005. DAVIDSSON, ÅKE. "Die Literatur zur Geschichte des Notendruckes." In his Musikbibliographische Beiträge. Uppsala, A. B. Lundequistska Bokhandeln, 1954. p. 91-115. (Uppsala Universitets Arsskrift, 1954:9)

A survey of the writings on the history of music printing, with a bibliography of 268 items on the subject.

Review by Edward N. Waters in Notes, 12 (1955) p. 604; by Vincent Duckles in The Library Quarterly, 26 (1956) p. 73-74.

1006. DAVIDSSON, ÅKE. Studier rörande svenskt musiktryck före år 1750. Studien über schwedischen Musikdruck vor 1750. Uppsala ⌐Almqvist & Wiksells ⌐ 1957. 167 p. (Studia musicologica upsaliensia, 5)

Part I (Allmän del) is a general survey of early Swedish music printing; Part II (Speciell del) is a bibliography of 124 Swedish imprints issued between 1585 and 1750, in chronological order. Text in Swedish; summary in German. General bibliography, and index of persons.

Review by Rudolph Gjelsness in Notes, 15 (1958) p. 569-70.

1007. DAY, CYRUS L. and E. B. MURRIE. English songbooks, 1651-1702; a bibliography with a first-line index of songs. London, Bibliographical Society, 1940 ⌐ for 1937⌐ 439 p.

Lists and describes the contents of 252 secular song books published in England and Scotland. Arrangement is chronological, non-extant works included. First-line index of 4,150 songs by about 250 composers. Also indexed by composer, author, performer, tunes and airs, source, collection title, printer, publisher and book-seller. A model of descriptive bibliography, particularly valuable for its coverage of the publishing activity of John and Henry Playford and their contemporaries.

1008. DEUTSCH, OTTO E. Musikverlags Nummern. Eine Auswahl von 40 datierten Listen. Zweite, verbesserte und erste deutsche Ausgabe. Berlin, Merseburger, 1961. 32 p.

Revision and expansion of a list originally published in the Journal of Documentation, 1 (1946), under the title "Music Publishers' Numbers, A Selection of 40 Dated Lists, 1710-1900." Treats 20 German, 14 Austrian, 3 Dutch, 1 English, 1 French, and 1 Swiss firm. Index of places and individual publishers. Supplemented by "Musikverlags-Nummern, ein Nachtrag," by O. E. Deutsch, in Die Musikforschung, 15 (1962) p. 155." Review by Donald W. Krummel in Notes, 19 (1961) p. 76-77.

Music publishers' numbers are useful in establishing dates for undated music publications. For other contributions to this field, see nos. 1017, 1032, 1050.

1009. DONÀ, MARIANGELA. La stampa musicale a Milano fino all'anno 1700. Firenze, Olschki, 1961. 167 p. (Biblioteca di bibliografia italiana, 39)

Milanese music publishers given in alphabetical order, with chronological listing of their publications. Copies located in major European libraries. Index of composers and works; index of persons to whom works are dedicated.

1010. EITNER, ROBERT. Buch- und Musikalienhändler, Buch- und Musikaliendrucker nebst Notenstecher, nur die Musik betreffend, nach den Originaldrucken verzeichnet von R. Eitner. Leipzig, Breitkopf & Härtel, 1904. 248 p. (Monatshefte für Musikgeschichte. Beilage)

Compiled as a by-product to his Quellen-Lexikon; limited to material before 1850. Alphabetical listing of publishers, printers, and dealers, their dates of location at various addresses, changes in name, branches if any. International coverage.

1011. FISHER, WILLIAM A. 150 years of music publishing in the U. S.; an historical sketch with special reference to the pioneer publisher, Oliver Ditson Co., 1783-1933. Boston, Oliver Ditson ⌐ 1934 ⌐ 146 p.

A revision and extension of portions of the author's Notes on Music in Old Boston (Boston, 1918).

1012. GAMBLE, WILLIAM. Music engraving and printing; historical and technical treatise ... London, New York, Pitman, 1923 ⌐ 1922 ⌐ 266 p.

Discusses the technical processes of music printing and engraving, with emphasis on contemporary practice. Illustrated.

1013. GERICKE, HANNELORE. Der Wiener Musikalien-handel von 1700 bis 1778. Graz, H. Böhlaus Nachf., 1960. 150 p. (Wiener musikwissenschaftliche Beiträge, 5)

Contents: Wiener Buchhändler als Verkäufer von Musikalien; Privatverkäufer; Kopisten; Kupferstecher; Verzeichnis der Wiener Musikdrucke von 1700-1778; Liste der verbotenen Musikbücher; Zusammenfassung; Literaturverzeichnis.

Review by Donald W. Krummel in <u>Notes</u>, 18 (1961) p. 229-30.

1014. GOOVAERTS, ALPHONSE J. M. A. Histoire et bibliographie de la typographie musicale dans les Pays-Bas. Anvers, P. Kockx, 1880. 608 p. (Extrait des Mémoires de l'Académie Royale de Belgique, Collection in-8º, tome XXIX)

Part I (historical): a chronological discussion of music publishing in the Netherlands from 1539. Part II (bibliographical): chronological list of 1,415 music publications from 1539 to 1841. Full descriptions. Index of personal names, titles, and places.

1015. GRAND-CARTERET, JOHN. Les titres illustrés et l'image au service de la musique. Turin, Bocca frères, 1904. 269 p.

<u>Première partie</u> (p. 3-120): Le titre de musique sous la Révolution, le Consulat et le premier Empire (1500-1800). <u>Deuxième partie:</u> Le titre de musique et la lithographie, 1. 1817-1830, 2. 1830-1850

Abundantly illustrated with facsimiles of title pages, printers' devices, etc.

1016. HEARTZ, DANIEL. "La chronologie des recueils imprimés par Pierre Attaingnant." In <u>Revue de musicologie</u>, 44 (1959) p. 178-92

Brief survey of Attaingnant's activity as a music printer, followed by a chronological tabulation of all collections published by him from 1528 to 1537.

1017. HILL, RICHARD S. "The plate numbers of C. F. Peters' predecessors." In <u>Papers ... of the American Musicological Society</u> ... Dec. 29 and 30, 1938. ⌐c. 1940⌐ p. 113-34

A history of the publishing activities of F. A. Hofmeister and A. Kühnel, 1784-1814, with a detailed analysis of their production in 1801-02, plate numbers 1-102.

1018. HOPKINSON, CECIL. A dictionary of Parisian music publishers, 1700-1950. London, Printed for the author, 1954. 131 p.

Describes some 550 publishers, tabulating their forms of name and addresses where they were active during specific periods. A useful tool in determining dates of undated publications.

Review by Inger M. Christensen in Notes, 11 (1954) p. 550-51; by Vincent Duckles in JAMS, 8 (1955) p. 62-64.

See no. 1020 for another approach to the same material.

1019. HUMPHRIES, CHARLES and WILLIAM C. SMITH. Music publishing in the British Isles from the earliest times to the middle of the 19th century; a dictionary of engravers, printers, publishers and music sellers, with a historical introduction. London, Cassell and Co. ⌐1954⌐ 355 p.

Covers more than 2,000 persons and firm names associated with British music publishing. Introductory essay of 42 pages, an excellent survey of the field. 25 plates. Indexes of firms outside of London, and of makers and repairers of musical instruments.

Supersedes Kidson (no. 1021 below).

Review by J. M. Coopersmith in Notes, 11 (1954) p. 549-50.

1020. JOHANSSON, CARI. French music publishers' catalogues of the second half of the eighteenth century. Uppsala, Almqvist & Wiksell, 1955. 2 v.

Vol. 1: Textband. 228 p. (octavo)

Vol. 2: Tafeln. 145 facsimiles of catalogs by French music publishers (folio)

Vol. 1 is an analysis and description of the contents of the catalogs, their use for dating purposes. Index of names, of titles, and of catalogs chronologically under name of firm.

Review by Donald W. Krummel in Notes, 17 (1960) p. 234-35; by A. Hyatt King in Music & Letters, 37 (1956) p. 376-77; by Wolfgang Schmieder in Die Musikforschung, 10 (1957) p. 180-82.

1021. KIDSON, FRANK. British music publishers, printers

and engravers ... From Queen Elizabeth's reign to George IV, with select bibliographical lists of musical works printed and published within that period. London, W. E. Hill & Sons, 1900. 231 p.

The pioneer work in this area; not as comprehensive as Humphries and Smith (no. 1019), but many of the entries are fuller and accompanied by lists of publications. Arranged alphabetically by place. No index.

1022. KING, A. HYATT. "English pictorial music title-pages, 1820-1885, their style, evolution and importance." In The Library, ser. 5, 4 (1949/50) p. 262-72

1023. KINKELDEY, OTTO. "Music and music printing in incunabula." In Bibliographical Soc. of America Papers, v. 26 (1932) p. 89-118

For discussions of music incunabula see also nos. 1033, 1035, 1060.

1024. KINSKY, GEORG. "Beethoven-Erstdrucke bis zum Jahre 1800." In Philobiblon, 3 (1930) p. 329-36

1025. KINSKY, GEORG. "Erstlingsdrucke der deutschen Tonmeister der Klassik und Romantik." In Philobiblon, 7 (1934) p. 347-64

Also printed separately. Wien, H. Reichner, 1934.

1026. KINSKY, GEORG. Die Originalausgaben der Werke Johann Sebastian Bachs; ein Beitrag zur Musikbibliographie. Wien, H. Reichner ⌈1937⌉ 134 p.

This, and the two preceding items, are contributions by one of the leading specialists in 18th- and 19th-century music bibliography.

1027. KRUMMEL, DONALD W. "Graphic analysis, its application to early American engraved music." In Notes, 16 (1959) p. 213-33. 7 plates.

Discussion of the history of early American music publishing in terms of the printing processes used, with special reference to the work of Blake and Willig.

1028. LENZ, HANS U. Der Berliner Musikdruck von seinen Anfängen bis zur Mitte des 18. Jahrhunderts ... Kassel, Bärenreiter, 1933. 116 p

Also issued as a dissertation, Rostock, 1932. Discussion of Berlin music printers, their output, their techniques. P. 27-35: chronological listing of 126 prints.

1029. LESURE, F. et G. THIBAULT. Bibliographie des éditions d'Adrian le Roy et Robert Ballard (1551-1598). Paris, Société française de musicologie, Heugel et Cie., 1955. 304 p. 9 facsimile plates (Publications de la Société française de musicologie. 2. sér., t. 9)

An exemplary bibliography of 319 musical editions by the Le Roy-Ballard press, cited chronologically with full bibliographical descriptions, lists of contents, and locations in public and private collections. Brief historical introduction, and an anthology of the most important prefaces, dedications, and other documents. First-line index of texts, index of titles and of personal names.

Review by Kenneth Levy in JAMS, 8 (1955) p. 221-23; and by Vincent Duckles in Notes, 15 (1957) p. 102-03.

1030. LESURE, F. et G. THIBAULT. "Bibliographie des éditions musicales publiées par Nicolas Du Chemin (1549-1576)." In Annales musicologiques, 1 (1953) p. 269-373

Bibliography similar in scope and format to the preceding work. Covers 100 editions published by Du Chemin, with full descriptions, listings of contents, and locations of copies. Numerous facsimiles of title pages. First-line index of Latin and French texts, and of titles and names.

1031. LITTLETON, ALFRED H. A catalog of one hundred works illustrating the history of music printing from the 15th to the end of the 17th century, in the library of Alfred Henry Littleton ... London, Novello, 1911. 38 p. 12 facsimiles

Includes both musical and theoretical works, grouped by nationality, with annotations directing attention to their interest as examples of music printing.

1032. MEYER, KATHI and INGER M. CHRISTENSEN. "Artaria plate numbers." In Notes, 15 (1942) p. 1-22.

1033. MEYER-BAER, KATHI. Liturgical music incunabula, a descriptive catalog. London, The Bibliographical Society, 1962. 63 p.

257 entries, arranged alphabetically by title, which treat some 800 items. Reference made to the standard bibliographies of incunabula, and to locations of copies in major libraries. 12 facsimile plates illustrating types of notation. Chronological index, and index of printers and places.

See also the author's preliminary study, "Liturgical music incunabula in the British Museum," in The Library, 4th ser., 20 (1939) p. 272-94

Review, anon., in The Times Literary Supplement, Nov. 16, 1962, p. 880.

1034. MEYER, KATHI and E. J. O'MEARA. "The printing of music, 1473-1934." In The Dolphin, 2 (1935) p. 171-207

A well-illustrated survey of the history of music printing. Includes a bibliography of works on the subject.

1035. MOLITOR, P. RAPHAEL. Deutsche Choral-Wiegendrucke, ein Beitrag zur Geschichte des Chorals und des Notendruckes in Deutschland. Regensburg, Pustet, 1904. 77 p. 26 facsimiles

A study of German liturgical music incunabula. Consideration of notation forms, and a survey of the work of some 33 printers.

1036. MOLITOR, P. RAPHAEL. "Italienische Choralnoten-drucke." In his Die Nach-Tridentinische Choral-Reform zu Rom. v. 1, p. 94-119. Leipzig, 1901.

A general discussion of Italian printers of liturgical books of the late 15th and 16th centuries.

1037. NOVELLO (Firm, Music Publishers, London). A century and a half in Soho; a short history of the firm of Novello, publishers and printers of music, 1811-1961. London, Novello ⌐ 1961 ⌐ 85 p.

A popular history of the music publishing house which exercised a wide influence on public taste through the printing of inexpensive editions of the classics.

Review by Donald W. Krummel in Notes, 19 (1961) p. 60-61.

1038. OLDMAN, CECIL B. Collecting musical first editions. London, Constable, 1938. ⌐ 29 p. ⌐ (Aspects of book collecting)

Reprinted from New Paths in Book Collecting, ed. by John Carter, London, 1934, p. 95-124

An informal and inviting discussion of the pleasures of music collecting. Bibliography, p. 120-24.

1039. PATTERSON, BRUCE. "Notes on early music printing." In The Library, ser. 4, 19:4 (1939) p. 389-421

1040. REDWAY, VIRGINIA L. Music directory of early New York City; a file of musicians, music publishers and musical instrument makers listed in N. Y. directories from 1786 through 1835, together with the most important New York music publishers from 1836 through 1875 ... New York, The New York Public Library, 1941. 102 p

Three main sections: musicians and teachers; publishers, printers, lithographers, and dealers, with names and addresses as they appeared in successive years; instrument makers and dealers. Appendices include chronological list of firms and individuals, 1786-1811, and a list of musical societies, 1789-99.

1041. RICORDI (Firm, Music Publishers, Milan). Casa Ricordi, 1808-1958; profile storico a cura di Claudio Sartori ... Milano, G. Ricordi, 1958. 116 p. 48 plates

16 of the plates are facsimile pages of composers' autographs; the remainder are chiefly reproductions, in color, of cover designs for noteworthy Ricordi music publications.

Review by Donald W. Krummel in Notes, 17 (1960) p. 400-01.

1042. ROBERT, HENRI. Traité de gravure de musique sur planches d'étain et des divers procédés de simili gravure de musique ... précédé de l'historique du signe, de l'impression et de la gravure de musique. 2nd ed. Paris, Chez l'auteur, 1926. 151 p.

First published in 1902.

Sketchy historical survey of music writing, printing, and engraving, followed by a description of the technical processes involved in preparing engraved plates.

1043. SARTORI, CLAUDIO. Bibliografia delle opere musicali stampate da Ottaviano Petrucci. Firenze, L. S. Olschki, 1948. 217 p. (Biblioteca di bibliografia italiana, 18)

Chronological bibliography of Petrucci's work, with full descriptions, contents of each publication. Index of titles, lists of libraries and their holdings of Petrucci prints. Bibliography.

1044. SARTORI, CLAUDIO. Dizionario degli editori musicali italiani (tipografi, incisori, librai-editori). Firenze, L. S. Olschki, 1958. 215 p. (Biblioteca di bibliografia italiana, 32)

Italian music printers, editors, and publishers from the 16th century to the present. Some bibliographical references given. 8 plates of early title pages. The principal issues of the publishers noted, but complete catalogs not given.

Index of names, but no chronology.

Review by Dragan Plamenac in Notes, 16 (1959) p. 242-43; by

Gerhard Croll in Die Musikforschung, 12 (1959) p. 255-56.

1045. SCHMID, ANTON. Ottaviano dei Petrucci da
Fossombrone, erste Erfinder des Musiknotendruckes mit
beweglichen Metalltypen, und seine Nachfolger im sechzehnten
Jahrhunderte ... Wien, P. Rohrmann, 1845. 342 p.

Schmid's work on Petrucci has long since been superseded,
but the discussion of his successors in Italy, Germany, France,
and the Netherlands (p. 111 to end) is still valuable.

1046. SMITH, WILLIAM C. A bibliography of the musical
works published by John Walsh during the years 1695-1720.
London, The Bibliographical Society, 1948. 215 p. 38 plates

622 Walsh publications cited for the period under consideration, with numerous descriptive annotations. Index of titles
and works, and general index.

Review by J. Coopersmith in Notes, 7 (1949) p. 104-06; by
A. Hyatt King in Music & Letters, 30 (1949) p. 273-76.

1047. STEELE, ROBERT. The earliest English music
printing; a description and bibliography of English printed music
to the close of the 16th century. London, Printed for the
Bibliographical Society, 1903. 102 p. (Illus. monographs issued
by the Bibliographical Soc., 11)

Brief introduction covers methods of printing and early
English printers of music. The bibliography, 197 items arranged
chronologically from 1495 to 1600, gives full title and collation,
library location, and notes on typography. Bibliography of 34
items on music printing.

1048. STELLFELD, J. A. Bibliographie des éditions
musicales plantiniennes. ⌐ Bruxelles, Palais des Académies,
1949 ⌐ 248 p. (Acad. royale de Belgique. Classe des beaux-arts.
Memoires, T. 5, fasc. 3)

Brief historical account of the Plantin press, with detailed
bibliographical description and discussion of the 21 music items

printed by the press at Antwerp and Leiden. 21 plates.

TOLEDO (OHIO). MUSEUM OF ART. The printed note ...
See no. 926.

1049. VOL'MAN, B. Russkie pechatnye noty XVIII veka.
Leningrad, Gosudarstvennoe muzykal'noe izdatel'stvo, 1957.
293 p.

Russian printed music of the 18th century.

1050. WEINMANN, ALEXANDER. BEITRÄGE ZUR
GESCHICHTE DES ALT-WIENER MUSIKVERLAGES, 1948-

A series of studies related to Viennese music publishing of
the late 18th and early 19th centuries. They appear under varied
imprints and in two sub-series: Reihe 1, Komponisten; Reihe 2,
Verleger. They are listed below in series order.

1051. Reihe 1, Folge 1: Verzeichnis der im Druck
erschienenen Werke von Joseph Lanner, sowie Listen der
Plattennummern der Originalausgaben für alle Besetzungen
... Wien, Leuen ⌐1948 ⌐ 31 p.

Tables listing the work of Lanner (1801-43) in opus number
order, with plate numbers of the first editions. Alphabetical index of the works by title.

1052. Reihe 2, Folge 1: Verzeichnis der Verlagswerke des
Musikalischen Magazins in Wien, 1784-1802. "Leopold
Kozeluch." Ein bibliographischer Behelf. Wien,
Österreichischer Bundesverlag ⌐1950⌐ 31 p.

Works without plate numbers, and with questionable plate
numbers, in chronological order; works with plate numbers
in numerical order, followed by an alphabetical list, by
composer, of Kozeluch's catalog, 1800.

1053. Reihe 2, Folge 2: Vollständiges Verlagsverzeichnis
Artaria & Comp. Wien, Ludwig Krenn ⌐1952⌐ 179 p.

A history of the Artaria firm, with a classified list, chronological within classifications, of its publications, giving in
most cases exact dates of publication. Index by composers.

Review by Richard S. Hill in Notes, 10 (1953) p. 449-50.

1054. Reihe 2, Folge 3: "Vollständiges Verlagsverzeichnis
des Musikalien des Kunst- und Industrie Comptoirs in Wien,
1801-1819." In Studien zur Musikwissenschaft; Beihefte
der DTOe, 22 (1955) p. 217-52

Contains a listing of 802 plate numbers in numerical order,
with composer, title, and date of publication of the corre-
sponding works. Composer index.

Review by William Klenz in Notes, 14 (1956) p. 117.

1055. Reihe 2, Folge 4: "Verzeichnis der Musikalien des
Verlages Johann Traeg in Wien, 1794-1818." In Studien
zur Musikwissenschaft; Beihefte der DTOe, 23 (1956)
p. 135-83

Lists all works published by the firm in chronological order.

1056. Reihe 2, Folge 5: Wiener Musikverleger und
Musikalienhändler von Mozarts Zeit bis gegen 1860; ein
firmengeschichtlicher und topographischer Behelf. Wien,
Rohrer, 1956. 72 p. (Oesterreichische Akademie der
Wissenschaft ... Veröff. der Kommission für
Musikforschung, 2)

Lists and discusses 38 music dealers and publishers, and 19
related general book dealers and publishers. Tables
showing early and existing addresses of the firms. Useful
in dating Viennese musical imprints.

Review by Richard S. Hill in Notes, 15 (1958) p. 396-97.

1057. Reihe 2, Folge 6: Verzeichnis der Musikalien aus dem
K. K. Hoftheater-Musik-Verlag. Wien, Universal [1961]
130 p. (Wiener Urtext Ausgabe)

Brief history of the firm, and biographical notes on the men associated with it. Listing of publications from 1796 to c. 1820, with plate numbers and dates of issue if known.

Review by Donald W. Krummel in <u>Notes</u>, 19 (1961) p. 76

1058. Reihe 2, Folge 7: Kataloge Anton Huberty (Wien) und Christoph Torricella. ⊏ Wien ⊐ Universal Edition, 1962. 135 p.

Brief historical discussions of the firms, followed by detailed listings of their publications, giving composer, title, date of publication if known, location of copies in European libraries.

1059. Reihe 2, Folge 8: Verlagsverzeichnis F. A. Hofmeister (Wien). (Not published as of February, 1964.)

1060. WOLF, JOHANNES. "Verzeichnis der musik-theoretischen Inkunabeln mit Fundorten." In Caza, Francesco, <u>Tractato vulgare de canto figurato</u> ... (Veröffentlichungen der Musik-bibliothek Paul Hirsch, no. 1) Berlin, M. Breslauer, 1922. p. 64-92

Lists 104 incunabula in the field of music theory, with locations where copies are preserved.

1061. ZUR WESTEN, WALTER VON. Musiktitel aus vier Jahrhunderten; Festschrift anlässlich der 57 jährigen Bestehens der Firma C. G. Röder. Leipzig ... ⊏ 1921 ⊐ 116 p. 96 facsimile illustrations

A study of musical title pages from the Renaissance to the end of the 19th century.

DISCOGRAPHIES

Within the last few decades the field of recorded sound has given rise to an abundance of documentation of interest to librarians, teachers, research scholars, and private collectors. It is an area which has a particular attraction for the collector whether his interests lie in the direction of early vocal discs or cylinders, or in jazz recordings. There has been a proliferation of record reviews, listeners' guides, manufacturers' catalogs and numerical lists, and journals devoted almost exclusively to discography. Some indication of the scope and variety of the bibliographical coverage is suggested by "A Bibliography of Discographies," by Carl L. Bruun and John Gray, in Recorded Sound, Journal of the British Institute of Recorded Sound (Summer 1962) pp. 206-13. A field of this kind requires its own "guide to reference materials." No effort has been made here to list more than a few representative examples of the major types of reference works available to the specialist in recorded sound.

In the following organization, "Encyclopedias of Recorded Music" have been distinguished from "Collectors' Guides." The distinction is perhaps an arbitrary one, but it is intended to separate the few all-inclusive discographies from those directed toward collectors of classical music, jazz, or early discs.

Encyclopedias of Recorded Music

1062. CLOUGH, FRANCIS F. and G. J. CUMING. The World's encyclopedia of recorded music. London, Sidgwick & Jackson, 1952. 890 p.

Second Supplement ⌐1951-52⌐ London, 1952. 262 p.

Third Supplement ⌐1953-55⌐ London, 1957. 564 p.

The First Supplement (April 1950 to May-June 1951) bound with main volume.

The World's Encyclopedia is the indispensable reference tool for record collectors. Arrangement is alphabetical by composer, with a sub-classification of works under prolific composers. Full information given as to contents and labels. Special section for anthologies.

Review by Philip L. Miller in Notes, 10 (1952) p. 94-95; and of the Third Supplement by Richard S. Hill in Notes, 14 (1957) p. 357-59.

1063. GRAMOPHONE SHOP, INC., NEW YORK. The Gramophone Shop encyclopedia of recorded music. New York, The Gramophone Shop, Inc., 1936. 574 p.

Compiled by R. D. Darrell. 2nd ed., New York, Simon & Schuster, 1942. George C. Leslie, Supervising editor. 558 p. 3rd ed., rev. and enl., New York, Crown, 1948. Robert H. Reid, Supervising editor. 639 p.

The prototype for encyclopedias of recorded music in its organization and coverage. Works arranged alphabetically under composer and partially classified. Brief biographical accounts of composers given. All three volumes must be consulted, since the later editions are not fully cumulative. Coverage restricted to 78 rpm discs.

1064. JOHNSON, WILLIAM W. The gramophone book, a complete guide for all lovers of recorded music. London, Hinrichsen ⌐1954⌐ 169 p.

A compendium of miscellaneous information useful to record collectors. British emphasis. Lacks an index.

1065. MYERS, KURTZ and RICHARD S. HILL. Record ratings, the Music Library Association's index of record reviews. New York, Crown Publishers, 1956. 440 p.

"Record Ratings is essentially a guidebook pointing the way to a tremendous body of critical writing about recordings" (preface). Two main sections: (1) composer and subject list; (2) composite releases. By means of a system of symbols the user is given a summary of critical opinion concerning the discs. Full description of each recording, including composer, title, label, number, and price. Contents listed for composite recordings. The editors have taken great pains to clarify and verify information about the discs and their contents. A major reference work in the field of discography. See also the current listing which appears in each issue of Notes under the title "Index of Record Reviews" (no. 1101).

Collectors' Guides to Classical Music

Books of this kind, of which there are an increasing number, can be described as compilations of brief record reviews in which observations on the technical quality of the recordings are combined with comments on the work recorded and on its performance. The listings below are confined to the more comprehensive English-language works in this category. Specialized guides of this kind are available in abundance. See, for example, the useful set of paperback editions published by J. B. Lippincott in the series of Keystone Books in Music: Cornelius G. Burke, The Collector's Haydn ⌐1959⌐ 316 pp.; John Briggs, The Collector's Tchaikowsky and the Five ⌐1959⌐ ; Harold C. Schonberg, The Collector's Chopin and Schumann ⌐1959⌐ 256 pp., etc.

1066. THE GUIDE TO LONG PLAYING RECORDS. New York, Knopf, 1955. 3 v.

Vol. 1: Irving Kolodin. Orchestral Music. 268 p.

Vol. 2: Philip L. Miller. Vocal Music. 381 p.

Vol. 3: Harold C. Schonberg. Chamber and Solo Instrument Music. 280 p.

1067. HALL, DAVID. The record book, a music lover's guide to the world of the phonograph. New York, Smith & Durrell, 1940. 771 p.

Supplement. 1941. (continuing pagination, 777-886)

Second Supplement. 1943. (continuing pagination, 887-1013)

Complete Edition. New York, Citadel Press, 1946. 1063 p. (incorporating the two preceding supplements)

1068. HALL, DAVID. The record book. International
edition. New York, Durrell, 1948. 1394 p.

1069. HALL, DAVID. Records: 1950 edition. New York,
Knopf, 1950. 524 p. Hall's books are addressed to the private
collector with an interest in serious music. In the earlier
editions the material is classified by medium. Beginning with the
"International Edition," the arrangement is alphabetical by composer. Much general information for the record collector included. The 1950 edition is the first to direct attention to
long-playing discs.

1070. KOLODIN, IRVING. A guide to recorded music.
Garden City, N.Y., Doubleday, 1941. 495 p.

1071. KOLODIN, IRVING. New guide to recorded music.
Rev. ed. Garden City, N.Y., Doubleday, 1947. 512 p.

1072. KOLODIN, IRVING. International edition. Garden
City, N.Y., Doubleday, 1950. 524 p.

Kolodin has adhered to an alphabetical arrangement by
composer, with classification by form and medium under
composer. Index of performers and performing groups.

1073. SACKVILLE-WEST, EDWARD and D. SHAWE-
TAYLOR. The record guide. London, Collins, 1951. 763 p.

1074. SACKVILLE-WEST, EDWARD and D. SHAWE-
TAYLOR. The record guide ... with Andrew Porter and
William Mann. Rev. ed. London, Collins [1955] 957 p.

Supplement [1956] 191 p.

1075. SACKVILLE-WEST, EDWARD and D. SHAWE-
TAYLOR. The record year, a guide to the year's gramophone
records, including a complete guide to long playing records.
Assisted by Andrew Porter. London, Collins [1952] 383 p.

The Sackville-West guides are designed for British record

collectors. The commentary is literate and well informed. The discs are arranged by composer, with special sections devoted to collections, and a performer index.

1076. THE STEREO RECORD GUIDE. By Edward Greenfield, Ivan March, and Denis Stevens. London, The Long Playing Record Library Ltd., 1960-61. 2 v.

The main arrangement for each volume is by composer, followed by special sections devoted to concerts, recitals, light music, etc. Vol. 1 contains "a selection of 50 outstanding records for 1958/59"; Vol. 2, "a selection of 100 outstanding recordings of 1960/61." A third volume has been projected.

Collectors' Guides to Early Recordings

The collecting of early discs and cylinder recordings of the period from 1898 to 1925 has long been the province of private collectors. The emphasis is usually placed on the performer, particularly the vocalist, rather than on the composer. More recently the importance of this field has been recognized by libraries and research institutions throughout the world: The New York Public Library, the U.S. Library of Congress, the British Institute of Recorded Sound, the Stanford University Archive of Recorded Sound, etc.

1077. BAUER, ROBERT. The new catalogue of historical records, 1898-1908/09. London, Sidgwick and Jackson [1947] 494 p.

Recordings listed under performer, grouped under label and year of pressing. Serial numbers given. Brief entries for composer and title of work.

1078. BENNETT, JOHN R. Voices of the past, a catalogue of vocal recordings from the English catalogues of The Gramophone Company 1898-1899, The Gramophone Company Limited 1899-1900, The Gramophone & Typewriter Company Limited 1901-1907 and The Gramophone Company Limited 1907-1925 [v. 1, pt. 1][Lingfield, Surrey, The Oakwood Press, 1955?-] 48 p. Projected as the beginning of a series intended to cover the complete catalog of H. M. V. vocal recordings of 1898-1925.

1079. DEAKINS, DUANE D. Cylinder records; a description of the numbering systems, physical appearance, and other aspects of cylinder records made by the major American companies, with brief remarks about the earliest American companies and the foreign record manufacturers ⌐2nd ed.⌐ Stockton, Calif. ⌐1958⌐ 35 p.

1080. HURST, P. G. The golden age recorded, a collector's survey. London, Sidgwick and Jackson ⌐1946⌐ 175 p.

A manual for private collectors. General discussions of record collecting, followed by biographical notices of the major artists classified by voice. Appendix, p. 133-75, "a catalog of records of whose historical value there will be no dispute."

1081. MOSES, JULIAN M. Collectors' guide to American recordings, 1895-1925; foreword by Giuseppe de Luca. New York, American Record Collectors' Exchange ⌐1949⌐ 199 p.

Discs arranged under performers by serial or matrix number. P. 172-95: numerical guide, Columbia and other makes. Index of operas, and instrumental index.

1082. MOSES, JULIAN M. Price guide to collectors' records. New York, American Record Collectors' Exchange ⌐1952⌐ 31 p.

Discs identified by matrix number under performer, with estimates of value. Designed to accompany the preceding work.

Collectors' Guides to Jazz Recordings

The jazz collector lives in a world of his own and is well equipped with reference tools designed to meet his needs. The impetus toward documentation has come from European rather than American enthusiasts: see Delaunay and Panassié below. Most of the periodicals devoted to popular music include jazz record reviews and print occasional discographies of jazz musicians. See particularly The Record Changer, 1942-57.

1083. DELAUNAY, CHARLES. New hot discography, the standard dictionary of recorded jazz. Edited by Walter E. Schaap & George Avakian. New York, Criterion, 1948. 608 p.

First published in France in 1936.

Separates the "pioneers of jazz" from "post-1930 jazz." Subdivided by region. An elaborate classification system groups recordings by major jazz personalities. Complete index of names.

1084. HARRIS, REX and BRIAN RUST. Recorded jazz. ⌐Harmondsworth, Middlesex ⌐ Penguin Books, 1958. 256 p. (Pelican Books A417)

"It must not be regarded as a comprehensive discography, but nevertheless the authors have presented a reasonable cross-section of real jazz, together with biographical notes of performers and a critical assessment of the records listed" (preface).

1085. LANGE, HORST H. Die deutsche Jazz-Discographie. Eine Geschichte des Jazz auf Schallplatten von 1902 bis 1955. Berlin, Bote & Bock, 1955. 652 p.

One of several recent European compilations of jazz records. Includes a number of English and Continental performers.

1086. McCARTHY, ALBERT J. Jazz discography 1; an international discography of recorded jazz, including blues, gospel, and rhythm-and-blues for the year January-December 1958. London, Cassell, 1960. 271 p.

The first volume of a projected yearbook to cover all jazz recordings issued throughout the world. New releases are listed alphabetically by country. Full contents of each disc listed, with personnel, place, and date of recording if known.

1087. PANASSIÉ, HUGUES. Discographie critique des

meilleurs disques de jazz. Paris, Robert Laffont ⌐1958⌐ 621 p.

An earlier edition, Paris, Corrêa, 1951. 371 p.

The author is a prolific writer on jazz and one of the first important discographers in the field. Arrangement is by performer, with an analytical index by medium and an index of names.

1088. RUST, BRIAN. Jazz records A-Z, 1897-1931. 2nd ed. ⌐Hatch End, Middlesex, Published by the author, 1961⌐ 736 p.

Index ⌐with additions and corrections to the discography⌐ 1963. 62 p.

Performers and ensembles listed alphabetically, with their recordings identified by matrix numbers and titles. Introduction and preliminary listing of record labels. Index of names.

1089. SMITH, CHARLES E. The jazz record book ... with Frederic Ramsey, Jr., Charles Payne Rogers and William Russell. New York, Smith & Durrell, 1942. 515 p.

P. 1-125: a survey of the history of jazz in its various regional styles; p. 130-508: record listings by major performers and ensembles, with critical and descriptive commentary. Selected bibliography of jazz; index of bands.

Ethnic and Folk Music

The use of recorded materials is basic to the techniques of modern ethnomusicology. Here the scholar is concerned less with commercially recorded discs and tapes than he is with recordings made in the field by research institutions and by individual collectors. The problem of bringing these materials under "bibliographic control" is a difficult one. A good start has been made, with the cooperation of UNESCO, in two series under the general title Archives of Recorded Music. Series B is concerned with Oriental music; Series C, with ethnographical and folk music. (Series A, not under consideration here, is devoted to Occidental music and has produced a general discography of the works of Frederic Chopin.)

1090. ARCHIVES OF RECORDED MUSIC (ARCHIVES DE LA MUSIQUE ENREGISTRÉE). SERIES B: ORIENTAL MUSIC. A catalogue of recorded classical and traditional Indian music. General discography and introduction by Alain Danielou. Paris, UNESCO ⌐1952⌐ 236 p.

The main organization is by region, subdivided by instrumental and vocal music, and listed under the performing artists. Chapter V is devoted to the songs of Rabindranath Tagore. Index of names. Bi-lingual (English-French).

1091. ARCHIVES OF RECORDED MUSIC .... SERIES C: ETHNOGRAPHICAL AND FOLK MUSIC. 1. Collection Phonothèque nationale (Paris). Catalogue prepared by the International Commission on Folk Arts and Folklore. Paris, UNESCO ⌐1952⌐ 254 p.

Lists 4,564 discs in groups as acquired by the Phonothèque. Recordings for any particular national group are scattered throughout the volume. There is an index of countries, however. Bi-lingual (French-English).

1092. ARCHIVES OF RECORDED MUSIC .... SERIES C: ETHNOGRAPHICAL AND FOLK MUSIC. 2. Collection Musée de l'Homme (Paris). Catalogue prepared by the International Commission on Folk Arts and Folklore. Paris, UNESCO ⌐1952⌐ 74 p.

Catalog of a collection of 1,007 recordings, chiefly field recordings made in various parts of Asis and Africa. Grouped under the name of the collector or expedition.

1093. ARCHIVES OF RECORDED MUSIC .... SERIES C: ETHNOGRAPHICAL AND FOLK MUSIC. 3. Katalog der europäischen Volksmusik im Schallarchiv des Institutes für Musikforschung Regensburg ... Bearbeitet von Felix Hoerburger. Regensburg, Gustav Bosse ⌐1952⌐ 189 p.

Material grouped by country and province.

1094. ARCHIVES OF RECORDED MUSIC .... SERIES C:
ETHNOGRAPHICAL AND FOLK MUSIC. 4. International catalogue of recorded folk music ... Edited by Norman Fraser, with
a preface by R. Vaughan Williams and introduction by Maud
Karpeles. Prepared and published for UNESCO by The International Folk Music Council in association with Oxford University
Press, 1954. 201 p.

Part I: "Commercial Records," a listing of the commercially
recorded discs of ethnic and folk music, arranged by continent and
by country. Part II: "Recordings Held by Institutions," a survey
of the major collections of ethnic and folk music in libraries and
research institutions throughout the world. Statistical summary of
their holdings, addresses, names of chief administrators.

1095. HICKMANN, HANS et CHARLES GRÉGOIRE DUC DE
MECKLEMBOURG. Catalogue d'enregistrements de musique
folklorique Égyptienne. Strasbourg, Heitz, 1958. 78 p.
(Collection d'études musicologiques, 37)

Description and analysis of the contents of a recorded collection of Egyptian folk music assembled in 1955. 211 items,
preceded by a discussion of the music and instruments employed.

1096. LUMPKIN, BEN G. and N. L. McNEIL. Folksongs on
records ... Issue three, cumulative, including essential material
in issues one and two. Boulder, Colorado, Folksongs on Records,
1950. 98 p.

Lists 700 commercially recorded discs and albums of folk-
song and folk music, chiefly American. Contents of discs given,
with informal annotations. Useful indexes to English and Scottish
ballads, spirituals, work songs, Irish songs, Mexican and Latin-
American songs; numerical list of albums.

1097. U. S. LIBRARY OF CONGRESS. DIVISION OF MUSIC.
ARCHIVE OF AMERICAN FOLK SONG. Check-list of recorded
songs in the English language in the Archive ... to July 1940.
Washington, D. C., Library of Congress, Division of Music,
1942. 3 v. in 1

A guide to the holdings of one of the world's great folk song collections. Songs listed by title, with name of singer, collector, and date of recording. The 3rd volume is a geographical index.

1098. U.S. LIBRARY OF CONGRESS. DIVISION OF MUSIC. ARCHIVE OF AMERICAN FOLK SONG. Folk music: a selection of folk songs, ballads, dances, instrumental pieces, and folk tales of the United States and Latin America; catalog of phonograph records. ⌐ Washington⌐ Music Division—Recording Laboratory, Reference Dept., Library of Congress, 1959. 103 p.

A selection "representative of the best ... in the collection of the Archive of American Folk Song" (p. 1).

Earlier listings of the same nature appeared in 1948 and 1953.

Current or Annual

Current listings and record reviews are in abundant supply. There are periodicals, such as High Fidelity, the American Record Guide, and The Gramophone, devoted exclusively to the interests of record collectors. Other literary or professional journals, such as The Saturday Review, The Nation, and the Library Journal, have regular departments of record reviews and comment. See the list of periodicals indexed in Record Ratings (no. 1065). For a description of some 30 foreign periodicals devoted to recordings, see no. 407.

1099. GRAMOPHONE SHOP, INC., RECORD SUPPLEMENT. v. 1:1 (Jan., 1938)-v. 17:2 (Feb., 1954)

Title varies: 1939, Record Reviews (Cover title: Record Supplement)

Extensively annotated listings of the major releases in the field of serious music. A monthly publication.

1100. HIGH FIDELITY RECORD ANNUAL. 1955-   Edited by Roland Gelatt. Philadelphia, J. B. Lippincott ⌐ 1955 ⌐

Title varies: From 1957, Records in Review. Great Barrington, Mass., The Wyeth Press. Editor, 1957, Joan Griffiths; editor, 1958-60, Frances Newbury.

A yearly compilation of reviews from High Fidelity magazine. Recordings arranged alphabetically by composer, with a section of "Collections and Miscellany." Signed reviews by High Fidelity contributors.

1101. "INDEX OF RECORD REVIEWS, with symbols indicating opinions of reviewers." In Notes, 5 (March, 1948)-

Since its inception in March, 1948, a regular feature of Notes. Compiled chiefly by Kurtz Myers, with the assistance of various specialists from time to time. One cumulative volume appeared in 1956 (see no. 1065). A valuable guide to record selection for libraries and private collectors.

1102. SCHWANN LONG PLAYING RECORD CATALOG, monthly guide to mono and stereo records. v. 1:1 (Jan., 1949)-

Title varies: began as Schwann Record Catalog.

The standard guide to long playing records currently available for retail purchase.

Specialized Discographies

1103. AMERICAN MUSIC ON RECORDS. A catalogue of recorded American music currently available. Prepared in cooperation with the Committee on Recordings of American Music of the National Music Council. New York, American Music Center ⌐ 1956 ⌐ 39 p.

A composer listing in alphabetical order, with reference to published scores and parts if available.

1104. AMERICAN SOCIETY OF COMPOSERS, AUTHORS AND PUBLISHERS. 40 years of show tunes, the big Broadway hits from 1917-1957. New York, ASCAP ⌐ 1958? ⌐ 149 p.

Chronological list of recorded show tunes arranged alphabetically under year of production. Composer, publisher, performing artist, and record number given. Title index.

1105. COHN, ARTHUR. The collector's twentieth-century music in the Western Hemisphere. Philadelphia, Lippincott [1961] 256 p. (Keystone books in music, KB-23)

One of the best discographies of contemporary music. Well annotated; full coverage for American composers.

1106. INTERNATIONAL ROMAN CATHOLIC ASSOCIATION FOR RADIODIFFUSION AND TELEVISION. Catalogue du disque de musique religieuse. Préf. de J. Schneuwly; introd. de Jean-Michel Hayoz. Edite' par UNDA, Association catholique internationale pour la radiodiffusion et la télévision. Fribourg [1956] 300 p.

YEARBOOKS

Publications appearing under the general title "Yearbook" can take a variety of forms. They may be annual volumes issued by learned societies, as, for example, the Spanish Anuario musical (1946-), the British Proceedings of the Royal Musical Association (1875-), the Jahrbuch für Liturgik und Hymnologie (1955-), and the Schweizerisches Jahrbuch für Musikwissenschaft (1924-38). They may be annual volumes issued by music publishing houses, such as C. F. Peters, Simrock, Breitkopf & Härtel; or they may be directories or compilations of factual information covering a specific year. Works of the latter kind are often useful for reference purposes, since they provide data on current musical activities and personalities difficult to find elsewhere. The following list is selective.

1107. ANNUARIO DEL TEATRO LIRICO ITALIANO. 1940- Pubblicazione ufficiale della Federazione Nazionale Fascista dei Lavoratori dello Spettacolo. Milano, Edizioni Corbaccio, 1940- (737 p.)

A compendium of facts related to the Italian lyric theater, including opera companies, legal aspects, theaters, artists (with portraits), index of interpreters for the standard repertory, instrumentalists, statistics on performances.

1108. HINRICHSEN'S MUSICAL YEAR BOOK, 1944- London, Hinrichsen Edition Ltd., 1944- 11 vols. to 1961.

A series of volumes edited by Max Hinrichsen, issued at irregular intervals, remarkably varied in content. The articles range from trivia to substantial contributions by recognized authorities. Most of the volumes contain bibliographies of current music publications, as well as numerous lists, illustrations, chronologies. The more recent volumes have been organized about a central theme, i. e., Vol. 8, "The Organ of Bach and Matters Related to this Subject" (1956); Vol. 9, "John Gay and the

Ballad Opera" (1956); Vol. 10, "Organ and Choral Aspects and
Prospects" (1958). Vol. 11 (1961) contains the papers read at
the Joint Congress of the International Association of Music
Libraries and the Galpin Society, Cambridge, 1959 (1961).

1109. JAHRBUCH DER MUSIKWELT. The yearbook of the
music world. Annuarie du monde musical. 1. Jahrgang, 1949/
50. Bayreuth, Verlag Julius Steeger, 1949. 696 p.

Only one volume published. Contains a vast amount of information regarding musicians and musical institutions throughout
the world. Contents include a classified listing of German music
dissertations, 1885-1948; a chronology of music dictionaries and
encyclopedias; European music periodicals, 1945-48; a bibliography of German music and writings on music, 1945-48; etc.
The volume also contains an 89-page study, by H. J. Moser,
of the German-American theorist Bernhard Ziehn.

1110. THE MUSIC MAGAZINE/MUSICAL COURIER. The
annual directory of the concert world. Evanston, Summy-
Birchard, 1962- Preceded by Musical Courier. Directory
Issue of the Musical Arts and Artists. 1957-

The 1963 edition, edited by Max D. Jones, contains pertinent
information on American and foreign music organizations, artist
and concert managers, artist availability, current series and
associations, orchestras, opera producing organizations,
festivals, foundations, schools of music, music publishers,
music periodicals, recording firms, music dealers.

1111. MUSICAL AMERICA. ⸢Annual directory or annual
booking edition⸣⸢New York, Music Publications, Ltd.⸣

While the annual directory or booking edition of this periodical is primarily intended for advertising performing artists,
editions of recent years contain many special articles and lists
of various kinds.

1112. THE MUSICIAN'S GUIDE; the directory of the world of
music. 1957 ed. New York, Music Information Service, 1957.

864 p. First annual edition, 1954.

A classified directory of names connected with all phases of commercial music activity.

Review by Richard S. Hill in Notes, 14 (1957) p. 111-13.

1113. OPERA ANNUAL. Ed. by Harold Rosenthal. No. 1- London, John Calder, 1953/54-

Opera Annual no. 7 (1959/60), like the others, contains many articles providing an overview of the opera world for the year under consideration.

1114. PIERRE KEY'S MUSIC YEAR BOOK, the standard music annual, 1924/25-1938. New York, Pierre Key, Inc., 1925-38. 6 v.

A directory of musical organizations and musicians, chiefly performers; issued irregularly over a period of 13 years. The earlier volumes are international in scope, the later are restricted to U.S. coverage.

1115. THE PURCHASER'S GUIDE TO THE MUSIC INDUSTRIES. Annual edition, 1897-   New York, The Music Trades, 1897. Title varies: after 1958, Directory Issue ...

Annual classified directory of instrument manufacturers; music publishers, engravers, and printers; retail music stores; dealers in music merchandise; etc. Excludes performing artists and groups.

1116. THE YEAR IN AMERICAN MUSIC, 1946/47-1947/48. New York, Allen, Towne & Heath ⌈ 1947-48 ⌉ 2 v.

1946/47 edition by Julius Bloom; 1947/48, by David Ewen.

The first part of each volume is a chronological survey of the important musical events of the year; followed by a miscellany of factual information, biographical and bibliographical.

1117. THE YEAR'S WORK IN MUSIC, 1947/48-1950/51. Edited by Alan Frank. London, New York, Published for the

British Council by Longmans, Green & Co., 1948-51.   3 v.

Each volume contains a series of essays by various specialists on aspects of British musical life during the current year:
musical research, the making and playing of instruments, the
B. B. C. and contemporary music, etc. Contains an annual
bibliography of published music and musical literature, compiled by A. Hyatt King.

MISCELLANEOUS BIBLIOGRAPHICAL TOOLS

In this section will be found listed the few existing bibliographies of music bibliography, together with a selected group of statements on the nature and current status of the field. The principal codes for music cataloging have been included, as well as manuals and discussions of music library practice. Among the remaining miscellany will be found two works concerned with the vexing problem of music copyright (nos. 1147 and 1149).

1118. ALLEN, WARREN D. "Bibliography of literature concerning the general history of music in chronological order." In his Philosophies of Music History. New York, American Book Co., 1939. p. 343-65

Reissued as paperback, New York, Dover, 1962.

317 titles arranged chronologically from 1600 to 1939. Not all can be described as histories in the modern sense, but they have bearing on the development of music historiography.

1119. BESTERMAN, THEODORE. "Music; Musical instruments." In his A World Bibliography of Bibliographies ... 2nd ed. London, T. Besterman, 1947-49. 3 v. Columns 1972-2008

An excellent basic list of music bibliographies. The user should also consult the entries under "Opera" and "Song, " and under the names of specific musicians.

1120. BOBILLIER, MARIE (Michel Brenet, pseud.). "Bibliographie des bibliographies musicales." In L'année musicale, 3 (1913) p. 1-152

One of the few specialized bibliographies of music bibliography. Outdated but still useful. Lists general works, including periodical articles, by author, individual bibliographies, catalogs of libraries, public and private, catalogs of dealers and publishers.

1121. THE BRITISH CATALOGUE OF MUSIC CLASSIFICA-
TION. Compiled for The Council of the British National Bibliog-
raphy, Ltd. , by E. J. Coates. Pub. by The Council of the British
National Bibliography, Ltd. , British Museum, London, 1960. 56 p.

The classification developed for The British Catalogue of
Music. See no. 551.

1122. BRYANT, E. T. Music librarianship; a practical
guide. London, James Clarke ⌐1959⌐ 503 p.

Part I, p. 3-285, is a discussion of the administration,
services, and technical processes of music libraries. Part II,
p. 289-450, is a series of annotated bibliographies of basic materials, chiefly scores, for a public library collection. The
emphasis is on British practices.

Review by Rita Benton in Notes, 17 (1960) p. 397-98.

1123. CODE INTERNATIONAL DE CATALOGAGE DE LA
MUSIQUE. I. Der Autoren-Katalog der Musikdrucke. The
author catalog of published music. ⌐By⌐ Franz Grasberger.
Trans. by Virginia Cunningham. Frankfurt/London, C. F.
Peters, 1957. 47 p.

1124. CODE INTERNATIONAL DE CATALOGAGE DE LA
MUSIQUE. II. Code restreint. Redige´par Yvette Federoff.
Kurzgefasste Anleitung. Limited code. Ubersetzung von Simone
Wallon. Trans. by Virginia Cunningham. Frankfurt/London,
C. F. Peters, 1961. 53 p.

These two volumes are the result of the work of the Commission of Music Cataloging of the International Association of Music
Libraries. Later volumes call for a complete code, and a code
for cataloging music manuscripts.

Vol. 1 reviewed by Richard S. Angell in Notes, 15 (1957)
p. 110-11; Vol. 2, by Minnie Elmer in Notes, 19 (1961) p. 247-49.

1125. COOVER, JAMES B. "The current status of music
bibliography. " In Notes, 13 (1956) p. 581-93

A survey of the accomplishments, progress, and lacunae in music bibliography as of 1956. The paper takes its point of departure from A. Hyatt King's statement in The Library (1945). See no. 1137.

1126. COOVER, JAMES B. Music lexicography, including a study of lacunae in music lexicography and a bibliography of music dictionaries. Denver, Bibliographical Center for Research, Denver Public Library, 1958. 126 p.

The 2nd edition of the author's A Bibliography of Music Dictionaries. Denver, 1952.

A comprehensive bibliography of music dictionaries, 1,335 items, including all known editions of the works cited. Preceded by a general discussion of the history of music lexicography and of existing lacunae.

Review by Irene Millen in Notes, 16 (1959) p. 383-84.

1127. DETROIT STUDIES IN MUSIC BIBLIOGRAPHY. No. 1- Detroit, Information Service, Inc., 1961-

A series of manuals, diverse in character and content, but each concerned with some aspect or area of music bibliography.

1128. No. 1: Reference Materials in Ethnomusicology, by Bruno Nettl. 1961. 46 p.

A bibliographic essay on primitive, oriental, and folk music which organizes, describes, and evaluates books and articles on the subjects.

Review by William Lichtenwanger in Notes, 19 (1962) p. 428-30. Also entered as no. 452.

1129. No. 2: Sir Arthur Sullivan: an Index to the Texts of his Vocal Works, by Sirvart Poladian. 1961. 91 p.

A comprehensive index to first lines, titles, and refrains of the composer's vocal works, sacred and secular.

Review by William Lichtenwanger in Notes, 19 (1962) p. 428-30.

1130. No. 3: <u>An Index to Beethoven's Conversation Books</u>, by Donald W. MacArdle. 1962. 46 p.

Review by Fred Blum in <u>Notes</u>, 20 (1963) p. 225-27.

1131. No. 4: <u>General Bibliography for Music Research</u>, by Keith E. Mixter. 1962. 38 p.

A survey of the non-musical aids to musical research, with emphasis on such reference works as general bibliographies of bibliographies, national and trade bibliographies, dictionaries, encyclopedias, union lists, and library catalogs.

Review by Fred Blum in <u>Notes</u>, 20 (1963) p. 225-27.

1132. DEUTSCH, OTTO E. "Music bibliography and catalogues." In <u>The Library</u>, 23:4 (Mar. 1943) p. 151-70.

1133. DUCKLES, VINCENT, ed. Music libraries and librarianship. ⌐ A special issue of⌐ <u>Library Trends</u>, 8 (April 1960) p. 495-617

15 specialists discuss various aspects of music librarianship, covering the areas of training for music librarianship, bibliography and selection, cataloging, services, and administration.

Review by Vladimir Fédorov in <u>Fontes artis musicae</u>, 8 (1961) p. 30-31.

1134. FISCHER, WILHELM. "Verzeichnis von bibliographischen Hilfswerken für musikhistorische Arbeiten." In Adler, Guido, <u>Methode der Musikgeschichte</u>. Leipzig, Breitkopf & Härtel, 1919. p. 200-22

Classified list, including general bibliographical works, general musical works, and bibliographies of single aspects of music history. Some inaccurate dates and incomplete titles for French and English works, which are less well covered.

1135. HOBOKEN, ANTHONY VAN. "Probleme der musikbibliographischen Terminologie." In <u>Fontes artis musicae</u>, 1958:1, p. 6-15.

A discussion centered in the difficulties of establishing music bibliography as an "exact science" in view of the variety and complexity of the materials with which it is concerned.

1136. HOPKINSON, CECIL. "The fundamentals of music bibliography." In Fontes artis musicae, 1955:2, p. 122-31.

An attempt to stimulate discussion of some basic points as to the nature, content and procedures of music bibliography as it serves the needs of collectors, musicians, and historians.

1137. KING, A. HYATT. "Recent work in music bibliography." In The Library, 26:2 (Sept.-Dec. 1945) p. 99-148

Also reprinted separately, London, Bibliographical Society, 1945.

1138. KROHN, ERNEST C. "The bibliography of music." In Musical Quarterly, 5:2 (Apr. 1919) p. 231-54

Narrative style. Gives an excellent idea of the state of music bibliography at the time of publication. Incomplete citations.

1139. KRUMMEL, DONALD W. and JAMES B. COOVER. "Current national bibliographies, their music coverage." In Notes, 17 (1960) p. 375-88

Surveys the music coverage in national bibliographies in the Western Hemisphere, Western and Eastern Europe, Africa, Asia, and Oceania.

1140. LAFORTE, CONRAD. Le catalogue de la chanson folklorique française. Québec, Les Presses Universitaires Laval, 1958. 397 p. (mimeographed) (Publications des archives de folklore, Université Laval)

Demonstrates a method for establishing an alphabetical catalog, by title, of French folk songs, with appropriate cross-references to permit the grouping of variants under a common title. Based on material in Canadian archives and collections.

1141. LUTHER, WILHELM MARTIN. "Bibliographie ...
Literatur." In MGG. Kassel, Bärenreiter Verlag, 1949-
v. 1, col. 1837-39

Surveys the history and concepts of music bibliography, with
an extensive listing of titles pertaining to the field.

1142. McCOLVIN, LIONEL R. and HAROLD REEVES.
Music libraries; their organization and contents, with a bibliography of music and musical literature. London, Grafton, 1937.
2 v.

A manual of music library practice, British emphasis, with
extensive bibliographies of music literature and musical scores
as guides to selection. Vol. 2, p. 213-92, devoted to a descriptive list of music collections throughout the world.

1143. MUSIC LIBRARY ASSOCIATION. Code for cataloging
music and phonorecords. Prepared by a Joint Committee of the
Music Library Association and the American Library Association,
Division of Cataloging and Classification. Chicago, American
Library Association, 1958. 88 p.

The five major divisions of the code are: entry, description,
phonorecords, simplified rules, and filing rules for conventional
titles. Glossary and index.

1144. MUSIC LIBRARY ASSOCIATION COMMITTEE ON
THEMATIC INDEXES. A check list of thematic catalogues,
prepared by a Committee of the Music Library Association. New
York, The New York Public Library, 1954. 37 p.

Reprinted from the Bulletin of The New York Public Library,
Jan.-March 1953. Preface signed: Helen Joy Sleeper. 350
numbered entries, including catalogs of 129 individual composers,
63 collections, 22 libraries, and 13 publishers.

Index of composers, and general index.

Review by Vincent Duckles in Notes, 11 (1954) p. 552-53; by
Scott Goldthwaite in JAMS, 8 (1955) p. 58-59.

1145. "MUSIC ... MUSICOLOGY." In The Bibliographic Index, a cumulative bibliography of bibliographies. New York, H. W. Wilson, 1937-   p. 1087-97, and in subsequent issues.

1146. NEW YORK PUBLIC LIBRARY. REFERENCE DEPARTMENT. Music subject headings, authorized for use in the catalogs of the Music Division.

Boston, G. K. Hall, 1959. 512 p.

Reproduced from cards in the subject headings file of The New York Public Library. An important tool for music catalogers, since it represents the practice of one of the great American music collections.

1147. POHLMANN, HANSJÖRG. Die Frühgeschichte des musikalischen Urheberrechts (ca. 1400-1800). Neue Materialien zur Entwicklung des Urheberrechtsbewusstseins der Komponisten. Kassel, Bärenreiter, 1962. 315 p. (Musikwissenschaftliche Arbeiten. Herausgegeben von der Gesellschaft für Musikforschung, 20)

A pioneer study in the history of music copyright, treating the sociological and psychological aspects of composers' rights, plagiarism, the history of honoraria for composers. An appendix gives 31 original documents in transcription. Bibliography (p. 299-309) covers both legal and musical aspects of the subject.

1148. REGELN ZUR KATALOGISIERUNG DER IN DER DEUTSCHEN BÜCHEREI EINGEHENDEN MUSIKALIEN. Entwurf. Leipzig, Deutsche Bücherei, 1959. 35 p.

Review by Virginia Cunningham in Notes, 16 (1959) p. 567,

1149. ROTHENBERG, STANLEY. Copyright and public performance of music. The Hague, Martinus Nijhoff, 1954. 188 p.

A survey of the current status of music copyright and performers' rights in the United States and in Europe.

1150. U.S. LIBRARY OF CONGRESS. Classification,

Class M: Music and books on music. 2nd edition, with supplementary pages.

Washington, D.C., Govt. Printing Office, 1957. 157, 85 p. First issued in 1904; revised, 1917.

Largely the work of O. G. Sonneck, this classification schedule has been accepted, with various modifications, in a great number of American music collections.

1151. U.S. LIBRARY OF CONGRESS. SUBJECT CATALOGING DIVISION. Music subject headings used on printed catalog cards of the Library of Congress. Washington, 1952. 133 p.

1152. WINCHELL, CONSTANCE M. "Music." In her Guide to Reference Books. 7th ed. Chicago, American Library Association, 1951. p. 346-56.

See also appropriate sections in later supplements.

1153. BREITKOPF & HÄRTEL (Publishers) Das Musik-Buch,
eine nach Gruppen und Gattungen geordnete Zusammenstellung
von Büchern über Musiker, die Musik und Instrument, mit
Einführungen ... aus dem Verlage von Breitkopf und Härtel.
Leipzit, Breitkopf & Härtel, 1913. 390 p. Nachtragsband, 1926.
149 p.

A trade catalog of Breitkopf & Härtel books on music.
Illustrated. Gives detailed descriptions of the works and their
contents. The book provides a useful survey of German music
literature as issued by the leading music publisher of the first
third of the 20th century.

1154. BÜCHTING, ADOLF. Bibliotheca musica.
Verzeichnis aller in Bezug auf die Musik ... 1847-1866 im
deutschen Buchhandel erschienenen Bücher und Zeitschriften.
Nebst Fortsetzung 1: die Jahre 1867-1871 umfassend.
Nordhausen, 1867-72. 2 v.

A bibliography of music literature covering German
publications from 1847 to 1871. The work takes its place
chronologically after that of Becker (no. 352) in the history of
music bibliography. The gap of 8 years in coverage between
Becker and Büchting has been filled by Robert Eitner. See
no. 360.

1155. ARCHIVIO MUSICALE. "I manoscritti musicali
gregoriani dell'archivio di Montecassino." ⌐ By Paolo M.

Ferretti ꓤ In <u>Casinensia: miscellanea di studi Cassinesi</u> ...
v. 1 (1929) p. 187-203.

Detailed descriptions of 11 manuscript sources of Gregorian chant, the 11th comprising a group of fragments from various sources. Two facsimile plates.

INDEX

The abbreviation "rev" before a number refers to a review. The numbers themselves refer to entry number--not to page number.